D1369437

Spanish-American War

Spanish-American War

Daniel E. Brannen Jr.

Julie L. Carnagie and Allison McNeill, Project Editors

Detroit • New York • San Diego • San Francisco • Cleveland • New Haven, Conn. • Waterville, Maine • London • Munich

THOMSON
™
GALE

Spanish-American War
Daniel E. Brannen Jr.

Project Editors
Julie L. Carnagie, Allison McNeill

Permissions
Shalice Shah-Caldwell

Imaging and Multimedia
Kelly A. Quin, Luke Rademacher

Product Design
Pamela A. E. Galbreath, Cynthia Baldwin, Jennifer Wahi

Composition
Evi Seoud

Manufacturing
Rita Wimberley

LIBRARY OF CONGRESS CATALOGING-IN-PUBLICATION DATA

Brannen Jr., Daniel E., 1968 -
 Spanish-American War / Daniel E. Brannen Jr. ; Allison McNeill, editor.
  p. cm.
 Summary: A comprehensive overview of the Spanish-American War, including biographies and full or excerpted memoirs, speeches, and other source documents.
 Includes bibliographical references and index.
 ISBN 0-7876-6561-4
 1. Spanish-American War, 1898–Juvenile literature. [1. Spanish-American War, 1898.] I. McNeill, Allison. II. Title.
 E715.B83 2003
 973.8'9–dc21   2002154459

Contents

Primary Sources

Reader's Guide

The Spanish-American War, fought from April to August 1898, was a short but brutal war between Spain and its colony of Cuba, which was supported by the United States. It was a continuation of Cuba's Second War for Independence, which had begun in 1895. Cubans sought freedom from Spain and the right to govern themselves to improve their lives economically and socially. Initially the United States stayed out of the conflict in Cuba, but upon hearing of Spain's harsh treatment of Cuban civilians, a majority of the American public came to favor war with Spain. The explosion of an American battleship, the U.S.S. *Maine,* in a Cuban harbor on February 15, 1898, killing more than 250 of the soldiers aboard, also fueled the call to war.

After entering the conflict on Cuba's side on April 21, 1898, the United States fought against Spain in land and sea battles in the Spanish colonies of Cuba, Puerto Rico, and the Philippines until the two countries called a truce in August 1898. Having defeated Spain at almost every turn, the United States dominated the peace negotiations that resulted in the Treaty of Paris in December 1898. Under the terms of the treaty, the United States assumed control of Puerto Rico, Guam, and the Philippines and established influence over newly independent Cuba.

Features

Spanish-American War presents a comprehensive view of the war, the events leading up to it, and its aftermath in three sections: Almanac, Biographies, and Primary Sources.

The Almanac contains six chapters that each focus on a particular aspect of the war, including Cuba's struggle for independence from Spain, U.S. entrance into the conflict, battles waged at Guam, Puerto Rico, and the Philippines, and the end of the war and peace negotiations.

The Biographies section profiles ten individuals who played key roles during the Spanish-American War. Readily recognizable figures such as the leader of the Rough Riders, Theodore Roosevelt, U.S. president William McKinley, and Red Cross relief worker and nurse Clara Barton are featured, as well as lesser-known people such as U.S. journalist Richard Harding Davis and Cuban military officer Máximo Gómez y Báez.

The Primary Sources section presents seven full and excerpted primary source documents that tell the story of the war in the words of the people who lived it. Included is Cuban general Calixto García's letter of protest to U.S. general William R. Shafter after his troops were excluded from the negotiations for the surrender of Santiago; and an excerpt from "The Report of the *Vizcaya*" sent by Spanish captain Antonio Eulate, whose ship was among those destroyed near Santiago harbor at the hands of the U.S. Navy.

Sidebar boxes highlighting people and events of special interest are sprinkled throughout the text, and each chapter, biography, and primary source entry offers a list of additional sources students can go to for more information. The volume begins with a timeline of important events in the history of the Spanish-American War, and a "Words to Know" section introduces students to difficult or unfamiliar terms (terms are also defined within the text). More than fifty-five black-and-white photographs and maps illustrate the material. The volume concludes with a general bibliography and a subject index so students can easily find the people, places, and events discussed throughout *Spanish-American War*.

Advisors

A note of appreciation is extended to the *Spanish-American War* advisors who provided invaluable suggestions when the work was in its formative stages:

Elaine Ezell
Media Specialist
Bowling Green Junior High School
Bowling Green, Ohio

Ann West LaPrise
Media Specialist
Renton Junior High School
New Boston, Michigan

Angela Leeper
Educational Consultant
North Carolina Department of Public Instruction
Raleigh, North Carolina

Comments and Suggestions

We welcome your comments on *Spanish-American War* and suggestions for other topics to consider. Please write: Editors, *Spanish-American War*, U•X•L, 27500 Drake Rd., Farmington Hills, Michigan 48331-3535; call toll-free: 1-800-877-4253; fax to 248-699-8097; or send e-mail via http://www.gale.com.

Spanish-American War Timeline

1492 Italian explorer Cristoforo Colombo (Christopher Columbus) takes Cuba from natives for Spain.

July 4, 1776 Thirteen American colonies reject imperialism with the Declaration of Independence, in which they claim, "Governments are instituted among Men, deriving their just Powers from the Consent of the Governed."

1823 United States of America, under President John Quincy Adams, offers to buy Cuba from Spain.

1848 United States of America, under President James K. Polk, offers to buy Cuba from Spain.

1854 United States of America, under President Franklin Pierce, offers to buy Cuba from Spain. In a communication that becomes known as the Ostend Manifesto, three U.S. diplomats in Europe urge U.S. secretary of state William L. Marcy to support seizure of Cuba if Spain refuses to sell.

1861 Outbreak of the American Civil War distracts American interest in acquiring Cuba.

October 10, 1868 Ten Years' War between Spain and Cuban rebels begins with the *Grito de Yara* (the Cry of Yara) in Cuba.

1878 Ten Years' War between Spain and Cuban rebels ends in a stalemate with the Pact of Zanjón.

August 1879 The *Guerra Chiquita* (Little War) begins and ends quickly, failing to revive the revolution against Spanish control of Cuba.

December 1879 Antonio Cánovas del Castillo replaces Arsenio Martínez Campos as the premier of Spain, dashing hopes for post-war reform of Spain's government of Cuba.

1883 Joseph Pulitzer purchases the *New York World* and develops the sensational style of newspaper journalism.

1890 First U.S. Congress to spend one billion dollars uses some of the money to add three new battleships, a cruiser, and a torpedo boat to the U.S. Navy.

1890 U.S. Census Bureau announces that the American frontier is closed, as Americans have settled in all areas of the continent.

January 5, 1892 Exiled Cuban philosopher José Julián Martí y Pérez helps form *El Partido Revolucionario Cubano* (the Cuban Revolutionary Party) in New York City to work for Cuban independence from Spain.

September 1892 José Martí recruits Ten Years' War veteran Máximo Gómez to lead the army in the upcoming Cuban revolution against Spain.

1893 United States of America enters worst economic depression since its birth.

March 1893 Grover Cleveland takes office as the twenty-fourth president of the United States of America.

June 1893 José Martí recruits Antonio Maceo to be second-in-command of the army in the upcoming Cuban revolution against Spain.

February 25, 1895 Juan Gualberto Gómez launches the Second Cuban War for Independence with the *Grito de Baire* (the Cry of Baire) in Cuba.

March 31, 1895 Antonio Maceo reaches the island of Cuba to join the revolutionary forces.

March 31, 1895 Spain sends Ten Years' War veteran General Arsenio Martínez Campos to Cuba to crush the revolution.

April 11, 1895 José Martí and Máximo Gómez reach the island of Cuba to join the revolutionary forces.

May 4, 1895 José Martí, Máximo Gómez, and Antonio Maceo meet to plot rebel strategy and appoint Gómez head of the Liberating Army, Maceo chief of operations in Oriente Province, and Martí head of the revolution outside Cuba.

May 19, 1895 José Martí dies in his first battle, near Don Rios, Cuba.

June 1895 U.S. president Grover Cleveland announces the United States of America will remain neutral in the conflict between Spain and the Cuban rebels. Cleveland, however, refuses to give international recognition to the Cuban rebels. This effectively allows Americans to help Spain, with whom the United States has normal diplomatic relations, while making it illegal for Americans to assist the Cubans.

July 1, 1895 General Máximo Gómez issues the order to stop sugarcane production and to prevent the shipment of industrial and agricultural goods to Spanish-controlled areas of Cuba.

November 6, 1895 General Gómez orders the destruction of sugarcane plantations and mills and their railroad connections in Cuba.

November 7, 1895 William Randolph Hearst publishes his first issue of the *New York Journal,* a newspaper he bought with inherited money to compete with Joseph Pulitzer and the *New York World.* The Cuban revolution and the Spanish-American War become the source of much material for a circulation war between the newspapers. Both publishers wanted the United States to go to war with Spain, and historians credit the newspapers with stirring up public support for war.

November 29, 1895 General Gómez, Antonio Maceo, and Liberating Army troops cross the main Spanish *trocha*, a barrier preventing the rebel forces from reaching the wealthy, western end of Cuba.

January 17, 1896 The governor and leader of the Spanish army in Cuba, Arsenio Martínez Campos, resigns. Spanish Premier Antonio Cánovas del Castillo selects General Valeriano Weyler y Nicolau to replace Martínez Campos.

January 22, 1896 Antonio Maceo and the Invading Army reach Mantua, the westernmost town in Cuba, marking the high point of the rebel effort.

February 1896 Spanish general Valeriano Weyler orders his troops to relocate Cuban civilians from the countryside into concentration camps in Spanish-controlled cities to prevent the civilians from assisting the Cuban rebels.

March 10, 1896 General Gómez and Antonio Maceo meet for the last time, agreeing that Maceo should continue invading the west while Gómez continues economic destruction in central Cuba.

December 7, 1896 Antonio Maceo dies in unusual nighttime battle at San Pedro de Hernández, Cuba.

January 1897 Journalist Richard Harding Davis and illustrator Frederic Remington travel to Cuba to cover the revolution for William Randolph Hearst and the *New York Journal*. When Remington telegraphs Hearst to say he sees no fighting and wants to come home, Hearst allegedly replies, "Please remain. You furnish the pictures and I'll furnish the war."

March 1897 William McKinley takes office as the twenty-fifth president of the United States of America.

May 1897 Over 300 American bankers, merchants, manufacturers, and steamship owners ask President McKinley to intervene in Cuba, where the revolutionary destruction of the sugar industry and other commerce is hurting their businesses.

June 1897 Judge William J. Calhoun, who visited Cuba at the request of President William McKinley, reports on the destruction he saw and his belief that Spain is not strong enough to defeat the Cuban rebels.

July 1897 Clara Barton, head of the American Red Cross, meets with President McKinley to suggest that her organization travel to Cuba to help the starving, dying Cuban civilians in concentration camps.

August 1897 Spanish premier Antonio Cánovas dies from an assassin's bullet. The queen regent of Spain makes Práxedes Mateo Sagasta the new premier, and Sagasta replaces Valeriano Weyler with General Ramón Blanco y Erenas as leader of the Spanish army in Cuba.

August 1897 William Randolph Hearst and the *New York Journal* launch campaign to pressure Spain to release Evangelina Cisneros from jail. Niece of the president of the Cuban Republic, Cisneros was charged with disloyalty to Spain and reportedly had resisted the sexual advances of a Spanish military officer. Hearst sends a journalist with money to bribe guards to release Cisneros, but prints a story saying the journalist freed Cisneros in a jailbreak.

September 1897 Assistant Naval Secretary Theodore Roosevelt uses political influence to have Commodore George Dewey appointed to lead the U.S. Asiatic Squadron.

December 1897 Rebels led by Emilio Aguinaldo end revolution against Spain in the Philippines. Aguinaldo agrees to be exiled from his country in return for a payment of money, which he saves for a future revolution.

December 1897 In his annual State of the Union message, President McKinley pressures Spain to end the Cuban revolution and recommends public assistance to Cuban civilians suffering in Spain's wartime concentration camps.

January 1, 1898 Central Cuban Relief Committee forms in New York to raise money for supplies for the Red Cross to distribute in Cuba.

January 24, 1898 In response to riots in Havana, Cuba, days earlier, President McKinley orders the U.S. warship *Maine* to port there.

February 9, 1898 The *New York Journal* publishes a stolen letter in which the Spanish minister to the United States, Enrique Dupuy de Lôme, calls President William McKinley "weak" and a "low politician." Dupuy de Lôme also says the only acceptable result for Spain in Cuba is military victory over the rebels, suggesting that recent governmental reforms there are not genuine.

February 15, 1898 U.S. warship *Maine,* stationed at Havana, Cuba, to protect American interests and pressure Spain to end the Cuban revolution, explodes, killing more than 250 men.

February 17, 1898 Headline in *New York Journal* announces, "Destruction of Warship *Maine* Was the Work of An Enemy." (Investigations failed ever to prove the cause of the explosion, whether accidental or intentional.)

February 25, 1898 Temporarily in charge in his boss's absence, Assistant Naval Secretary Theodore Roosevelt telegrams Commodore George Dewey with instructions to prepare the Asiatic Squadron for war with Spain in the Philippines.

March 1898 Commodore George Dewey arrives with the U.S. Asiatic Squadron in Hong Kong to prepare for battle in the Philippines in case of war with Spain.

March 6, 1898 While negotiating for peace, McKinley tells Congressman Joe Cannon that he needs money for war, which now seems inevitable to the president.

March 17, 1898 Senator Redfield Proctor, who had visited Cuba, gives speech to U.S. Senate on the conditions he observed. Proctor's speech adds to the momentum for war with Spain.

March 25, 1898 U.S. naval court of inquiry led by Admiral William T. Sampson reports that an external mine ignited ammunition on the *Maine,* resulting in two deadly explosions. The court, however, is unable to identify who is responsible for the incident.

April 9, 1898 U.S. war secretary Russell A. Alger sends Lieutenant Andrew S. Rowan on a mission to gather military information from Cuban general Calixto García.

April 11, 1898 President William McKinley asks Congress for authority to end the revolution in Cuba with American naval and military forces.

April 19, 1898 Congress votes to give President William McKinley authority to end the revolution in Cuba with American naval and military forces. The Congressional resolutions include the Teller Amendment, by which the United States promises to leave Cuba to govern itself after expelling Spain and securing peace on the island. The United States makes no such promise with respect to other Spanish colonies.

April 21, 1898 President William McKinley orders a naval blockade of Cuba and severs diplomatic relations with Spain.

April 24, 1898 U.S. Navy secretary John D. Long sends telegram to U.S. commodore George Dewey ordering the U.S. Asiatic Squadron to capture or destroy the Spanish squadron in the Philippines led by Admiral Patricio Montojo y Pasarón.

April 25, 1898 U.S. Congress declares war on Spain.

April 27, 1898 In the first military engagement of the war, Spanish artillery at Matanzas, Cuba, fires upon U.S. battleship *New York,* which returns fire and ends the attack in twenty minutes.

April 29, 1898 Spanish admiral Pascual Cervera y Topete departs Cape Verde Islands for an unknown destination, raising fears that the squadron might attack cities on the east coast of the United States.

May 1, 1898 U.S. commodore George Dewey defeats Spanish admiral Patricio Montojo y Pasarón in a five-hour battle in Manila Bay, Philippines, that kills hundreds of Spaniards.

May 1, 1898 Authorities in New York City prevent the Socialist Labor party from holding an antiwar parade.

May 1, 1898 U.S. lieutenant Andrew S. Rowan meets with Cuban general Calixto García, who agrees to assist with an American invasion of Spain in Cuba.

May 7, 1898 McKinley receives official telegram from Dewey announcing naval victory in the Philippines.

May 11, 1898 United States suffers its first defeat when Spain fires upon and disables a torpedo boat, the *Winslow,* as it enters the harbor at Cárdenas on the northwest coast of Cuba, killing five Americans.

May 11, 1898 Cuban general Calixto García informs General Gómez that the United States will land on the northern coast of Cuba with arms and ammunition for a joint operation against Spain in the city of Holguín.

May 12, 1898 In light of a crushing defeat at the Philippines on May 1, Spain orders that Admiral Cervera return to Europe to protect the homeland. At sea, Cervera does not see the order until he arrives at Cuba.

May 19, 1898 Unprepared for war, Admiral Cervera avoids the U.S. Navy and slips into port at Spanish-controlled Santiago de Cuba near the southeastern end of the island. Days later, Admiral Sampson's blockade arrives at the mouth of the harbor to shut Cervera in.

May 19, 1898 Filipino rebel Emilio Aguinaldo returns to the Philippines and organizes an army to attack Spain in the city of Manila, all with newly promoted Admiral Dewey's approval and perhaps at his request.

May 25, 1898 U.S. expedition led by Brigadier General Thomas Anderson leaves San Francisco to help Admiral Dewey take the city of Manila from Spain in the Philippines.

June 3, 1898 President McKinley outlines peace proposal, demanding that Spain give up Cuba, Puerto Rico, a port in the Philippines, and a port in the Ladrone (or Marianas) Islands.

June 7, 1898 U.S. Fifth Army Corps (V Corps) led by General William R. Shafter boards transport vessels at Tampa Bay, Florida. Alleged sightings of Spanish vessels nearby prevents the V Corps from heading to Cuba for another week.

June 10, 1898 U.S. Marines land at Guantánamo on the southeastern tip of Cuba and take the area in battles with Spanish soldiers.

June 12, 1898 Aguinaldo and Filipino rebels declare Philippine independence from Spain.

June 14, 1898 V Corps leaves Tampa, Florida, for Cuba.

June 20, 1898 Clara Barton and the American Red Cross leave Tampa, Florida, to provide wartime relief in Cuba.

June 20, 1898 General Shafter and Admiral Sampson meet with Cuban general Calixto García to select landing point for the V Corps near Santiago de Cuba.

June 21, 1898 Unaware that Spain is at war, Spaniards at Guam surrender the island after Americans en route to the Philippines arrive to fight the day before.

June 22 and 23, 1898 The V Corps lands on Cuba at Daiquirí and then Siboney, about twelve miles southeast of Santiago, which the army intends to capture. The shift of plans from the north to the south coast prevents the Cuban rebels from participating fully.

June 24, 1898 Regiments from the V Corps begin march toward Santiago and battle Spaniards at Las Guásimas until Spaniards retreat.

July 1898 Congress votes to take the independent nation of Hawaii for the United States of America.

July 1, 1898 The V Corps and Cuban rebels engage in bloody, day-long battle with Spaniards at El Caney and San Juan Heights, Spain's last line of defense before Santiago. In the battle at San Juan Heights, Theodore Roosevelt and the volunteer regiment known as the Rough Riders make their famous charge up Kettle Hill with two regular army regiments of African Americans. By day's end, Spain retreats toward Santiago.

July 3, 1898 Under orders to flee, Admiral Cervera leaves harbor at Santiago to be defeated by Commodore Winfield S. Schley.

July 17, 1898 The Spanish commander at Santiago, José Torál, surrenders Santiago and all troops in the region to the United States. General Shafter insults the Cuban republic by declining to invite Generals Gómez or García to the surrender ceremony. General García resigns from the Liberating Army to protest the insult.

July 25, 1898 American troops commanded by General Nelson A. Miles land on Guánica on the southern coast of Puerto Rico.

July 31, 1898 Fighting commences between United States and Spain for control of the city of Manila in the Philippines.

August 3, 1898 General Shafter's officers write the Round-Robin Letter, urging the U.S. Army to remove its troops from Cuba before they all die from yellow fever and malaria.

August 9–12, 1898 Americans troops in Puerto Rico fight six major battles with Spanish soldiers while marching toward the capital of San Juan.

August 12, 1898 United States secretary of state William R. Day and French ambassador Jules Cambon (acting for Spain) sign peace protocol to end the fighting. Under the agreement, Spain promises to set Cuba free and to leave Guam and Puerto Rico to the United States. The fate of the Philippines rests in treaty negotiations to begin in Paris on October 1.

August 13, 1898 Unaware of the peace protocol, thanks to a severed telegraph cable, Spain and the United States stage a fake battle before Spain surrenders at Manila in the Philippines.

October 1, 1898 Peace commissions from Spain and the United States begin meetings in Paris, France, to craft a treaty to end the war officially.

October 1, 1898 Philippine native Felipe Agoncillo meets with President McKinley to remind him that U.S. officials promised independence for the Filipinos in exchange for military assistance against Spain at Manila during the war. McKinley rejects this notion and instructs the peace commissioners in Paris to exclude the Filipinos from negotiations that will determine the fate of their country.

December 10, 1898 Peace commissioners sign Treaty of Paris in France. In the document, Spain frees Cuba, gives Puerto Rico and Guam to the United States to cover war costs, and sells the Philippines to the United States for $20 million.

January 1899 Filipino rebels set up republic by adopting the Malolos Constitution and sever diplomatic relations with the United States.

January 1, 1899 United States occupies Cuba with a military government.

February 4, 1899 Fighting breaks out between Filipino rebels and U.S. military occupation. The war lasts until April 1902, ending with American control of the Philippines.

February 6, 1899 Amidst rumors, perhaps inaccurate, that the Filipinos had fired the first shot two days earlier, the U.S. Senate ratifies (approves) the Treaty of Paris.

March 19, 1899 The queen regent of Spain approves the Treaty of Paris after the *Cortes,* Spain's legislative body, rejects it.

November 5, 1900 Cuban Constitutional Convention meets for the first time to begin drafting a constitution for an independent Cuba.

February 11, 1901 Cuban Constitutional Convention adopts a constitution for Cuba.

February 27, 1901 Unhappy that the Cuban constitution did not give the United States the right to intervene in Cuban affairs, the U.S. Senate adopts the Platt Amendment, saying the American military will not leave Cuba until the United States gets the power it wants.

June 12, 1901 Pressured by America's strength and bribed by a favorable trade agreement, the Cuban Constitutional Convention adopts a new constitution giving the United States the right to intervene in Cuban affairs.

May 20, 1902 U.S. military turns the government of Cuba over to newly elected Cuban president Tomás Estrada Palma.

1917 Puerto Ricans get U.S. citizenship, but not the right to vote in federal elections.

1935 Under the Tydings–McDuffie Act, the Philippines begins a trial period of self-government as a commonwealth of the United States.

1946 The Philippines gets complete independence from the United States.

1947 Puerto Rico gets right to select governor with popular elections.

1968 Guam gets right to select governor with popular elections.

1976 A U.S. naval investigation of the destruction of the U.S. warship *Maine* concludes that an accidental internal explosion in the ammunition magazines was the most likely cause of the disaster.

1997 Computer analysis by the National Geographic Society concludes that either an internal or external explosion could have caused the *Maine* disaster in February 1898.

2002 United States still holds Puerto Rico as a commonwealth and Guam as a territory, precluding the residents of both colonies from electing the president of the United States or voting representatives in Congress.

Words to Know

A

ambassador: A person who represents one country in diplomatic relations with another country.

anarchy: A state of society without government or law.

annexation: The act of taking a foreign land and making it part of another country.

artillery: Mounted, as opposed to portable, guns and missile launchers.

autonomy: The right of self-government.

B

brigade: A unit of organization in the U.S. Army made up of two or more regiments.

C

cable: A message sent through an electrical wire.

carbine: A light rifle.

casualties: People who are injured or killed in fighting.

cavalry: A unit of soldiers on horses. In the Spanish-American War, most of the American cavalry that fought in Cuba fought on foot because transport ships did not have enough room for the horses.

ciudadano: The Spanish word for citizen.

colony: A land ruled by a foreign power without governmental representation.

commonwealth: A self-governing territory of the United States of America.

consul: A government official who looks out for the welfare of her country's commerce and citizens in another country.

correspondent: A person who gathers news for a newspaper or other media organization.

Cortes: The legislative, or law-making, body of government in Spain.

Creoles: People of European (especially Spanish) descent who are born in the West Indies, including Cuba.

customs duties: Government charges on goods coming into or leaving a country.

D

debark: To go ashore from a ship.

democracy: A state in which all people exercise governmental power through elected representatives.

dinghy: A small boat.

diplomacy: The conduct of negotiations and other relations between nations.

discrimination: Treating people differently on the basis of their race, color, religion, national origin, gender, sexual orientation, or other category of humanity.

division: A unit of organization in the U.S. Army made up of two or more brigades.

E

embark: To board a ship and start on a journey.

exile: Being expelled from one's homeland by the government.

G

garrison: A military post, or the body of troops stationed there.

gruel: A cooked cereal made by boiling grain meal, especially oatmeal, with water or milk.

guerilla warfare: A military tactic that involves hit-and-run attacks from hidden positions.

I

imperialism: The act of controlling a foreign country without giving its people equal participation in government.

Invading Army: The rebel Cuban army lead by Antonio Maceo that invaded western Cuba during the Second Cuban War for Independence (1895–1898).

J

jingo: A person who strongly supports war and foreign conquest.

***Junta*:** A group organized in New York City in 1892 to support Cuban independence from Spain.

L

latrine: A trench in the earth used as a toilet.

Liberating Army: The rebel army that controlled the eastern end of Cuba during the Second Cuban War for Independence (1895–1898).

lynch mobs: Gangs of citizens that attacked and killed people, especially African Americans, in the decades following the American Civil War (1861–1865).

M

magazines: A supply chamber that holds ammunition for war ships or other weaponry.

malaria: A disease that destroys red blood cells and is caused by parasites transmitted by mosquitoes.

mambises: Rebel forces fighting against Spain in Cuba.

N

new journalism: A style of journalism invented by Joseph Pulitzer in the 1880s. New journalism catered to working-class people and immigrants with sensational stories about crime and corruption in business and government.

P

pacificos: Cuban civilians who did not fight with the rebels during the Second Cuban War for Independence (1895–1898).

parliament: The name for the government in Spain and other countries.

Peninsulares: Spanish natives who settled in Cuba.

prejudice: Unreasonable, sometimes hostile opinions about a racial group.

premier: The prime minister, or head of government, in Spain.

protectorate: An arrangement under which one nation protects and controls another.

protocol: An original agreement from which a treaty is prepared.

Q

quarantine: An isolation of people, designed to prevent disease from spreading.

queen regent: A person who rules on behalf of the queen, often until the queen reaches a particular age.

R

racism: The belief that one race of humans is superior to others.

ratify: To approve governmental action officially, as when the U.S. Senate approves a treaty signed by the president.

reconcentrados: Cuban civilians herded into concentration camps by Spain during the Second Cuban War for Independence (1895–1898).

regiment: The basic unit of organization for U.S. Army soldiers in the Spanish-American War.

republic: A state in which all people exercise governmental power through elected representatives.

S

sanitarium: A health resort.

secede: To withdraw from a union of states.

sentry boxes: Small structures for sheltering a sentry, or guard, from bad weather.

socialism: A system under which income and property are distributed by the government instead of by economic markets.

sovereign nation: A nation that governs itself.

squadron: A part of a naval fleet.

stereotypes: Common, often inaccurate notions about a group of people.

T

tariffs: Government charges, or taxes, on goods coming into or leaving a country.

telegram: A message sent through an electrical wire.

treaty: A formal, official agreement between nations.

trochas: Military barriers built with barbed-wire-choked trenches and defended by guard stations.

turret: An armored, rotating gun aboard a vessel.

V

V Corps: The abbreviated name for the Fifth Army Corps, the portion of the U. S. Army that landed on Cuba in June 1898 and fought its way to the gates of Santiago, which surrendered on July 17.

W

West Indies: A collection of islands in the North Atlantic Ocean, including Cuba, stretching from North to South America.

Y

yellow fever: A serious, often deadly infection caused by a virus transmitted by mosquitoes in warm climates.

yellow journalism: A sensational style of journalism in the 1890s that involved shocking stories, sometimes false, written to increase readership without regard to accuracy.

Spanish-American War

Almanac

Cuba's Struggle
for Independence

The Spanish-American War, fought from April to August 1898, was a short but brutal war between Spain and its colony of Cuba, which was supported by the United States. It was a continuation of Cuba's Second War for Independence, which had begun in 1895. Cubans sought freedom from Spain and the right to govern themselves to improve their lives economically and socially.

Initially the United States stayed out of the conflict in Cuba. Still recovering from an economic depression that had begun around 1893, the United States depended upon good foreign relations to promote international trade and revive its economy. Outraged by newspaper articles describing Spain's brutal treatment of Cuban civilians, however, a majority of the American public came to favor war with Spain. U.S. president **William McKinley** (1843–1901; served 1897–1901; see entry in Biographies section) found it hard not to resist these wishes after an American battleship, the U.S.S. *Maine,* mysteriously blew up in a Cuban harbor on February 15, 1898, killing more than 250 of the soldiers aboard. After prominent U.S. business leaders signaled their support for war in March 1898, McKinley agreed.

The explosion that destroyed the U.S.S. *Maine* in February 1898, which many in America blamed on the Spanish, played a big part in the United States's decision to go to war with Spain. *Hulton Archive/Getty Images. Reproduced by permission.*

After entering the conflict on Cuba's side in April 1898, the United States fought against Spain in land and sea battles in the Spanish colonies of Cuba, Puerto Rico, and the Philippines until the two countries called a truce in August 1898. Having defeated Spain at almost every turn, the United States dominated the peace negotiations that resulted in the Treaty of Paris in December 1898. Under the terms of the treaty, the United States assumed control of Puerto Rico, Guam, and the Philippines and established influence over newly independent Cuba. The former colonies's residents were not allowed to participate in crafting the treaty.

Near the end of hostilities, John Hay (1838–1905), the American ambassador to Great Britain, called it a "splendid little war." While this assessment may have reflected popular opinion at the time, it ignored the horror that war is. Around 5,500 Americans died, mostly from yellow fever and other diseases caught in the tropical battle zones.

In addition to the Cuban struggle for independence and the battles and bloodshed, the Spanish-American War is the story of how the United States officially became an imperialist nation. Imperialism is the act of exercising governmental control over foreign people. Although it had spent the nineteenth century conquering Native Americans, the United States officially spoke out against imperialism in favor of democracy, which means governmental control by the people being governed. By acquiring Spain's remaining colonies, the United States abandoned democracy in order to govern people who lacked representation in their nation's capital. The story of the war began on a beautiful Caribbean island whose people wanted to break the shackles of Spanish imperialism and undertake local self-government.

Spain's Cuban colony

Cuba is part of the Antilles island chain, which stretches in an arc around the Caribbean Sea. Located ninety miles south of Florida, "the pearl of the Antilles" was home to a favorable climate and rich soils that made it valuable for farming. In 1492, Cuba's inhabitants were descendants of natives from South America, including tribes such as the Arawaken (called the Taino in Cuba), Guanahatabey, and Ciboney. Cuba hosted a native population of around fifty thousand when Cristoforo Colombo (Christopher Columbus, 1451–1506) arrived on October 27, 1492, and seized the island for Spain.

Cuba first served as a base for Spain's exploration of the New World, as the Americas were formerly called. Over the next fifty years, the conquistadors's expeditions, disease, and mistreatment of the natives reduced the island's population to around five thousand by 1550. For the next century and a half, disease, piracy, and competition between Spain and other European invaders continued to plague Cuba. During the eighteenth century, Spain increased the island's agricultural output, primarily sugarcane production. By importing human beings from Africa and forcing them into slavery on the sugarcane plantations, the Spanish motherland planted the seeds of revolution.

In the nineteenth century, sugarcane production began to be mechanized by technology created during the Industrial Revolution. The Industrial Revolution was a period beginning around 1760 during which raw materials such as iron and steel and energy sources such as coal and electricity

Cuba, approximately ninety miles off the coast of Florida, was home to a favorable climate and rich soils that made it valuable for farming. *UPI/Corbis. Reproduced by permission.*

led to the replacement of human handiwork by automated machines. Wealthy emigrants from Spain controlled both these new means of production as well as Cuba's colonial government, resulting in policies and taxes that oppressed small landowners, laborers, and slaves. Meanwhile, from 1810 to 1825, Spain's remaining colonies in the New World revolted against the empire and achieved their independence, leaving only Cuba and Puerto Rico under Spanish control.

The Ten Years' War

In 1842, Cuba's population of around one million included 436,495 black slaves, 152,838 free blacks, and 448,291 whites. The white population had two main social classes—the *Peninsulares* and the *Creoles*. Peninsulares were Spanish natives who had settled in Cuba. Creoles were people of Spanish descent who had been born in Cuba. Generally speaking, Peninsulares controlled commerce, held most positions in the colonial government, and were naturally loyal to Spain. Creoles were primarily landowners, farmers, and professional people.

Spanish taxes and restrictions on trade with other countries oppressed the Creoles. Corrupt government by the Peninsulares for the benefit of Spanish industries also dissatisfied the Creoles. Although they wanted more political influence and economic freedom, they relied on the government and the military for a different kind of oppression—the maintenance of slavery. This dependence prevented the Creoles from mounting a serious movement for independence until the 1860s.

By 1865, the end of the American Civil War (1861–65) in the United States showed that slavery could be defeated. Meanwhile, economic and social unrest in Cuba worsened, causing Spain to create a Colonial Reform Commission to discuss proposals for reform (improvement of economic and social policies) in Cuba and Puerto Rico. Opposition to reform by the conservative element of Spain's legislature in Madrid—the Cortes—caused the reform efforts to fail. Then in 1867, Spain enacted new real estate, income, and business taxes in Cuba, adding to the already excessive customs duties—government charges on goods coming in and out of the colony. Spain simply refused to stop using its colonies for its own economic benefit.

In response to the hardship, revolution broke out on Cuba in October 1868 with the *Grito de Yara* (Cry of Yara). Led by military leaders such as **Máximo Gómez y Báez** (1836–1905; see entry in Biographies section) and Antonio Maceo (1845–1896), the rebels fought for independence for the next ten years. Busy with its period of Reconstruction (1865–1877) following the Civil War, the United States chose not to get involved. Instead, America hoped Spain would decide to sell the colony.

Cuba's first revolution for independence failed for a number of reasons. Racism prevented many rebels from rejecting slavery and welcoming blacks into the struggle. Similarly, the revolutionaries could not agree on whether they were fighting for complete independence or just political reform. Furthermore, many of the twenty thousand *mambises,* as the rebel forces were called, fought only with machetes (large knife with a wide blade), while the Spaniards used modern rifles.

José Julián Martí y Pérez (1853–1895)

Cuba's famous revolutionary patriot was born in Havana on January 28, 1853. His parents, Leonor Pérez Martí and Mariano Martí y Navarro, were *Peninsulares*. Peninsulares were natives of Spain who had settled in Cuba. Young José's father taught him to be strictly loyal to Spain in honor of tradition. The boy, however, chose a different path.

Around 1865, Martí met Rafael María de Mendive, a teacher, principal, and poet at the Havana Municipal High School for Boys. Mendive became Martí's mentor, teaching him that Cuban independence was the only acceptable solution to the troubles caused by Spain's economic policies. When Cuba's First War for Independence—the Ten Years' War—broke out in 1868, Martí wrote revolutionary poetry and formed a boys' club to support the rebels.

When the authorities found one of Martí's poems while searching Mendive's house in January 1869, they threw Martí in jail. He remained there for nine months before facing charges. At his trial, Martí said Cuba had a right to be free from Spain and to operate its own government. Convicted of disloyalty, Martí faced six years of hard labor in a limestone quarry while imprisoned at Havana's *Presidio* (Spanish military post).

Martí never finished his sentence. Herniated, half-blind, and scarred with whiplashes, he was exiled from Cuba, first on the nearby Isle of Pines and later in Spain, arriving there in 1871. In Spain, Martí continued his education and writing, receiving degrees in law and philosophy from the University of Zaragosa in 1874. He then spent a few years in France, Mexico, Guatemala, Cuba (using a different name), Spain, France, New York City, and then Venezuela before finally settling in New York City in 1881. During this time Martí continued political writing and activity that would lead to Cuba's second revolution for independence in 1895. In 1890, for example, Martí and Rafael Serra formed *La Liga* (The League), a club for poor, black Cuban exiles. Martí believed poor people should lead the coming revolution.

On January 5, 1892, Martí created *El Partido Revolucionario Cubano,* the Cuban Revolutionary Party. The party's goal was to generate and organize support and sympathy for an independent Cuba. At first, the party focused on organizing within Cuban communities in the United States, especially in Florida. Later, it attracted support from the American press and labor organizations. Martí opposed efforts within the

An ongoing military stalemate (deadlock), however, made it necessary to end the war in 1878 with a truce called the Pact of Zanjón. Famously, Maceo refused to sign the pact, largely because it failed to end slavery in Cuba. Over two hundred thousand people had died during the uprising.

Jose Martí. ©Bettmann/CORBIS. Reproduced by permission.

party to discriminate against blacks and socialists—people who believe that income and property should be distributed by society instead of market forces. When serving as the party's leader, Martí chose to be called delegate instead of president.

When Cuba's Second War for Independence broke out on February 25, 1895, Martí traveled with General Máximo Gómez y Báez (1836–1905) and others to fight in Cuba, where they landed on April 11. Some supporters felt Martí would better serve the revolution as an organizer in the United States. Critics wondered whether the skinny man was up to fighting. In a letter written on the eve of his departure for Cuba, according to Philip S. Foner in *The Spanish-Cuban-American War and the Birth of American Imperialism,* Martí said, "I called up the war; my responsibility begins rather than ends with it.... But my one desire would be to stand beside the last tree, the last fighter, and die in silence. For me, the hour has come."

The hour came sooner than Martí probably expected. Fighting atop a white horse in Don Rios in his first battle, on May 19, 1895, Martí was shot and killed, becoming a martyr to inspire the rebels. A hymn written for the revolution in November 1895 by Enrique Loynaz del Castillo began, "The adored memory of Martí/Presents Honor to our lives."

Martí's inspiration lives on in his essays and poems about freedom. These include *Versos libres,* a collection of poetry written between 1878 and 1882, and *Our America: Writings on Latin America and the Cuban Struggle for Independence,* an English translation of Martí's writing published in 1978.

Spanish General Arsenio Martínez de Campos (1834–1900), who had led the defense in Cuba starting in 1876, became the premier, or prime minister, of Spain after signing the Pact of Zanjón. Many hoped he would introduce reforms that would end Cuba's revolutionary problems, as he had promised to do when negotiating with the rebels for peace. Resistance to reform by the conservative members of the Cortes, however, prevented Martínez de Campos from keeping his promise.

Many rebels who had signed the Pact of Zanjón launched another revolt in August 1879 on the eastern end of Cuba, where the poorest communities were located. Spain quickly ended this revolt, giving it the name *Guerra Chiquita,* or Little War. In December 1879, Martínez de Campos's government failed, leading to his replacement by Premier Antonio Cánovas del Castillo (1828–1897), a conservative who ended hopes for a solution to Cuba's troubles.

Preparing for independence

By the early 1890s, Cubans began organizing for another revolution. In New York City on January 5, 1892, exiled Cuban poet and philosopher José Julián Martí y Pérez (1853–1895) helped form *El Partido Revolucionario Cubano,* the Cuban Revolutionary Party. The party's council operated from New York to organize support for the coming revolution. Martí also launched the newspaper *Patria,* meaning Fatherland, to spread information supporting Cuba's right to be free.

Although the Cuban Revolutionary Party sought financial and philosophical support from Americans, Martí and others wanted the revolution to be at the hands of Cubans alone. Martí had watched pineapple producers in Hawaii grow interested in United States's control of that island republic. He was well aware that American businesses had invested around $50 million in Cuba and engaged in $100 million of trade annually with the colony. Martí feared that the United States might want to replace Spain as the foreign power controlling his homeland. "Cuba must be free from Spain and the United States," said Martí, according to Ivan Musicant in *Empire by Default.*

After getting the party up and running, Martí set out to organize military leadership for the revolution. In September 1892, he asked Ten Years' War veteran Máximo Gómez to be the rebel army's general. Gómez agreed, receiving his official appointment to the position in January 1893. Later that year, in June, Martí approached Antonio Maceo. Called the Bronze Titan, Maceo was living in Costa Rica, and he initially resisted joining the party for fear of another failure. After learning how well Martí had organized everything, however, Maceo agreed to join him.

By late 1894, Martí was anxious to launch his revolution. Some rich planters in Cuba offered their support if the rebels would delay the fighting until after the sugarcane harvest. Martí did not believe this promise of help, however. saying, again according to Musicant, "the rich people will never enter the Revolution."

Economic conditions in Cuba continued to worsen for the middle and lower classes. The United States had enacted a steep tariff—or tax—on sugar imported from Cuba into America. In response, Spain raised tariffs on American goods sold in Cuba, raising the already oppressive cost of living in the colony. The growing wealth gap there made revolution seem inevitable.

Cuba's second revolution begins

Led by former slave Juan Gualberto Gómez, the revolution began with the *Grito de Baire,* or Outcry of Baire, on February 25, 1895. Named for the small town in which the fighting began, the *Grito de Baire* initially looked like it might turn into another little war. Spanish authorities crushed the revolutionaries and captured their leaders quite easily, leading to small press reports in Spain and the United States that the revolt would lead to nothing.

Things changed, however, after Maceo reached Cuba on March 31 and Martí and Gómez reached the island on April 11. These three leaders finally met on May 4 at La Mejorana to formulate a strategy for reviving the revolution. Gómez announced a scorched-earth policy for military conduct. Believing that the inequality of wealth created Cuba's troubles, Gómez said the solution was to strike at that wealth by destroying sugarcane plantations and other wealthy businesses. This strategy would deplete the Spanish revenue that

Cuban military leader **Antonio Maceo.** *Courtesy of the Library of Congress.*

came from taxing the businesses. Gómez felt that making the war expensive for Spain would even the rebels's odds against the large, well-equipped Spanish army.

Back in Spain, as the government planned its response to the rebellion, a scandal involving newspaper criticism of the Spanish military forced Premier Práxedes Mateo Sagasta (1825–1903) to resign. His replacement, Antonio Cánovas del Castillo, decided to send Ten Years' War veteran Arsenio Martínez de Campos to be Cuba's governor and military general. Martínez de Campos intended to end the revolution while implementing new laws to give minimal relief to Cuba's political and economic concerns.

Martínez de Campos planned a military strategy similar to the one that he had used in the Ten Years' War. First, he divided the army into two parts. One part remained in the cities and towns to defend them against rebel attack. The second part roamed the countryside to engage the rebels in battle. Using Spanish *trochas*—fortified barriers that at one point crossed the entire island between Mariel and Majana—Martínez de Campos hoped to corner, surround, and then overwhelm the rebel army with large numbers of Spanish troops.

The rebel army, which was strongest on the poorer eastern end of the island, set out to dominate the countryside with its scorched-earth policy. With support from rural residents, the Cuban rebels planned to break through the main *trocha,* spread over the western end of the island, and starve the country to death with economic destruction. Fighting without Martí, who died in his first battle on May 19, 1895, the rebel army implemented this strategy in June of that year. Gómez ordered his soldiers to kill plantation owners and workers who resisted the army's economic tactics. He also prohibited the transportation of goods, such as leather, wood, tobacco, coffee, and honey, into towns held by the Spanish army.

By January 1896, the Liberating Army, as the rebels came to be called, had achieved its greatest military success. Forces led by both Gómez and Maceo had broken through the main *trocha* and spread westward. Martínez de Campos declared a state of war in Cuba's capital of Havana, which faced threats from rebel forces.

Spain had deployed 186,000 soldiers to fight rebel forces that roamed in bands of hundreds and thousands of men. Despite this huge numerical advantage, the Spanish army faced a military stalemate (deadlock) due to its soldiers's poor marksmanship, its habit of withdrawing into town garrisons (military posts) after victories to avoid ambushes, and especially the tropical summertime diseases of Cuba. When asked to name his best generals, Gómez identified June, July, and August, according to Philip S. Foner in *The Spanish-Cuban-American War and the Birth of American Imperialism.*

Enter "the butcher"

Back in Spain, discontent with Martínez de Campos had reached the breaking point. Many felt he was being too easy on the rebels. Faced with this pressure, Martínez de Campos resigned on January 17, 1896. Premier Cánovas replaced him with General Valeriano Weyler y Nicolau (1838–1930), whom the *Chicago Times-Herald* called "the most brutal and heartless soldier to be found in a supposedly civilized country."

Spanish general Valeriano Weyler y Nicolau, also known as "the butcher" for his harsh treatment of the Cubans. ©*Corbis. Reproduced by permission.*

Soon after arriving in Cuba, Weyler issued the first of many *reconcentración,* or reconcentration, orders. His strategy was to starve the rebels of the food, shelter, and other support they received from civilians living in the countryside. Weyler ordered the *pacíficos,* as the non-rebels were called, to leave their homes and move into Spanish-occupied cities and towns. The Spanish army then destroyed the food and shelter the pacificos had left behind.

Weyler's reconcentration policy turned out to be an international public relations disaster for Spain. Food and shelter already was scarce in the cities and towns occupied by Spanish troops. The relocated pacificos ended up hungry and dirty, living in filthy conditions that spelled death for hundreds of thousands of them. The American press, already tending to support the Cuban rebels, criticized Weyler's inhumane policies and called him "the butcher." Yet the media usually failed to condemn the inhuman tactics used by the rebel army. Such biased coverage helped to generate public support in the United States for its eventual war with Spain.

In the Cuban countryside, Maceo's dwindling army kept the Spanish forces on the run. Maceo complained to the revolutionary government, however, that he was not receiving his fair share of arms and ammunition, a problem he blamed on racism. Maceo managed to last for almost one year against Weyler's forces. Then, on December 7, 1896, after crossing around a *trocha* by sea, Maceo's rebels faced an unusual nighttime battle at San Pedro de Hernández. Sleeping in a hammock and weak from many war wounds, Maceo was unprepared to fight because the Spanish usually retreated into the safety of their garrisons at night. Battling while atop a horse, Maceo received two bullets that ended his life.

Without Maceo, who led the most effective assaults on Spanish-occupied towns during the revolution, the war continued to be a military stalemate. Weyler controlled the cities, ports, and military forts. Gómez and the rebels controlled the countryside. As early as October 1896, there was pressure in Spain to recall Weyler, who was generating bad international press while failing to end the revolution.

In August 1897, Premier Cánovas died by an assassin's bullet. The queen regent of Spain soon put the liberal Sagasta back into the office of premier, and Sagasta replaced Weyler with General Ramón Blanco y Erenas (1831–1906). Under Sagasta, the Spanish government eventually agreed to end the reconcentration camps, stop fighting, and make Cuba a free unit of government under Spain. Cuba, however, wanted complete independence, and events in early 1898 brought Spain to war with the United States.

For More Information

Collins, Mary. *The Spanish-American War.* New York: Children's Press, 1998.

Dolan, Edward F. *The Spanish-American War.* Brookfield, CT: Millbrook Press, 2001.

Foner, Philip S. *The Spanish-Cuban-American War and the Birth of American Imperialism.* New York: Monthly Review Press, 1972.

Gay, Kathlyn, and Martin K. Gay. *Spanish-American War.* New York: Twenty First Century Books, 1995.

Golay, Michael. *The Spanish-American War.* New York: Facts On File, Inc., 1995.

Graves, Kerry A. *The Spanish-American War.* Mankato, MN: Capstone Books, 2001.

Langellier, John P. *Uncle Sam's Little Wars: The Spanish-American War, Philippine Insurrection, and Boxer Rebellion, 1898–1902.* Philadelphia, PA: Chelsea House, 2002.

Linderman, Gerald F. *The Mirror of War: American Society and the Spanish-American War.* Ann Arbor, MI: The University of Michigan Press, 1974.

Musicant, Ivan. *Empire by Default: The Spanish-American War and the Dawn of the American Century.* New York: Henry Holt and Company, 1998.

O'Toole, G. J. A. *The Spanish War: An American Epic–1898.* New York: W. W. Norton & Company, 1984.

Smith, Angel, and Emma Dávila-Cox, eds. *The Crisis of 1898: Colonial Redistribution and Nationalist Mobilization.* New York: St. Martin's Press, Inc., 1999.

Somerlott, Robert. *The Spanish-American War: Remember the Maine!* Berkeley Heights, NJ: Enslow Publishers, Inc., 2002.

Wukovits, John F. *The Spanish-American War.* San Diego, CA: Lucent Books, 2001.

Zinn, Howard. *A People's History of the United States: 1492–Present.* 20th anniversary ed. New York: HarperCollins, 1999.

The United States Declares War

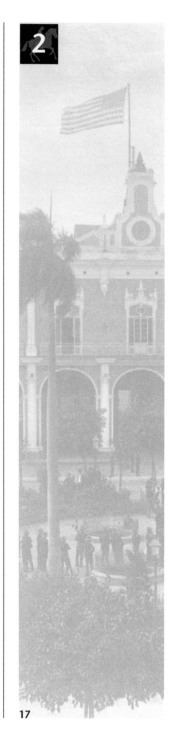

2

The United States was formed under the belief that people have a natural right to control their government. Some people think this right comes from God, while others believe it comes from being human. The Declaration of Independence, written by Thomas Jefferson (1743–1826) when the American colonies separated from Great Britain in 1776, reflects this principle by saying, "Governments are instituted among Men, deriving their just Powers from the Consent of the Governed." The Tenth Amendment to the U.S. Constitution, written in 1789 to restrict the power of the newly formed federal government, also supports this belief by saying that all power not given to the federal government stays with the states and with the people.

In spite of these democratic principles, America still allowed slavery. Shortly after the United States adopted a constitution in 1789, the slavery states in the South expressed interest in acquiring the colony of Cuba from Spain. The colony sat just ninety miles from the tip of what would become the state of Florida. Cuba's agriculture, slave trade, and location in the Caribbean made it valuable to America's economy and military strategic interests. When several revolutions occurred in the early 1800s throughout Latin America, the U.S. slavery states were not disappointed that Cuba failed to win its independence.

During the nineteenth century, the United States offered to buy Cuba from Spain three times: in 1823 through Secretary of State John Quincy Adams (1767–1848), in 1848 through President James K. Polk (1795–1849), and in 1854 through President Franklin Pierce (1804–1869). Spain refused all three offers. In 1854, three U.S. diplomats in Europe issued the Ostend Manifesto, urging U.S. secretary of state William L. Marcy (1786–1857) to support seizure of Cuba if Spain would not sell it. Their advice stemmed from a wish to avoid Cuban slave revolts, such as those that had occurred in nearby Haiti, and to extend slave territory for the United States.

The Ostend Manifesto provoked anger among American antislavery Republicans, primarily in the North. Spain, however, still refused to sell Cuba, and U.S. interest in the island decreased as the United States entered the Civil War (1861–65) in 1861.

American social conditions

Five years before the Spanish-American War (April–August 1898), the United States had undergone its worst economic crisis ever. After decades of expansion, over six hundred banks failed and sixteen thousand businesses closed in 1893, unable to sustain the rapid growth. Twenty percent of working Americans were unemployed that year.

The depression came at a time when two groups of American workers—laborers and farmers—were organizing as they never had before. Members of unions such as the American Federation of Labor, the Knights of Labor, and the American Railway Union sought higher pay and better working conditions from the steel, railroad, textile, and other industries that had become wealthy from the laborers's hard work. Farmers formed a political party—the Populist Party—to seek relief from oppressive economic conditions that caused land, equipment, loan, and transportation prices to rise while food prices dropped.

Many racial and ethnic minority Americans faced human and civil rights abuses during this time. The federal government, which had pushed Native Americans into the western part of the continent, waged war against them to take their land for railroads and forced them onto reservations. African Americans, entitled to equal treatment under the law according to the Thirteenth, Fourteenth, and Fifteenth Amendments to the U.S. Constitution—passed after the Civil War—still found themselves discriminated against, especially in the South. In fact, during the first forty-four years after the Fourteenth Amendment was ratified in 1868, the U.S. Supreme Court cited the amendment in only twenty-eight cases involving African Americans but in 312 cases concerning the rights of corporations. Between 1889 and 1903, an average of two African Americans were lynched—killed, often by hanging—by mobs each week.

Oppression in Cuba

These oppressed Americans empathized with the Cubans' desire for independence when Cuban rebels began to organize revolts against Spain in the 1860s. Cuba had been a colony of Spain since Cristoforo Colombo (Christopher Columbus, 1451–1506) had landed there on October 27, 1492. By the mid-1800s, Cuba had developed a thriving agricultural economy based mainly upon sugar, tobacco, and coffee plantations worked by African slaves.

Corruption was commonplace in the Cuban government. Local officials and Cuban representatives in the Spanish parliament operated the island's government to benefit Spanish businesses. Spain's tariff and tax policies made trade with other countries very expensive for small farmers and small businesses in Cuba. Middle-class civilians, laborers, and the slaves all wished to break free from Spain to improve their respective economic and social conditions.

In 1868, Cuban rebels launched their first war for independence. The war lasted for ten years before both sides signed a truce in 1878. The rebels organized a second revolution in February 1895. Unable to crush the rebellion early on, Spain assigned a vicious general named Valeriano Weyler y Nicolau (1838–1930) to take over military operations in Cuba in February 1896.

At the time, Spain controlled Cuba's main cities and ports while the rebels dominated the countryside. To starve the rebels of food, shelter, and support, Weyler decided to re-

locate all rural civilians into the cities and to burn what they left behind. Crowded, unhealthy conditions and scarce food in the concentration camps led to death for hundreds of thousands of relocated civilians. Meanwhile, volunteers in the Spanish army committed gross deeds of torture and murder after capturing Cuban rebels.

America's "Yellow Press"

Weyler's conduct of the war and Spain's refusal to give the Cubans freedom both received intense American newspaper coverage. Two papers in particular, the *New York World* and the *New York Journal,* used the conflict to wage their own circulation war for greater readership. Joseph Pulitzer (1847–1911), whose name accompanies the prestigious Pulitzer Prize for Literature, controlled the *World,* which he had purchased in 1883. Using sensational journalism to cover scandals such as governmental corruption and the plight of the poor, Pulitzer had significantly increased the paper's circulation and profitability by 1895.

Owner of the *New York World* Joseph Pulitzer used sensational stories in his newspaper to motivate the United States to take action in Cuba. *©Bettmann/Corbis. Reproduced by permission.*

That year, a young man named **William Randolph Hearst** (1863–1951; see entry in Biographies section) used inherited money to purchase the competing *Journal.* Hearst immediately developed his own sensationalism to compete with Pulitzer. In early 1896, Pulitzer cut the price of the *World* in half, to one cent, to battle his new rival. Both newspapers published shocking stories without checking facts and sometimes by inventing them. The tactic came to be called "yellow journalism" after a popular comic strip character from the *World* called the Yellow Kid.

The Cuban revolution of 1895–98 and America's war with Spain in 1898 were the primary sources of material for the newspapers' circulation war. Pulitzer found it easy to side with the rebels, who sought freedom from economic and social oppression. Hearst used the conflicts to develop publicity stunts that made his paper famous. In their coverage, both men sought to motivate the United States to take some form of action to support the Cuban rebels, leading to the term "the journalism that acts," according to Charles H. Brown in *The Correspondents' War.*

When a Spanish ship mistakenly fired on an American merchant vessel in March 1895, Pulitzer's *World* announced "Our Flag Fired Upon," according to Ivan Musicant in *Empire By Default.* Other papers urged the United States to teach Spain a lesson with a military response.

In August 1897, Spain imprisoned Evangelina Cisneros, a niece of the president of the Cuban rebel republic. Upon learning of the case, Hearst immediately launched a campaign to have Cisneros released. After she escaped, with the assistance of *Journal* correspondents and some bribery money, Cisneros came to America. She attended a rally of one hundred thousand people at Madison Square Garden in New York City and visited with President **William McKinley** (1843–1901; served 1897–1901; see entry in Biographies section). These events boosted morale for those Cubans who wanted the United States to support their efforts.

Public opinion on Cuba's cause

Newspapers were Americans' primary connection to the outside world in the 1890s, so press coverage shaped public opinion of the Cuban revolution. Historians suggest that newspapers led most Americans to sympathize with the rebels, and this is easy to believe. The nation of the United States was founded in 1776 with a colonial revolution against an oppressive motherland. In the 1890s, American farmers, laborers, African Americans, and Native Americans all could relate to the plight of their counterparts in Cuba. In 1897, American Federation of Labor president Samuel Gompers said, "The sympathy of our movement with Cuba is genuine, earnest, and sincere," according to Howard Zinn in *A People's History of the United States.* Virtually all Americans, including those in the upper and middle classes, eventually came to understand and support the Cuban desire for self-government.

There was, however, a less noble force shaping American public opinion—prejudice. Many Americans ignorantly viewed

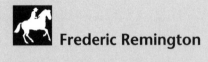

Frederic Remington

Historians often describe newspaper coverage of the Second Cuban War for Independence (1895–98) and the Spanish-American War as a battle in print. Competing for readership, the *New York World* and the *New York Journal* featured stories written to shock Americans into supporting the Cuban cause. One of the most famous of these sensationalistic journalists was a man named Frederic Remington (1861–1909).

Remington was born in Canton, New York, on October 4, 1861. The son of a journalist, Remington set out to become an illustrator, enrolling at Yale University's School of Fine Arts in 1878 and the Art Students League in 1886. In between his student days, Remington spent some time out West, where he began to paint portraits of America's dying frontier, depicting cowboys, Native Americans, and horses.

In late 1896, during the Second Cuban War for Independence, Spanish General Valeriano Weyler y Nicolau (1838–1930) was wreaking havoc by relocating Cuban civilians into dirty, overcrowded, concentration camps in the cities to prevent them from helping the Cuban rebels in the country. William Randolph Hearst, publisher of the *New York Journal,* sent Remington and fellow reporter **Richard Harding Davis** (1864–1916; see entry in Biographies section) to Key West, Florida, in December 1896 to cover the war. Remington and Davis were supposed to make their way to Cuba and report from the front alongside rebel leader General **Máximo Gómez y Báez** (1836–1905; see entry in Biographies section) and his troops.

Travel problems prevented the team from reaching Gómez and the rebels, however. Landing in Spanish-controlled Havana instead, Davis and Remington met with Spanish general Weyler, who gave Davis a pass to travel throughout Cuba's western provinces to cover the fighting. Weyler sent spies to follow Davis.

Stuck in Havana, Remington soon became bored. According to Charles H. Brown in *The Correspondent's War,* Remington sent a telegram to Hearst that said: "Everything is quiet. There is no trouble. There will be no war. I wish to return." As reported by Brown, some historians say Hearst replied, "Please remain. You furnish the Spaniards as naturally savage. According to Gerald F. Linderman in *The Mirror of War,* historian Charles Francis Adams said in 1898, "No single good thing in law, or science, or art, or literature…has resulted to the race of men…from Spanish domination in America…. I have tried to think of one in vain."

According to Linderman, the president of the University of Wisconsin also used these themes in his address to

Frederic Remington. *©Bettmann/Corbis.*
Reproduced by permission.

penned by Remington and reflecting many prejudices of the day:

> *The acts of the terrible savages, or irregular troops called 'guerrillas,' employed by the Spanish, pass all understanding by civilized man. The American Indian was never guilty of the monstrous crimes that they commit. The treatment of women is unspeakable and as for the men captured by them alive, the blood curdles in my veins as I think of the atrocity, of the cruelty, practiced on these helpless victims. My picture illustrates one case where the guerrillas saw fit to bring their captives into the lines, trussed up at the elbows.*

Remington delivered his illustrations to the *Journal* himself, choosing to leave Cuba despite Hearst's request. He later returned to the island to cover the mysterious destruction of the *Maine* on February 15, 1898, the U.S. naval blockade in April, and the U.S. Army's siege of El Caney on July 1. According to Brown, after the siege at El Caney, Remington recalled "men half naked, men sitting down on the roadside utterly spent, men hopping on one foot with a rifle for a crutch, men out of their minds from heatstroke, men dead, men dying."

the pictures and I'll furnish the war." Hearst, however, denied the statement.

On January 17, 1897, the *Journal* falsely reported that Remington and Davis had joined the insurgents. One week later, the paper printed Remington's first illustrations from the island. As told by Brown, a drawing published on page three of the *Journal* contained the following caption,

graduating seniors in June 1898, saying, "What has Spain ever done for civilization? What books, what inventions have come from Spain? What discoveries in the laboratories or in scientific fields? So few have they been that they are scarcely worth mentioning." Later in the speech he continued, "Examination of the Spanish character shows it to be the same as it was centuries ago. Wherever the Spaniard has endeavored to rule he has shown an unrivaled incapacity for government.

And the incapacity was such and the cruelty was such that all their colonies and provinces have slipped away."

The Cleveland administration

When the Cubans launched their second revolution in February 1895, Grover Cleveland (1837–1908; served 1885– 1889 and 1893–1897) was president of the United States. Initial reports accurately reflected that Spain had come very close to ending the rebellion from the start. By June, however, the rebels had recovered and were taking control of the countryside on the eastern end of the island, where large numbers of poor people eagerly joined the cause. The Cuban rebels were following a strategy of destroying plantations, sugarcane mills, and other business property in order to starve Spain financially by depriving it of revenue from taxes on trade.

With the revolution growing, President Cleveland had to let the world know where the United States stood on the dispute. Siding with the rebels would destroy diplomatic relations with Spain. Siding with Spain would make the United States appear insensitive to Spain's harsh treatment of the colony. In June 1895, Cleveland announced that the United States would remain neutral, officially favoring neither side in the revolution. More significantly, however, Cleveland refused to give official recognition to the rebels and their government under international law.

Cleveland's decision was unpopular with Cuban Americans and many members of Congress. With the United States remaining neutral, American businesses could still sell weapons and other military equipment to Spain, with whom the United States had normal diplomatic relations. Refusing to recognize the Cuban republic made it illegal for Americans to supply arms to the rebels. This annoyed members of Congress who were imperialists—people who wanted the United States to begin acquiring colonies of its own. It also displeased U.S. representatives who had Cuban Americans in their districts.

Cleveland's stance on the revolution did satisfy big business interests in the United States, however. American business leaders that had survived the economic hard times of 1893 did not want to see war disrupt their recovery. They were unsure whether a rebel Cuban government would continue to support policies that had resulted in $50 million of U.S. investment in Cuban plantations, sugar mills, and other businesses, and $100 million of trade with the island each year. According to journals of the time, most businesses wanted the federal government to focus on negotiating trade agreements to provide foreign markets for American goods and otherwise to avoid all conflict.

Racial prejudice also may have played a role in Cleveland's stance on the revolution. His secretary of state, Richard B. Olney, expressed concern that a free Cuba would descend into a war between blacks and whites "until the one had been completely vanquished and subdued by the other," according to Philip S. Foner in *The Spanish-Cuban-American War and the Birth of American Imperialism.*

Under the administration of President Grover Cleveland, the U.S. remained neutral in the conflict between Spain and its Cuban colony.
Courtesy of the Library of Congress.

The McKinley administration

When President William McKinley succeeded Cleveland in March 1897, he adopted a similar approach to the Cuban revolution. As a Christian who had served in the American Civil War (1861–65), McKinley simply hated war. "I shall never get into a war, until I am sure that God and man approve. I have been through one war; I have seen the dead piled up, and I do not want to see another," McKinley said in February 1898, according to Musicant.

In May 1897, McKinley received a plea from over three hundred American business leaders—bankers, merchants, manufacturers, and steamship owners—who said that the destruction of the Cuba's sugar industry and commerce was hurting the U.S. economy. Then in June 1897, McKinley received a report from Judge William J. Calhoun, who had visited Cuba to survey the situation. Viewing the effects of Spanish reconcentration and rebel economic destruction in

In a letter published in the *New York Journal,* Spanish minister to the United States Enrique Dupuy de Lôme heightened tensions between the U.S. and Spain by stating, among other things, "McKinley is weak." *Granger Collection. Reproduced by permission.*

the countryside, Calhoun said, "Every house had been burned, banana trees cut down, cane fields swept with fire, and everything in the shape of food destroyed," according to Musicant. Calhoun continued, "The country was wrapped in the stillness of death and the silence of desolation." The judge told McKinley that Spain could not win the war, suggesting that American support for the rebels would tilt the conflict in the rebels' favor.

Historians disagree on the motives for McKinley's conduct at this point. Some say he still held out for peace because of his Christian faith. Others say that when Spain removed General Weyler from Cuba in August 1897 and promised to enact economic and social reform on the island, McKinley wanted to give those efforts time to work. In *A People's History of the United States,* Howard Zinn suggests that McKinley strove for peace only until the business community spoke out in favor of war in March 1898. Foner charges McKinley with responding to Calhoun's report by pressuring Spain to secure peace only so the United States could later take over Cuba.

American insult and tragedy

McKinley himself left little written record of his thoughts and beliefs, so it is impossible to be certain of what he was thinking. History does, however, record two events in February 1898 that made the American public cry out for war with Spain. On February 9, Hearst's *Journal* published a letter that had been written by the Spanish minister to the United States, Enrique Dupuy de Lôme. In it, Dupuy de Lôme told a friend in Havana that "McKinley is weak and catering to the rabble and, besides, a low politician who desires to leave a door open to himself and to stand well with the jingos of his party," according to Foner. (Jingo was a term used to describe

The remains of the U.S.S. *Maine,* which exploded in Havana harbor on February 15, 1898, and triggered the United States's entry into the Spanish-American War. *Hulton Archive/Getty Images. Reproduced by permission.*

people who wanted to wage war in order to expand the territory of the United States.) In the letter, Dupuy de Lôme also said that Spain had promised reform in Cuba only to buy time for its army to crush the rebellion.

Six days later, the American warship *Maine* exploded and sank in the harbor at Havana, Cuba, killing more than 250 sailors onboard. The yellow press devoured the catastrophe. Within days, the *Journal* had accused Spain of the crime, saying "the *Maine* was destroyed by treachery" and was "split in two by an enemy's secret infernal machine," according to Foner. Hearst offered a fifty-thousand-dollar reward for conviction of the people responsible. Pulitzer's *World* said there was evidence that a mine had destroyed the vessel. Across the country, "Remember the *Maine*, to hell with Spain!" became a rallying cry.

McKinley appointed a naval commission to investigate the explosion. In late March, the commission reported that a mine outside the ship had set off some of the ammunition in the *Maine's* magazines. The naval commission could not determine who had planted the mine, but many Americans already blamed Spain. (In 1976, a naval investigation concluded that spontaneous combustion of coal inside the ship was really the most likely cause of the whole disaster. But a National Geographic Society study in 1997 said that computer analysis pointed equally to an internal or external explosion as the cause.)

The letter from Dupuy de Lôme and the destruction of the *Maine* created momentum for war with Spain. That momentum increased when McKinley received messages through Senator Henry Cabot Lodge (1850–1924) and others that the business community finally supported military action by the United States to end the conflict. U.S. minister to Spain Stewart L. Woodford (1835–1913) spent April negotiating with Spain for peace, but his efforts may have been a mere formality. On April 21, 1898, McKinley ordered a naval blockade of Cuba and severed diplomatic relations with Spain. Four days later, Congress declared war on Spain and the country prepared to fight.

For More Information

Blow, Michael. *A Ship to Remember: The* Maine *and the Spanish-American War.* New York: William Morrow and Company, 1992.

Brown, Charles H. *The Correspondents' War: Journalists in the Spanish-American War.* New York: Charles Scribner's Sons, 1967.

Collins, Mary. *The Spanish-American War.* New York: Children's Press, 1998.

Dolan, Edward F. *The Spanish-American War.* Brookfield, CT: Millbrook Press, 2001.

Foner, Philip S. *The Spanish-Cuban-American War and the Birth of American Imperialism.* New York: Monthly Review Press, 1972.

Gay, Kathlyn, and Martin K. Gay. *Spanish American War*. New York: Twenty First Century Books, 1995.

Golay, Michael. *The Spanish-American War*. New York: Facts On File, , 1995.

Graves, Kerry A. *The Spanish-American War*. Mankato, MN: Capstone Books, 2001.

Langellier, John P. *Uncle Sam's Little Wars: The Spanish-American War, Philippine Insurrection, and Boxer Rebellion, 1898–1902*. Philadelphia, PA: Chelsea House, 2001.

Linderman, Gerald F. *The Mirror of War: American Society and the Spanish-American War*. Ann Arbor, MI: The University of Michigan Press, 1974.

Musicant, Ivan. *Empire by Default: The Spanish-American War and the Dawn of the American Century*. New York: Henry Holt and Company, 1998.

O'Toole, G. J. A. *The Spanish War: An American Epic–1898*. New York: W. W. Norton & Company, 1984.

Rosenfeld, Harvey. *Diary of a Dirty Little War: The Spanish-American War of 1898*. Westport, CT: Praeger Publishers, 2000.

Smith, Angel, and Emma Dávila-Cox, eds. *The Crisis of 1898: Colonial Redistribution and Nationalist Mobilization*. New York: St. Martin's Press, 1999.

Somerlott, Robert. *The Spanish-American War: Remember the Maine!* Berkeley Heights, NJ: Enslow Publishers, Inc., 2002.

Wukovits, John F. *The Spanish-American War*. San Diego, CA: Lucent Books, 2001.

Zinn, Howard. *A People's History of the United States: 1492–Present*. 20th anniversary ed. New York: HarperCollins, 1999.

Manila Bay and Assembling the U.S. Army

3

Spain had been fighting against a rebel Liberating Army in its colony of Cuba since 1895 when it came to war with the United States in April 1898. Spain's colonial empire then included the Caribbean islands of Cuba and Puerto Rico, the Pacific island of Guam, and the Asian islands of the Philippines. By the end of the Spanish-American War in August 1898, the United States had taken all but Cuba for itself and was officially in control of that island by early 1899. The United States prevailed thanks to the efforts of its navy and the Cuban Liberating Army, and in spite of many problems experienced by its own army.

Except for battles fought to conquer Native Americans, the United States had not been at war since the American Civil War (1861–65). In early 1898, the U.S. Army had only 28,000 soldiers, compared to the 180,000 regulars that Spain had stationed in Cuba. U.S. secretary of war Russell A. Alger (1836–1907), who oversaw the army, was still devising his plan of attack when war began. (The U.S. Department of Defense was called the Department of War until 1947; from 1947 until 1949, it was referred to as the Department of the Army.)

Spanish admiral Patricio Montojo y Pasarón, whose six-vessel squadron was soundly defeated by the U.S. squadron at Manila Bay on May 1, 1898. *Granger Collection. Reproduced by permission.*

The U.S. Navy, which was separate from the War Department and thus was disconnected from the army, was in better shape. In December 1889, Navy secretary Benjamin F. Tracy (1830–1915) issued an annual report that said naval war, "though defensive in principle, may be conducted most effectively by being offensive in its operations," according to Ivan Musicant in *Empire By Default.*

In 1890, Captain Alfred Thayer Mahan (1840–1914) published a book called *The Influence of Sea Power upon History, 1660–1783.* Mahan, then president of the U.S. Naval War College, argued that a strong navy with overseas bases was essential for the United States to open and protect foreign markets for goods manufactured at home. That year, the first U.S. Congress to spend one billion dollars used some of the money to add three new battleships, a cruiser, and a torpedo boat to the navy. When war came with Spain in 1898, the U.S. Navy was ready.

Battle of Manila Bay

U.S. president **William McKinley** (1843–1901; served 1897–1901; see entry in Biographies section) went to war on April 21, 1898, by ordering a naval blockade of Cuba and severing diplomatic relations with Spain. Cuba was the immediate source of the conflict. Spain's treatment of the colony had sparked a revolution on the island in February 1895. The United States meant to send the Spanish troops back to Europe and end the fighting, which was hurting American investment in and trade with the island.

On the other side of the world, Spain had just called a truce in December 1897 with rebels in the Philippines fighting for their own freedom. When the war with the United States began the following April, Spain still had a six-vessel

naval squadron deployed near the Philippines under the command of Admiral Patricio Montojo y Pasarón. Six hundred miles to the north, in British-ruled Hong Kong, U.S. commodore **George Dewey** (1837–1917; see entry in Biographies section) commanded the seven-vessel Asiatic Squadron aboard the flagship U.S.S. *Olympia.* Dewey had arrived in Hong Kong in March 1898, in case U.S. participation in the war in Cuba should require action against Montojo's fleet.

On April 24, 1898, U.S. Navy secretary John D. Long (1838–1915) sent a telegram to Dewey saying, "War has commenced between the United States and Spain. Proceed at once to Philippine Islands. Commence operations at once, particularly against Spanish fleet. You must capture vessels or destroy. Use utmost endeavors," according to Harvey Rosenfeld in *Diary of a Dirty Little War.* Three days later, the Asiatic Squadron began steaming toward Manila, the capital city of the Philippines on its large island of Luzon.

The Spanish warship *Reina Christina,* Admiral Montojo's flagship, was destroyed by U.S. commodore Dewey's squadron on May 1, 1898. *©Corbis. Reproduced by permission.*

Dewey's lookouts spotted Luzon on April 30. By the morning of May 1, his vessels were within one mile of the Manila shoreline in Manila Bay. Expecting to find Montojo's squadron guarding the capital city, Dewey was surprised to find it anchored instead at the nearby Cavite naval station. At 5:41 A.M. on May 1, after watching Spanish bombs fall short of his vessels, Dewey turned to the captain of the *Olympia* and said, "You may fire when you are ready, Gridley," according to Laurin Hall Healy and Luis Kutner in *The Admiral.*

The ensuing battle was very one-sided, for Dewey's ships carried fifty-three guns compared to Montojo's thirty-one. Montojo surrendered his wrecked vessels with around four hundred casualties (dead or severely wounded) less than seven hours after the battle began. Dewey's ships incurred little damage and his crews suffered few injuries. Historians say that not a single American died, but a newspaper reported that Dewey lost one man to heatstroke.

Anxious to send news of the victory to McKinley, Dewey sought Spain's permission to use the telegraph office in Manila. When the commander there refused, Dewey ordered his men to dredge the underwater telegraph cable from the bay floor and cut it. As a result, Dewey had to send a messenger by boat to telegraph Washington, D.C., from Hong Kong. Waiting anxiously amid unconfirmed reports from the Spanish capital of Madrid and elsewhere, McKinley finally received Dewey's victory announcement on May 7.

McKinley decided to seize the Philippines with an expeditionary force to be assembled and shipped out from San Francisco, California. According to Rosenfeld, Americans thought the Philippines would be a great base from which to prevent Japan from trying to take over Hawaii, which was an independent country at the time. (The United States ended up taking Hawaii for itself in July 1898.) Meanwhile, the United States was busy trying to scrounge together an army to fight in Cuba and Puerto Rico.

Assembling the U.S. Army

In February 1898, before the Spanish-American War began, McKinley proposed to some senators that the United States try to buy Cuba from Spain. When the senators rejected

the idea, McKinley told U.S. representative Joe Cannon on March 6, "I must have money to get ready for war. I am doing everything possible to prevent war, but it must come, and we are not prepared," according to Musicant. Two weeks later the U.S. minister to Spain, Stewart L. Woodford (1835–1913), wrote to McKinley, "I am thus, reluctantly, slowly, but entirely a convert to the early American ownership and occupation of the Island. If we recognize independence, we may turn the Island over to part of its inhabitants against the judgment of many of its most educated and wealthy residents.... If we have war we must finally occupy and ultimately own the Island," according to Philip Foner in *The Spanish-Cuban-American War and the Birth of American Imperialism.*

These designs set the stage for war with Spain. Publicly, the United States called its intervention a humanitarian effort to free Cuba from Spain's brutal control. But a large part of the motivation was America's effort to grow into a global economic powerhouse.

Crew members aboard the U.S.S *Raleigh* show off a Spanish warship gun captured at the battle of Manila Bay. *Courtesy of the Library of Congress.*

**U.S. minister to Spain
Stewart Woodford.** *Hulton
Archive/Getty Images.
Reproduced by permission.*

To get there, the United States needed an army. McKinley initially asked 125,000 American men to volunteer for military service to their country. One million answered the call. As Dewey defeated Montojo in the Philippines and word of the victory reached home, would-be soldiers crowded into recruiting offices and took physical examinations. By Monday, May 9, the army had plans to assemble a force of fifty to sixty thousand troops to attack Spain in Cuba. By the end of the month, it had designed a similar force for invading Puerto Rico. According to Rosenfeld, an army officer commented, "Napoleon took two years to get together transports for the…100,000 men which he proposed to invade England, and we were expected to get together transports for…50,000 men in two weeks."

The army for invading Cuba converged in Tampa, Florida, during the month of May. Assistant Secretary of the Navy **Theodore Roosevelt** (1858–1919; see entry in Biographies section) resigned from his office to become a lieutenant colonel in the army. He was a jingoist who scoffed at peace and celebrated war as manly and American. Roosevelt would lead a group of volunteers in the First U.S. Volunteer Regiment, which became known as the Rough Riders. According to Rosenfeld, the Rough Riders wrote a fight song that said, "Rough, tough, we're the stuff. We want to fight and we can't get enough."

Before the forces in Tampa could leave for Cuba, they had to be uniformed, armed, equipped, and trained. In this way, as in many others, the U.S. Army was terribly unprepared for war. Soldiers received heavy wool uniforms that were inappropriate for battle in tropical Cuba. Food arriving for meals included canned beef, some from bad batches that contained bits of gristle, rope, and dead maggots, according to Ivan Musicant in *Empire by Default*. African Americans volunteering to serve their country found that they were treated as second-class citizens; for example, they often could not receive service in Florida restaurants. Basic training emphasized long marches to harden bodies rather then drills and exercises in battle tactics, according to Gerald F. Linderman in *The Mirror of War*. Boredom spread and tempers flared as the troops waited over a month for the U.S. Navy to complete a blockade in Cuba that would eventually allow the army to leave for the island in late June.

Public opinion of the war

History books suggest that the American public was almost unanimous in supporting the Spanish-American War. According to Harvey Rosenfeld in *Diary of a Dirty Little War,* an article in the *New York Times* on May 18, 1898, said:

> It is a grand, patriotic impulse that unites [us]...for the dominant thought is that this is our country's war, 'our country—right or wrong.' It is this impulse, which does not [look back] for the establishment of the righteousness of our cause, that moves the majority...to uphold the action of the National Government.... The present generation has never witnessed such an outpouring of...patriotism.... Never before have the National colors been so profusely...displayed in city, town, and village ...[nor] the younger generation...so profoundly stirred by allusions to the country's cause.

Newspaper coverage of the war shaped public opinion greatly. During the Second Cuban Revolution, from 1895 to 1898, a circulation war between the *New York World* and the *New York Journal* had fed growing support for American intervention in Cuba. Early in May 1898, War Secretary Alger announced that 145 newspapers would receive passes for correspondents who wanted to cover the war alongside the U.S. Army. Journalists such as **Stephen Crane** (1871–1900; see entry in Primary Sources section) and **Richard Harding Davis** (1864–1916; see entry in Biographies section) joined illustrators such as Frederic Remington (1861–1909) to give Americans close-up accounts of the war. Small newspapers that could not afford to send correspondents used soldiers, who sent stories back for publication.

The antiwar sentiment

History books do not tell much of the antiwar element of public opinion. According to Michael Golay in *The*

"Tell Them I Died Like A Man "

On May 11, 1898, the United States suffered its first defeat in the Spanish-American War. That day, the Spanish fired upon and disabled the American torpedo boat *Winslow* after it entered the harbor at Cárdenas on the northwest coast of Cuba. Five Americans died in the fight. According to Harvey Rosenfeld in *Diary of a Dirty Little War*, *Winslow* fireman G. B. Meeks's last words were, "Tell them I died like a man." These words became a song that captured the nationalistic, masculine, and deadly aspects of war, as recorded by Rosenfeld:

On Cárdenas' *sunny bay*
In the thickest of the fray,
Was the Winslow, *fighting bravely, but in vain.*
For the foeman aimed too well
Every shot and every shell,
But still Yankee showed her teeth to Spain
Then we heard a sudden cry:

"Help us! Save us, or we die!"
Upon her deck had burst a murderous shell.
And we saw her heroes fall,
But above the noise and all
Came a moan from one poor lad as he fell.

Tell them I died like a man!
That I fell in the battle's van!
Tell them not to grieve or cry.
I was not afraid to die
'Twas my turn and I died like a man!

As we drew our boats away
Torn and bleeding there he lay—
By his side were other comrades gone to rest.
In the flag he loved so well
Did we wrap him where he fell.
And crossed his wounded hands upon his breast.
Ne'er again will call to arms
Summon him to war's alarms.
His soul has gone to seek its rest on high.
And when other heroes fall.
Answ'ring to their country's call.
That brave lad's words will cheer them as they die.

Spanish-American War, a cobbler in Kansas City hung a sign over his door that said, "Closed in memory of a Christian nation that descends to the barbarity of war." Rosenfeld tells of a Jewish man named Solomon Solis-Cohen, who opposed the war despite Spain's barbaric torture and murder of Jews during the Spanish Inquisition (1478–1834), saying, "If thine enemy hunger, give him food, and if he thirst give him to drink. The expulsion or ill-treatment of my fathers by…Spain gives me no right to murder Spaniards…even though I…march beneath a banner bearing stars and stripes."

Socialists—people who believe goods and property should be government owned and distributed instead of privately held—opposed the war in great numbers. Many of them felt that war benefits the rich and hurts the poor. Authorities in New York City prevented the Socialist Labor party from holding an antiwar parade on May 1, 1898. A socialist writing in the *Voice of Labor* said, "It is a terrible thing to think that the poor workers of this country should be sent to kill and wound the poor workers of Spain merely because a few leaders may incite them to do so," according to Howard Zinn in *A People's History of the United States.* Also according to Zinn, a labor leader named Bolton Hall told workers that war would only give them "the privilege of hating your Spanish fellow-workmen, who are really your brothers and who have had as little to do with the wrongs of Cuba as you have."

Some Americans even questioned whether the United States had good reason to act righteous (morally superior) compared to Spain. Referring to the weekly murder of African Americans by lynch mobs, Chaplain George W. Prioleau asked, "Is America any better than Spain?…Has [America] not subjects in her very midst who are murdered daily without a trial…whose children are half-fed and half-clothed, because their father's skin is black?," according to Rosenfeld. According to Zinn, the monthly journal of the International Association of Machinists resisted war before its outbreak, saying that the

> "…carnival of carnage that takes place every day, month and year in the realm of industry, the thousands of useful lives that are annually sacrificed to the Moloch of greed, the blood tribute paid by labor to capitalism, brings forth no shout for vengeance and reparation…. Death comes in thousands of instances in mill and mine, claims his victims, and no popular uproar is heard."

Still, young men marched off to war in Cuba, and their country cheered them on.

For More Information

Collins, Mary. *The Spanish-American War.* New York: Children's Press, 1998.

Dolan, Edward F. *The Spanish-American War.* Brookfield, CT: Millbrook Press, 2001.

Feuer, A. B. *The Spanish-American War at Sea.* Westport, CT: Praeger Publishers, 1995.

Foner, Philip S. *The Spanish-Cuban-American War and the Birth of American Imperialism.* New York: Monthly Review Press, 1972.

Gay, Kathlyn, and Martin K. Gay. *Spanish American War.* New York: Twenty First Century Books, 1995.

Golay, Michael. *The Spanish-American War.* New York: Facts On File, 1995.

Graves, Kerry A. *The Spanish-American War.* Mankato, MN: Capstone Books, 2001.

Langellier, John P. *Uncle Sam's Little Wars: The Spanish-American War, Philippine Insurrection, and Boxer Rebellion, 1898–1902.* Philadelphia, PA: Chelsea House, 2001.

Linderman, Gerald F. *The Mirror of War: American Society and the Spanish-American War.* Ann Arbor, MI: The University of Michigan Press, 1974.

Musicant, Ivan. *Empire by Default: The Spanish-American War and the Dawn of the American Century.* New York: Henry Holt and Company, 1998.

O'Toole, G. J. A. *The Spanish War: An American Epic–1898.* New York: W. W. Norton & Company, 1984.

Rosenfeld, Harvey. *Diary of a Dirty Little War: The Spanish-American War of 1898.* Westport, CT: Praeger Publishers, 2000.

Smith, Angel, and Emma Dávila-Cox, eds. *The Crisis of 1898: Colonial Redistribution and Nationalist Mobilization.* New York: St. Martin's Press, 1999.

Somerlott, Robert. *The Spanish-American War: Remember the Maine!* Berkeley Heights, NJ: Enslow Publishers, Inc., 2002.

Wukovits, John F. *The Spanish-American War.* San Diego, CA: Lucent Books, 2001.

Zinn, Howard. *A People's History of the United States: 1492–Present.* 20th anniversary ed. New York: HarperCollins, 1999.

The Siege at Cuba

4

The Spanish-American War (April–August 1898) began on April 21, 1898, when the United States decided to fight Spain for control of the Spanish colony of Cuba. Rebels on the island of Cuba had been fighting the Spanish army since February 1895 for freedom from Spain and the right to govern themselves. The Spanish tactic of relocating civilians into crowded concentration camps to prevent them from helping the rebels was killing hundreds of thousands of innocent Cubans through disease and starvation. And the Cuban Liberating Army's tactic of burning sugarcane fields and mills was destroying the island's economy, in which American businesses had invested $50 million. America eventually decided it had to intervene to protect its financial interests and the welfare of the Cuban people.

War strategy

Before the war began, the United States had planned to coordinate its military strategy with the Cuban Liberating Army. On April 9, 1898, U.S. war secretary Russell A. Alger (1836–1907) and U.S. Army general Nelson A. Miles (1839–

1925) sent Lieutenant Andrew S. Rowan on a mission to find Cuban general **Calixto García** (1839–1898; see entry in Primary Sources section). With assistance from rebels in Jamaica and on Cuba, Rowan found García in Bayamo, Cuba, on May 1, 1898. That same day, Commodore **George Dewey** (1837–1917; see entry in Biographies section) defeated a Spanish squadron in a naval battle at Manila Bay in the Philippines, giving the United States its first big victory.

After meeting with Rowan, García sent him back to Washington, D.C., with Cuban officers, maps, and military data. In a memorandum to Secretary Alger, García welcomed coordination with the U.S. Army. In a letter to Cuban general **Máximo Gómez y Báez** (1836–1905; see entry in Biographies section) on May 11, García said he had asked the United States to land troops on the northern coast of the island, along with arms and ammunition. That strategy would allow both armies to conduct joint operations designed to capture the city of Holguín in the province of Oriente in the eastern half of the island. From there, Cuba and the United States could make plans for defeating Spain in its strongholds in the west.

During the month of May, the United States assembled an army in Florida and other locations for its assault on Spain. When the war began, the U.S. Army had only 28,000 regular soldiers, compared to Spain's 180,000 military personnel in Cuba. Newly enlisted troops and volunteers would have to make up the difference needed for victory; as it turned out, more than one million men answered U.S. president **William McKinley's** (1843–1901; served 1897–1901; see entry in Biographies section) request for volunteers.

While the army prepared to do battle, two U.S. naval squadrons, led by Admiral William T. Sampson (1840–1902) and Commodore Winfield S. Schley (1839–1909), set out to form a blockade in Cuba. Spanish admiral **Pascual Cervera y Topete** (1839–1909; see entry in Biographies section) and his six-vessel fleet had sailed from the Cape Verde Islands south of Spain on April 29 for an unknown destination. This gave rise to fears that Cervera might be headed to bombard cities on America's eastern coast. The U.S. Navy eased tensions somewhat by sending vessels to defend major eastern ports, such as Portland, Maine, and by forming a squadron of fast vessels to patrol the East Coast.

Hobson the Hero

On May 19, 1898, a six-vessel Spanish fleet led by Admiral Pascual Cervera y Topete (1839–1909) sailed into harbor at Santiago de Cuba near the southeastern edge of the island. Richmond P. Hobson, a U.S. naval constructor, devised a plan to trap Cervera's fleet there. Hobson proposed to take six other men on the U.S.S. *Merrimac* and sink it in the narrowest part of the harbor, leaving Cervera no room for escape. The men planned to escape the sinking ship in a dinghy—a small boat—to be rescued by the warship *New York*.

Hobson wished to attempt the feat during daylight to navigate to the right position in the harbor. Admiral William T. Sampson (1840–1902), who commanded the U.S. Navy in Cuba, insisted that Hobson go at night to make detection more difficult. Shortly after midnight on June 3, Hobson and his crew began steaming through the harbor in the *Merrimac*. The men had cords tied to them so that by pulling on the cords at the right moment, Hobson could signal when to drop the anchors, flood the hull, and detonate the torpedoes that would sink the boat. As the crew approached its destination, it shut off the *Merrimac's* engines so the ship would glide into place.

Moments later, gunfire erupted from a small Spanish boat and from nearby forts, attacking the *Merrimac* under the light of the moon. Hobson tugged on cords amid the hostile fire and shouted instructions to bring the boat down. The surprise attack, however, prevented things from going as planned, and the *Merrimac* floated past the narrow part of the harbor before sinking where it would be ineffective as a blockade.

When daylight arrived, Cervera picked up Hobson and his men, who had survived and spent the night in their dinghy. Cervera applauded the crew's bravery and offered to exchange them for Spanish prisoners-of-war being held by the United States. Perhaps because the Americans had valuable information about harbor mines that had exploded during the event, Spain did not complete the exchange until after the U.S. Navy defeated Cervera's squadron on July 3. After being released, Hobson said Cervera called his feat "one of the most daring acts in naval history," according to Harvey Rosenfeld in *Diary of a Dirty Little War*.

Unbeknownst to the United States, Cervera's fleet was not in good working order, so the fifty-nine-year-old sailor wished to avoid the U.S. Navy. Steaming around the Caribbean Sea for a couple of weeks, Cervera avoided Sampson and Schley and slipped into port at Santiago de

U.S. troops landing at Daiquirí, June 22, 1898.
Granger Collection. Reproduced by permission.

Cuba on the southeast coast of the island on May 19. After Sampson and Schley set up a blockade to keep Cervera there, the U.S. Army decided to land troops near Santiago for their initial assault on the island. The change of plans disrupted coordination with General Gómez, who was expecting the United States to land somewhere on the other side of the island. This confusion set the stage for an American military effort that used and abused the Cuban Liberating Army.

Las Guásimas

On June 7, 1898, General Miles ordered General **William R. Shafter** (1835–1906; see entry in Biographies section) to board American transport vessels with troops enlisted in the Fifth Army Corps in Tampa, Florida. The V Corps, as the army called Shafter's men, broke camp and headed for the Tampa port. Regiments there fought with each other to get on the limited number of available transports—thirty-two vessels that could carry only sixteen thousand passengers plus horses, wagons, ambulances, and artillery. Fist fights and gun threats between fellow soldiers suggested the futility of trying to make peace in Cuba with war.

The V Corps sailed for Cuba one week later. A smaller U.S. expedition was then battling Spain at Guantánamo on the southeastern tip of the island. An American victory in that battle made landing there a safe bet. Upon conferring with García and Sampson, however, Shafter decided to land near Daiquirí twelve miles southeast of the stronghold at Santiago. Disembarking near Daiquirí would shorten the tough march to Santiago and also make it easier for García's forces to guard their American allies.

On June 22, the U.S. Navy bombed suspected Spanish defenses near the planned landing point. When Cuban rebels signaled that the Spanish had retreated, the V Corps began to disembark and assemble on the shore. The troops made their landing free of enemy fire thanks to protection from U.S. vessels at sea and Cuban rebels on land. Exploration revealed that the Spanish forces had burned and deserted not only Daiquirí but also the port city of Siboney, further up the coast, where more U.S. troops landed on June 23.

During the second day of landing, the V Corps discovered that Spain had retreated toward Santiago to an area called Las Guásimas. General Joseph Wheeler (1836–1906), a Confederate (Southern) general during the American Civil War (1861–65), commanded the U.S. cavalry division—troops who typically served on horses but fought in Cuba on foot because space restrictions had forced them to leave most of their horses in Tampa. Wheeler ordered an attack on Las Guásimas for June 24.

U.S. general Joseph Wheeler commanded the U.S. cavalry division. ©*Medford Historical Collection/CORBIS. Reproduced by permission.*

Members of African American volunteer units fighting at the Battle of Las Guásimas, June 24, 1898.
Hulton Archive/Getty Images. Reproduced by permission.

That morning, Wheeler led a regular army regiment along the main road to Las Guásimas, while American officers Colonel Leonard Wood (1860–1927) and Lieutenant Colonel **Theodore Roosevelt** (1858–1919; see entry in Biographies section) led the 1st U.S. Volunteer Cavalry—known as the Rough Riders—through the dense woods parallel to the road. Some Cubans went along as guards, but Cuban colonel González Clavell refused to send his troops on the mission, for he believed it was not carefully planned and was unnecessary for capturing Santiago. When deadly gunfire erupted, the reality of war set in as soldiers fell to the ground, injured or dead.

As it had done in its battles with the Cuban rebels since 1895, however, Spain retreated as soon as the U.S. Army reached its battle lines. According to Michael Golay in *The Spanish-American War*, Wheeler greeted the retreat by yelling, "We've got the damn Yankees on the run!" When the fight was over, the United States had sixteen casualties and fifty-two soldiers wounded, while Spain suffered ten fatalities and twenty-five wounded.

American news correspondents on the scene called the Cubans cowards for not participating in the battle. According to Philip Foner in *The Spanish-Cuban-American War and the Birth of American Imperialism,* however, Spain was retreating all the way to Santiago, so Clavell had been right that the dangerous, deadly ambush was unnecessary. An American Civil War veteran agreed with the Cuban general in a letter published in the *New York Times,* condemning the ambush as foolishly executed.

El Caney and San Juan Heights

Spain now dug in its heels at El Caney and San Juan Heights, its last defenses separating the U.S. and Cuban armies from Santiago. The American troops spent one week resting, restocking supplies and ammunition, and discussing plans. Then, at 6:30 A.M. on July 1, General Henry Lawton (1843–1899) and his division of 5,400 troops began an assault on El Caney. Although Lawton expected to capture the village in two hours, he had severely underestimated the difficulty of the task.

The attack on El Caney began on July 1 with U.S. general Henry Lawton and his division of 5,400 troops. *Hulton Archive/Getty Images. Reproduced by permission.*

Just hours into the El Caney charge, General Shafter ordered Wheeler and General Jacob Kent to begin attacking San Juan Heights. In this battle, Roosevelt's Rough Riders joined with African American soldiers in the 9th and 10th Cavalries for a famous charge up Kettle Hill (which got its name from a large iron sugar mill pot sitting atop it).

The battle was bloody and deadly. A balloon used by the U.S. Army to survey the situation made it easy for the Spaniards to know where to fire at the American and Cuban armies. Black powder clouds from the American soldiers's rifles added to this problem. By the time the United States had won the battle after eleven hours of killing, 205 of its troops were dead and 1,180 were wounded. For Spain, 215 were dead and 376 were wounded.

Americans again blamed the Cubans for failing to help in the effort, accusing them of watching the battle from a nearby hill. Foner counters these charges by noting that a contingent of twelve hundred Cubans helped General Adna R. Chaffee open the road to El Caney. General Clavell's contingent also participated in the attack, and rebels under General García's command helped with the final push to take El Caney. Other Cubans staked out positions north of Santiago to prevent Spain from sending reinforcements.

U.S. general Jacob Kent led his troops at the Battle of San Juan Heights. *Hulton Archive/Getty Images. Reproduced by permission.*

The Battle of Santiago Harbor

After the battle of San Juan Heights, Santiago and Admiral Cervera's fleet were all that stood between the United States and victory in Cuba. Admiral Sampson and General Shafter disagreed on how to proceed, however. Shafter wanted the navy to steam into the harbor and take out Cervera's fleet before the army stormed Santiago. This strategy would deprive the troops in Santiago of support from the guns onboard the Spanish vessels.

Sampson, on the other hand, wanted the army to storm Santiago first. He did not think it was safe for the navy to go into the harbor to take out Cervera's fleet. Mines in the harbor might destroy his vessels before they ever reached Cervera. According to Golay, naval officer Alfred Mahan summed up Sampson's thinking when he wrote, "If we lost ten thousand men, the country could replace them; if we lost a battleship, it could not be replaced."

On the Spanish side, a similar argument existed between Cervera and the Spanish military commander, Ramón

Blanco y Arenas (1831–1906). Blanco wanted the Spanish navy to leave port and try to escape Sampson and Schley's blockade. Cervera knew his fleet would not survive the effort, but Blanco felt it was better for morale and the honor of Spain to lose in battle than to be destroyed at anchor.

Blanco prevailed by ordering Cervera to make the run. On the morning of July 3, Cervera's fleet began to steam out of the harbor. Sampson was aboard the flagship *New York,* headed for a meeting with Shafter in Daiquirí. That left Commodore Schley responsible for preventing Cervera's escape.

Sampson had left orders for the Americans to rush Cervera's fleet to prevent it from escaping the harbor. When this tactic failed, the battle turned into a race along the Cuban coastline. Schley commanded thirteen vessels to Cervera's six, which moved slowly due to marine growth on their bottoms. Over the course of four hours, between 9:00 A.M. and 1:00 P.M., the American vessels overtook the Spanish ships and either destroyed them or bombed them into surrendering. Ironically, the last vessel to be defeated was the *Cristóbal Colon,* named for the Italian explorer (Christopher Columbus, 1451–1506) who claimed Cuba for Spain during his famous voyage of 1492.

The cold numbers of the battle made it look like a nice victory for Schley. The United States lost only one soldier, Yeoman George H. Ellis, while killing 323 Spaniards and capturing 1,800 prisoners.

Under the command of Commodore Winfield S. Schley, the U.S. naval squadron captured or destroyed all of the Spanish naval squadron involved in the Battle of Santiago Bay on July 3, 1898. *Hulton Archive/Getty Images. Reproduced by permission.*

Surrender in Cuba

The naval victory at Santiago put the United States in position to end the entire war. General Shafter asked the Spanish commander in Santiago, José Torál, to surrender.

Torál, however, refused, saying Spain would defend its honor by fighting to the death. Torál actually was waiting for four thousand reinforcements to arrive at Santiago from the west.

After more fighting and bombardment by the U.S. Navy over the next couple weeks, Torál finally agreed to surrender. He offered the United States not only Santiago but also all of the troops under his command, numbering around twelve thousand in the region surrounding the city. Shafter, Wheeler, and others attended a formal ceremony with Torál on Sunday, July 17. Later battles on Puerto Rico would bring the entire war to an end the following month.

America insulted the Cuban Liberating Army yet again during the surrender process. Shafter excluded the Cubans from negotiations and the ceremony on July 17. President William McKinley ordered that after victory, Spanish laws and public officials would remain in place until a new government could be set up. After fighting a revolution for three years and helping the United States win the war, the Cubans found themselves still governed, if only temporarily, by the very people they had fought to overthrow.

For More Information

Collins, Mary. *The Spanish-American War.* New York: Children's Press, 1998.

Dolan, Edward F. *The Spanish-American War.* Brookfield, CT: Millbrook Press, 2001.

Feuer, A. B. *The Santiago Campaign of 1898.* Westport, CT: Praeger Publishers, 1993.

Feuer, A. B. *The Spanish-American War at Sea.* Westport, CT: Praeger Publishers, 1995.

Foner, Philip S. *The Spanish-Cuban-American War and the Birth of American Imperialism.* New York: Monthly Review Press, 1972.

Gay, Kathlyn, and Martin K. Gay. *Spanish American War.* New York: Twenty First Century Books, 1995.

Golay, Michael. *The Spanish-American War.* New York: Facts On File, Inc., 1995.

Graves, Kerry A. *The Spanish-American War.* Mankato, MN: Capstone Books, 2001.

Langellier, John P. *Uncle Sam's Little Wars: The Spanish-American War, Philippine Insurrection, and Boxer Rebellion, 1898–1902.* Philadelphia, PA: Chelsea House, 2001.

Linderman, Gerald F. *The Mirror of War: American Society and the Spanish-American War.* Ann Arbor, MI: The University of Michigan Press, 1974.

Musicant, Ivan. *Empire by Default: The Spanish-American War and the Dawn of the American Century.* New York: Henry Holt and Company, 1998.

O'Toole, G. J. A. *The Spanish War: An American Epic–1898.* New York: W. W. Norton & Company, 1984.

Rosenfeld, Harvey. *Diary of a Dirty Little War: The Spanish-American War of 1898.* Westport, CT: Praeger Publishers, 2000.

Smith, Angel, and Emma Dávila-Cox, eds. *The Crisis of 1898: Colonial Redistribution and Nationalist Mobilization.* New York: St. Martin's Press,1999.

Somerlott, Robert. *The Spanish-American War: Remember the Maine!* Berkeley Heights, NJ: Enslow Publishers, Inc., 2002.

Wukovits, John F. *The Spanish-American War.* San Diego, CA: Lucent Books, 2001.

Zinn, Howard. *A People's History of the United States: 1492–Present.* 20th anniversary ed. New York: HarperCollins, 1999.

Guam, Puerto Rico, and the Philippines

The Spanish-American War began on April 21, 1898, when the United States decided to fight Spain for control of the Spanish colony of Cuba. Rebels had been fighting there since 1895 for independence from Spain. In April 1898, the United States declared war on Spain to end the revolution, which was hurting American business on the island. The United States said it wanted to secure freedom for Cuban civilians, who were dying by the hundreds of thousands in Spanish concentration camps. Many Americans, however, wanted to acquire Cuba and its rich farming economy.

What began as a war over Cuba, however, turned into an American campaign to strip Spain of its overseas colonies. In 1898, besides Cuba, the Spanish government controlled Guam, Puerto Rico, and the Philippines. Guam, a small island east of the Philippines in the Pacific Ocean, was interesting to the United States and European countries as a potential spot for military bases. Puerto Rico, southeast of Cuba in the Caribbean Sea, had a small agricultural economy. The Philippines, a collection of more than seven thousand islands south of China in the Pacific Ocean, had a rebel population that, like the Cubans, wanted freedom from Spain. America's war with Spain in 1898 took its military to each of these colonies.

The Philippines

The war's first major battle was fought in Manila Bay in the Philippines on May 1, 1898. Spanish admiral Patricio Montojo y Pasarón captained a six-vessel fleet that had opposed a Filipino revolution in 1897. When the United States declared war, U.S. naval secretary John D. Long (1838–1915) ordered U.S. commodore **George Dewey** (1837–1917; see entry in Biographies section) to sail from Hong Kong to Manila Bay with his seven-vessel Asiatic Squadron. Finding Montojo's fleet at anchor there, Dewey destroyed it in just a few hours on the morning of May 1.

In the wake of this early victory, U.S. president **William McKinley** (1843–1901; served 1897–1901; see entry in Biographies section) decided to maintain control of the Philippines until the war was over. The U.S. Army assembled an expedition to join Dewey and help him take the city of Manila. Commanded by Brigadier General Thomas Anderson, the expedition embarked from San Francisco, California, on May 25, 1898.

Guam

When Anderson left San Francisco, he had twenty-five hundred troops and four hundred tons of ammunition aboard three vessels—*City of Pekin, City of Sydney,* and *Australia.* When the expedition stopped in Honolulu, Hawaii, to get coal for its engines, the *Charleston* joined it for the voyage. By then, Captain Henry Glass of the *Charleston* had received orders to seize Guam on his way to the Philippines.

Glass's fleet arrived at Guam the morning of June 20. The Americans expected to find Spain ready to fight at the capital of Agaña and the harbor of San Luis D'Apra. Instead, Agaña was undefended and the forts at San Luis D'Apra were abandoned. When the fleet sailed into harbor and fired a few shots, Spain sent the port captain on a boat to speak with the Americans.

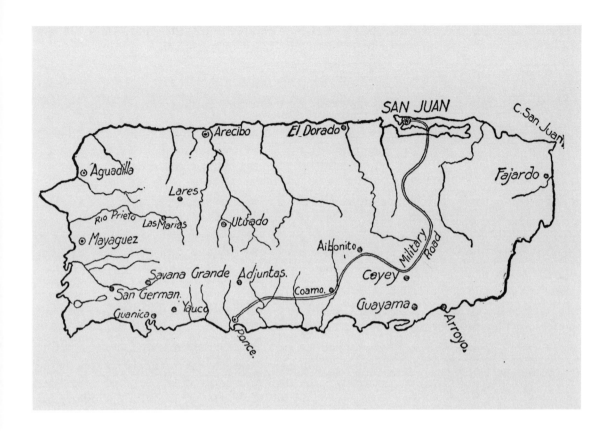

The Spaniard told Captain Glass that Guam did not know Spain was at war. Glass replied that the captain and his men were now prisoners-of-war and asked them to return to port to request a surrender by Guam's governor, Lieutenant Colonel Juan Marina.

Marina surrendered the next day because Guam lacked any ability to defend itself. Glass's expedition raised the American flag over Fort Santa Cruz and took Spain's military personnel aboard the *City of Sydney* as prisoners. Leaving behind a small occupation force, the expedition steamed back out of the harbor and headed for the Philippines.

Puerto Rico

Over the next two days, June 22 and 23, the U.S. Army landed on the southern coast of Cuba, east of the city of Santiago. Spanish admiral **Pascual Cervera y Topete**

Admiral William T. Sampson (1840–1902)

William T. Sampson was the officer in charge of the U.S. Navy in Cuba during the Spanish-American War. Born in Palmyra, New York, on February 9, 1840, Sampson did well enough in school to attend the U.S. Naval Academy. He graduated there first in his class in 1861.

Sampson served in the American Civil War (1861–65) aboard the monitor *Patapsco*. He was on the vessel's turret—armored gun—when the vessel exploded while removing mines in Charleston Harbor, South Carolina, on January 15, 1865. After the war, Sampson completed many successful assignments before becoming captain of the battleship *Iowa* in the North Atlantic squadron in 1897.

In January 1898, tensions between Spain and the United States over Spain's colony of Cuba were approaching the boiling point. America had $50 million invested in business on the island. Spain's three-year war with Cuban rebels seeking independence was destroying business. Late that month, the United States sent the warship *Maine* to Havana, Cuba, to pressure Spain to end the conflict.

Anchored in Havana harbor on February 15, 1898, the *Maine* blew up, killing more than 250 people onboard.

Many Americans suspected the Spanish were to blame. U.S. Navy secretary John D. Long (1838–1915) appointed Sampson to preside over a court of inquiry to determine the cause of the disaster. Sampson, who paid great attention to detail, finally signed the court's report on March 25. The report concluded that an external mine had detonated ammunition in the *Maine's* magazines. Sampson could not determine, however, who had planted the mine.

The United States was at war with Spain less than one month later. Because the commander of the North Atlantic squadron was recovering from illness, Long elevated Sampson to the post. On April 21, Sampson received orders to use the North Atlantic squadron to form a blockade at Cuba to prevent Spain from arriving there with a squadron of its own.

The blockade failed; Admiral Pascual Cervera y Topete (1839–1909) slipped into harbor at Santiago, Cuba, on May 19, 1898. Sampson quickly used his fleets to set up a blockade outside the harbor. The navy then protected the U.S. Army as it landed troops at Daiquirí and Siboney near Santiago on June 22 and June 23. Between then and July 1, the army marched and battled Spanish troops until it seized San

(1839–1909; see entry in Biographies section) was in port at Santiago, trapped there by U.S. Navy squadrons under the command of Admiral William T. Sampson (1840–1902). Cervera's fleet was Spain's main naval defense in Cuba.

William Sampson. *Hulton Archive/Getty Images. Reproduced by permission.*

Juan Heights and was in position to attack Santiago.

In danger of being captured while at anchor, Cervera received orders to leave port and run past Sampson's blockade. On July 2, Sampson's fleet saw smoke on the horizon, suggesting that Cervera's fleet was firing up its engines. That did not stop Sampson from leaving the blockade and heading east on the flagship *New York* for a meeting with U.S. Army commander General William R. Shafter (1835–1906) on July 3. As a result, Sampson was seven miles

away when Cervera's fleet appeared at the mouth of Santiago harbor that day.

Following orders that Sampson left behind, Commodore Winfield S. Schley (1839–1909) led the navy to victory over Cervera's fleet. Sampson heard the battle and turned the *New York* around to try to join it. Although he received fire from Spanish forts, Sampson never reached the battle, which had been a race westward along the Cuban coast.

After the last Spanish vessel surrendered, Schley signaled Sampson with the message, "A glorious victory has been achieved. Details later," according to Michael Golay in *The Spanish-American War.* Sampson replied with the stern command, "Report your casualties." In fact, one American had died.

Sampson's terse response to Schley's news foreshadowed a conflict between the two men. When Sampson telegraphed Washington, D.C., to report the victory, Americans disagreed over whether Sampson or Schley deserved the credit. Senior naval officers tended to say Sampson deserved the credit as head of the squadron. Schley observed that if the navy had lost the battle, there would have been no question that he was to blame.

By the end of the day on July 1, General **William R. Shafter**'s (1835–1906; see entry in Biographies section) troops had fought their way to San Juan Heights, just outside Santiago. On July 3, Sampson defeated Cervera's fleet as it tried to

General Nelson A. Miles commanded the war effort for the United States against Spain in Puerto Rico.

escape the blockade. The Spanish army surrendered at Santiago two weeks later because further defense of the island seemed futile.

General Nelson A. Miles (1839–1925), who commanded the war effort for the United States, decided to lead an expedition against Spain in Puerto Rico, one of Spain's colonies. Miles wanted to improve the army's image after the sloppy campaign in Santiago, where General Shafter had faced supply and disease problems while losing hundreds of American lives in poorly planned attacks.

On July 25, over one week after the surrender at Santiago, American troops landed on the southern coast of Puerto Rico at Guánica. The Spanish army quickly surrendered the town and fled toward the capital of San Juan. Spain meant to mount its final stand there on the northeastern coast of the island.

The United States landed a force of fifteen thousand men on Puerto Rico. Miles organized the troops into four columns to march northward toward San Juan from different points on the island. The march resulted in six primary battles from August 9 to August 12. On the twelfth, Miles learned that the United States and Spain had signed a peace agreement, so he called a cease-fire.

Peace protocol

The United States began suggesting terms for a truce as early as June 3. That day, U.S. president McKinley demanded that Spain give up Cuba, Puerto Rico, a port in the Philippines, and a port in the Ladrone (also called Marianas) Islands in the Pacific Ocean. McKinley raised the stakes by the end of July by asking for the entire island of Guam. He also asked Spain to give the United States the port and city of Manila until treaty negotiations decided the fate of the Philippines. Under McKinley's offer, treaty negotiations would begin in Paris no later than October 1.

Spain refused to consider these terms at first. By August, however, the United States had the military advantage in Cuba, Guam, and the Philippines, and was advancing on San Juan in Puerto Rico. The Spanish government feared the United States might even send a naval fleet to attack Spain itself in Europe. Under pressure, the government of Premier Práxedes Mateo Sagasta (1825–1903) approved the peace protocol on August 12 to temporarily end hostilities until the signing of a formal treaty, which happened on December 10. U.S. secretary of state William R. Day (1849–1923) and French ambassador Jules Cambon (who had permission to act for Spain) signed the agreement in Washington, D.C., on August 12, 1898.

General Wesley Merritt commanded the U.S. Army in the Philippines. *Courtesy of the Library of Congress.*

Fighting continues in the Philippines

After seizing Guam on June 21, 1898, Captain Henry Glass's expedition continued its mission, reaching Manila in the Philippines in late June. By then, Filipino rebels had declared independence from Spain and were attacking the Spaniards to capture the province surrounding the capital city. By the end of the month, General Wesley Merritt (1836–1910), who commanded the U.S. Army in the Philippines, had eleven thousand troops ready for attack.

The Filipino rebels presented a problem for the United States. After Dewey captured Manila Bay on May 1, he welcomed rebel assistance because he lacked the forces to attack Spain in Manila. Once Glass's transports reached the Philippines, however, McKinley decided to capture the city of Manila without assistance from the rebels. Pushing the rebels

Emilio Aguinaldo

Emilio Aguinaldo (1869–1964) was a revolutionary leader in the Philippines. Born there on March 23, 1869, Aguinaldo grew up in Cavite and went to college in the capital city of Manila at the University of Santo Tomás. In August 1896, Aguinaldo became the mayor of his hometown. Around that time he also served as leader of Katipunan, a group that fought for independence from Spain, which controlled the Philippines as a colony.

Spain and the rebels signed an agreement to end the revolution in December 1897. In return for governmental reform and a monetary payment, Aguinaldo agreed to be exiled with other rebel leaders. Aguinaldo left his homeland to live in nearby Hong Kong and Singapore.

Months later, in April 1898, war broke out between Spain and the United States over Spain's treatment of its colony of Cuba. Spanish Admiral Patricio Montojo y Pasarón was then in Manila Bay with a six-vessel fleet that Spain had used to fight the Filipino rebels. U.S. commodore George Dewey's (1837–1917) seven-vessel fleet in nearby Hong Kong would soon sail to defeat Montojo.

Before Dewey left, U.S. consul general E. Spencer Pratt contacted Aguinaldo in Singapore, asking him to organize his rebels to attack Spain in Manila. Aguinaldo asked what the Filipinos would get in return. According to Ivan Musicant in *Empire by Default,* Pratt's response led Aguinaldo to believe that the United States would support independence for the Philippines.

Dewey defeated Montojo easily on May 1, 1898. At the urging of his fellow rebels, Aguinaldo returned to Manila on May 19 on the American warship *McCulloch.* There he met with Dewey, who told Aguinaldo to "go ashore and start your army," according to Musicant. Also according to Musicant, Dewey told Aguinaldo, "America is exceedingly well off as regards territory, revenue and resources and, therefore needs no colonies."

Aguinaldo organized the rebels to capture the province of Cavite around Manila before attacking the city. On June 12 the Filipinos declared independence, an action later ratified—meaning approved—by a formal assembly of Filipino rebels in September.

By late July, Aguinaldo wondered whether the United States would really support independence for his country. According to Harvey Rosenfeld in *Diary of a Dirty Little War,* Aguinaldo wrote a letter to U.S. consul general Rounsvelle Wildmand that foreshadowed his future war with the United States:

> *I have read in the* [New York Evening] Journal *that I am getting the*

Emilio Aguinaldo. *Hulton Archive/Getty Images. Reproduced by permission.*

'big head' and not behaving as I promised you. In reply I ask, 'Why should America expect me to outline my policy, present and future, and fight blindly for her interests when America will not be frank with me?' Tell me this: Am I fighting for annexation, protection, or independence? It is for America to say, not me.

I can take Manila as I have defeated the Spanish everywhere, but what would be the use? If America takes Manila, I can save my men and arms for what the future has in store for me. Now, good friend, believe me, I am not both fool and rogue. The interests of my people are as sacred to me as are the interests of your people to you.

After fighting with Spain ended in August 1898, the United States decided to keep the Philippines for itself. U.S. president William McKinley (1843–1901) expressed the misinformed opinion that the Filipinos needed to be Christianized before they could govern themselves. America's desire to open foreign markets for its manufactured goods also influenced the president's decision.

American domination in the Philippines led to revolution again, however. In January 1899, Filipino rebels set up a republic by adopting a constitution. They then elected Aguinaldo president of their new government.

Fighting broke out with the United States the following month. Aguinaldo declared war and fled with the Filipino government north of Manila, which U.S. forces controlled. From there, the rebels waged a bloody guerilla war—a military tactic involving hit-and-run attacks from hidden positions. The United States captured Aguinaldo in March 1901 and forced him to take an oath of allegiance to the United States. Fighting continued, however, until the rebels agreed to a cease-fire in April of 1902.

The United States controlled the Philippines until finally giving the Filipinos their independence in 1946. Aguinaldo worked on veterans' affairs, democracy, and foreign relations issues throughout the years before dying on February 6, 1964.

from the trenches, U.S. forces commenced fighting against Spain when Spanish soldiers opened fire on July 31. Small battles continued over the next few days.

On August 6, the United States demanded that Spanish commander General Fermín Jaudenes y Alvarez surrender his troops in Manila. With Dewey's fleet in Manila Bay, there was no way Jaudenes could hope to win. Pride, however, prevented the commander from giving up without the appearance of a real fight. Jaudenes said he would surrender only after staging a fake battle, and only if the United States would prevent rebel forces from coming into Manila afterwards.

Merritt and Dewey agreed to the proposal. On August 13, unaware that Spain and the United States had signed the peace protocol in Washington, D.C., the day before, Dewey bombarded a Spanish fort while Merritt and Jaudenes's troops exchanged fire. (Unable to secure Spanish permission to use the telegraph cable at Manila for sending news of his victory on May 1, Dewey had dredged up the cable from the harbor floor and cut it. Because Dewey had cut the telegraph cable, nobody in the Philippines yet knew of the cease-fire.)

Six Americans and many Spaniards died in the fake battle. Jaudenes signed surrender papers the next day, and two days later a boat arrived from Hong Kong with news that the war was over. Treaty negotiations that October would decide the fate of the Philippines.

For More Information

Collins, Mary. *The Spanish-American War.* New York: Children's Press, 1998.

Dolan, Edward F. *The Spanish-American War.* Brookfield, CT: Millbrook Press, 2001.

Feuer, A. B. *The Santiago Campaign of 1898.* Westport, CT: Praeger Publishers, 1993.

Feuer, A. B. *The Spanish-American War at Sea.* Westport, CT: Praeger Publishers, 1995.

Foner, Philip S. *The Spanish-Cuban-American War and the Birth of American Imperialism.* New York: Monthly Review Press, 1972.

Gay, Kathlyn, and Martin K. Gay. *Spanish American War.* New York: Twenty First Century Books, 1995.

Golay, Michael. *The Spanish-American War.* New York: Facts On File, 1995.

Graves, Kerry A. *The Spanish-American War.* Mankato, MN: Capstone Books, 2001.

Langellier, John P. *Uncle Sam's Little Wars: The Spanish-American War, Philippine Insurrection, and Boxer Rebellion, 1898–1902.* Philadelphia, PA: Chelsea House, 2001.

Linderman, Gerald F. *The Mirror of War: American Society and the Spanish-American War.* Ann Arbor, MI: The University of Michigan Press, 1974.

Musicant, Ivan. *Empire by Default: The Spanish-American War and the Dawn of the American Century.* New York: Henry Holt and Company, 1998.

O'Toole, G. J. A. *The Spanish War: An American Epic–1898.* New York: W. W. Norton & Company, 1984.

Rosenfeld, Harvey. *Diary of a Dirty Little War: The Spanish-American War of 1898.* Westport, CT: Praeger Publishers, 2000.

Smith, Angel, and Emma Dávila-Cox, eds. *The Crisis of 1898: Colonial Redistribution and Nationalist Mobilization.* New York: St. Martin's Press, 1999.

Somerlott, Robert. *The Spanish-American War: Remember the Maine!* Berkeley Heights, NJ: Enslow Publishers, Inc., 2002.

Wukovits, John F. *The Spanish-American War.* San Diego, CA: Lucent Books, 2001.

Zinn, Howard. *A People's History of the United States: 1492–Present.* 20th anniversary ed. New York: HarperCollins.

Treaty and Imperialism

The Spanish-American War began on April 21, 1898, when the United States decided to fight Spain for control of the Spanish colony of Cuba. Though it initially stayed out of the conflict between Spain and Cuba, the United States eventually decided it had to intervene to protect its financial interests in Cuba and the welfare of the Cuban people, who were being severely mistreated at the hands of the Spanish.

When the United States went to war with Spain, Cuba had a thriving economy based primarily on sugarcane, tobacco, and coffee production. Americans had $50 million invested in businesses on the island. Such interests were the primary reason the United States intervened in the Cuban revolution.

A shift to imperialism

Imperialism is the act of controlling people in foreign lands. The United States of America owed its very existence to the spirit of anti-imperialism. In 1776, white men from thir-

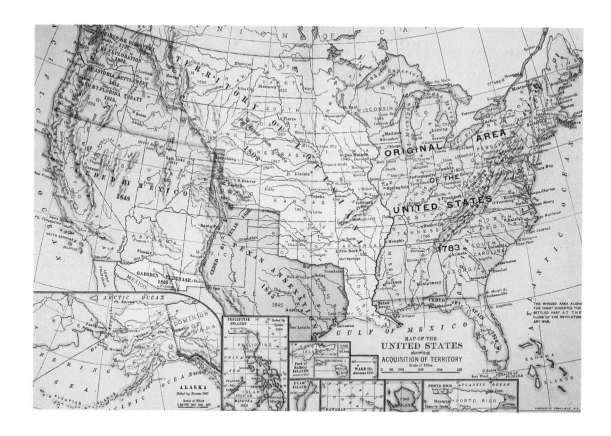

A 1905 map of the United States showing its expansion by purchase and conquest through the end of the Spanish-American War. *Granger Collection. Reproduced by permission.*

teen colonies declared independence from the empire of Great Britain and set out to govern themselves. The famous revolutionary cry against taxation without representation captured the unfairness of being governed without participating in the government. Owing their very freedom to anti-imperialism, early Americans were critical of several European countries' practice of holding foreign colonies.

Prior to 1898, the United States did not have any colonies. To be sure, the United States committed its own share of atrocities as it grew from thirteen colonies to span the North American continent. White Americans captured Africans and sold them into slavery. The federal government removed Native Americans from their homelands, forcing them onto reservations. The United States fought Mexico from 1846 to 1848 to acquire land stretching from Texas to California. Between 1798 and 1895, U.S. armed forces intervened no fewer than 103 times in the affairs of foreign nations.

In the late 1800s, Americans were starting a heated debate over imperialism. Imperialists believed the United States needed to acquire foreign colonies to provide markets for its goods. U.S. manufacturers already were producing $2 billion more products than Americans could consume each year. Imperialists also felt that having colonies made a country appear powerful. Great Britain, Germany, and Japan were building empires, so why shouldn't the United States?

Anti-imperialists believed America needed only to negotiate favorable trade agreements with foreign countries to provide markets for American goods. Many felt that acquiring colonies would burden the United States with financial responsibilities and foreign disputes. Some also clung to the honorable notion that colonies and imperialism are undemocratic.

When the United States prepared for war with Spain in April 1898, the national debate over imperialism led to a congressional document called the Teller Amendment, which promised Cuban independence. Senator Henry Teller of Colorado asked his country to pledge, "That the United States hereby disclaims [denies] any disposition or intention to exercise sovereignty, jurisdiction, or control over [Cuba] except for the pacification thereof, and asserts its determination when that is accomplished to leave the government and control of the island to its people." Imperialists in Congress did not have the courage to oppose the Teller Amendment, so they included it in the war resolutions that Congress passed on April 19.

Less than four months later, on August 12, the United States signed a peace protocol with Spain to end the fighting. U.S. forces had defeated Spain in Cuba and in Spain's other colonies of Puerto Rico, Guam, and the Philippines. In the peace protocol, Spain agreed to set Cuba free, give Puerto Rico and Guam to the United States, and decide the fate of the

Philippines during peace negotiations to be held in Paris beginning on October 1. The protocol set the stage for America to acquire its first colonies and become an imperialist nation.

Selecting the peace commissions

With treaty negotiations less than two months away, U.S. president **William McKinley** (1843–1901; served 1897–1901; see entry in Biographies section) quickly selected the American peace commissioners who would negotiate with Spain. McKinley asked William R. Day (1849–1923) to serve as chair of the group. Day, an attorney and U.S. secretary of state, believed the United States should purchase the Philippines rather than seize them outright. McKinley then stacked the commission with three Republican imperialists—Senators Cushman K. Davis and William P. Frye, and former ambassador to France Whitelaw Reid. One Democratic anti-imperialist—Senator George Gray—rounded out the team of five, meaning the commission leaned heavily in favor of acquiring the Philippines from Spain.

William R. Day served as the head of the American peace commissioners who negotiated the Treaty of Paris with Spain in October 1898. Granger Collection. Reproduced by permission.

In Spain, Premier Práxedes Mateo Sagasta (1825–1903) faced a political problem. Members of the Conservative Party (a political party) refused to participate in peace negotiations because they did not want the inevitably disastrous outcome to affect their reputation. That left Sagasta to appoint all the peace commissioners from his party, the Liberal Party. Sagasta chose party leader and Senate president Eugenio Montero Ríos as chair. Montero Ríos went to Paris along with Senator Buenaventura Abaruza, Justice José de Garnica y Díaz, Minister Wenceslas Ramírez de Villa-Urrutia, and Major General Rafael Ceroro y Sáenz.

The major question to be worked out in Paris was the fate of the Philippines, where local rebels had been fighting for independence from Spain. Spain wanted to keep the islands. Anti-imperialist Americans opposed taking the colony, especially with the dangerous situation posed by the Filipinos who wanted freedom for their country. McKinley was unsure what to do, but at the very least he wanted to retain a naval base and coaling station to help support American commerce in Asia.

Imperialists in Congress and across the nation, however, wanted to take the whole colony from Spain. Some Americans worried that Japan or Germany would seize the islands if the United States left the Filipinos to govern themselves. Many Christians said it was America's duty to educate and convert the Filipino natives to Christianity and prepare them for a "civilized" existence. McKinley, a man of great religious conviction, wrongly believing the natives to be incapable of self-government, eventually adopted this approach after much thought and prayer.

Spanish premier Práxedes Mateo Sagasta. *Hulton Archive/Getty Images. Reproduced by permission.*

Spain revealed its negotiating strategy before October 1 arrived. Because the United States had captured the Philippine city of Manila on August 13, one day after signing the peace protocol, Spain said the island still belonged to Spain. (U.S. commodore **George Dewey** [1837–1917; see entry in Biographies section] had cut telegraph cables in Manila Bay at the beginning of the war, so sending a telegraph message concerning the protocol had been impossible.) Contrary to both the law of war and the language of the protocol, the United States said the agreement did not take effect until a boat from Hong Kong arrived in Manila to deliver news of the cease-fire.

The Treaty of Paris

On October 1, as the peace commissioners began their meetings in Paris, a Filipino rebel named Felipe Ag-

Eugenio Montero Ríos was a member of the Spanish peace commission who negotiated the Treaty of Paris with the United States. *Granger Collection. Reproduced by permission.*

oncillo met with President McKinley to ask what the United States planned to do with his country. Agoncillo reminded McKinley that Commodore Dewey and U.S. consul general E. Spencer Pratt had promised rebel leader Emilio Aguinaldo (1869–1964) that the United States would support independence for the Philippines if the rebels would help with the war effort in the city of Manila, as they had done. McKinley rejected the notion that Dewey and Pratt had made such a promise, and the historical record is unclear. What is certain is that, with the knowledge that Agoncillo was headed for Paris, McKinley instructed the peace commissioners to prevent the Filipinos from joining the negotiations to decide the fate of their own country.

The peace commissioners finally signed the Treaty of Paris on December 10, 1898. The treaty confirmed Spain's obligation to leave Cuba to govern itself. Spain gave Puerto Rico and Guam to the United States to compensate it for the cost of the war. Under threats that the war might resume without a treaty, Spain agreed to sell the Philippines to the United States for $20 million.

Both countries had to ratify—approve—the Treaty of Paris before it became law. The Senate ratified the treaty in the United States on February 6, 1899, by a vote of 57 to 27. Debate over imperialism made the vote close—only two votes over the two-thirds majority required for approval.

Spain's legislative body, the Cortes, failed to approve the treaty by the required number of votes. Instead, the queen regent had to override the legislature and approve the treaty on March 19. Premier Sagasta's government fell soon afterwards; he was replaced by the opposition party, the Conservatives.

The Philippines

When it became clear that the United States meant to replace Spain as their governing body, Filipino rebels decided to fight their new enemy. On February 4, 1899, two days before the U.S. Senate ratified the Treaty of Paris, a bloody revolution began in the Philippines. American historians often call it the Philippine Insurrection, even though they call their own country's fight for freedom the American Revolution.

Conquering the islands in the three-year conflict cost the lives of over four thousand American soldiers, sixteen thousand Filipino rebels, and two hundred thousand Filipino civilians. Many of the civilians died as a result of disease and starvation in American concentration camps—crowded camps designed to prevent the civilians from assisting the rebels. Such tactics resembled those of Spanish general Valeriano Weyler y Nicolau (1838–1930)— tactics that had drawn the United States into war with Spain in Cuba in the first place.

U.S. troops in a trench near Manila during the Philippine Insurrection.
Hulton Archive/Getty Images. Reproduced by permission.

For example, on Samar, U.S. general Jacob Smith ordered his troops to convert the island to a "howling wilderness" by first removing civilians to concentration camps. All civilians who stayed behind and could carry arms, including Filipino boys over ten years of age, were to be shot and killed. "I want no prisoners. I wish you to kill and burn; the more you burn and kill the better it will please me," Smith said, according to Philip S. Foner in *The Spanish-Cuban-American War and the Birth of American Imperialism*. Eventually put on trial by the U.S. military, Smith's only punishment for his brutality was an early retirement.

The Filipino rebels finally surrendered to the United States in April 1902. For the next thirty-three years, a governor appointed by the president of the United States ruled over the Philippines. Under the Tydings-McDuffie Act in 1935, the United States allowed the Philippines to begin a trial period as a commonwealth under a popularly elected governor. In 1946, the Philippines finally became an independent, self-governing republic, with Manuel A. Roxas as its first president.

Puerto Rico

The United States was headed for a military victory in Puerto Rico when it signed the peace protocol with Spain on August 12, 1898. While Puerto Rico had a rich agricultural tradition built around small farms, it was more valuable to the United States as a coaling station for warships, and as a stepping stone to a canal the United States wanted to build in Central America to connect the Atlantic and Pacific Oceans.

At the time of the Spanish-American War, there was not a large movement for Puerto Rican independence from Spain. Most Puerto Ricans simply wanted more local control of their government. To pacify these desires, Spain set up a local government in 1897 to be supervised by a governor-general from Spain. This local government did not operate for very long before the United States attacked Puerto Rico in July 1898. In the aftermath of its victory in October, the United States put military governor General John R. Brooke in charge of the island.

At first, Puerto Ricans did not seem to be disappointed to be colonized by the United States. Their natural desire for self-government, however, caused unhappiness with the military arrangement. The United States responded to this over the years by giving Puerto Ricans U.S. citizenship in 1917, a popularly elected governor in 1947, and commonwealth status with a constitution in 1952. Puerto Ricans, however, still cannot vote in U.S. elections and have no voting representatives in Congress. By the end of the twentieth century, almost half of all Puerto Ricans wanted their island to remain a U.S. commonwealth, a slightly smaller number wanted it to become the fifty-first state, and just a small minority favored independence.

Guam

Guam, like Puerto Rico, operated under a military governor before becoming a territory with its own popularly elected governor in 1968. It has been of great importance to the United States because of its naval bases. By the end of the twentieth century, U.S. armed forces owned one-third of the land on the island. Citizens of Guam are citizens of the United States but, like Puerto Ricans, do not vote in presidential elections and lack a voting representative in Washington, D.C.

Cuba

The United States did not treat the Cuban revolutionaries respectfully either before or during the Spanish-American War. Presidents Grover Cleveland (1837–1908; served 1885–1889 and 1893–1897) and William McKinley refused to recognize the government set up by the rebels in 1895. McKinley maintained this position even as the United States declared war on Spain in April 1898, supposedly to fight for Cuban independence. When Spain surrendered at Santiago de Cuba in July 1898, U.S. military officers refused to include Cuban officers in the surrender negotiations and ceremonies. The Cubans, like the Filipinos, were not allowed to take part in the negotiations which resulted in the Treaty of Paris.

The United States continued to ignore Cuba's wishes when setting the country on the road to independence. As soon as the fighting ended in August 1898, American busi-

U.S. colonel Leonard Wood, a veteran of the Spanish-American War, took over military leadership in Cuba in late 1899. *Courtesy of the Library of Congress.*

nesses began buying their way into Cuba. According to historian Howard Zinn, the United Fruit Company entered the sugar industry by purchasing 1.9 million acres of agricultural land. American businesses, led by Bethlehem Steel, acquired 80 percent of Cuba's mineral export interests.

To protect these economic interests, the United States wanted preferential trade relations with Cuba, a naval base on the island, and the power to interfere in case another country threatened to take the island for itself. Cubans wanted absolute independence and freedom to run their country as they wished. The United States of America—the land of the free—was not about to let such a valuable island enjoy the same freedom.

On January 1, 1899, the United States occupied Cuba under the leadership of a military governor named General John Brooke. Brooke disbanded the Cuban army and tried to exclude Cubans from all government positions. Leonard Wood (1860–1927), who had fought in Cuba during the war, replaced Brooke by December 1899.

The Cuban Constitution

As of the spring of 1900, the United States had made no progress toward turning the government over to Cuba. Prominent anti-imperialists such as Augustus O. Bacon (1839–1914) accused the United States of stalling to allow memory of the Teller Amendment to fade so Americans could take Cuba for themselves. This accusation motivated the United States to form a convention to adopt a constitution for Cuba.

The Cuban Constitutional Convention first met on November 5, 1900, with thirty-one delegates elected by the people of Cuba. It drafted a constitution that largely resembled the U.S. Constitution on February 11, 1901. The document proposed to set up a republican form of government with three branches: executive, legislative, and judicial. It even went beyond the U.S. Constitution by giving all people, not just men, the right to vote. (Women did not obtain the right to vote in the United States until 1920.)

Contrary to President McKinley's wishes, however, the proposed Cuban constitution did not give the United States power to intervene in Cuban affairs to protect American interests. When the delegates signed the constitution on February 21, delegate Salvador Betancourt Cisneros even objected to sending it to the United States, saying America had no business approving the document.

The Platt Amendment

McKinley and War Secretary Elihu Root (1845–1937) devised a plan to extract what they wanted from Cuba. Through Senator Orville H. Platt (1827–1905), they attached language to an U.S. Army funding bill to outline the conditions under which the U.S. military would withdraw from Cuba. The Platt Amendment demanded that the United States retain the right to intervene in domestic affairs to protect Cuban independence and life, liberty, and property on the island; the right to review and approve Cuban treaties with foreign nations; and the right to buy or lease land for a naval base in Cuba (which would become the base at Guantánamo Bay). McKinley refused to withdraw the military from Cuba unless Cuba's new constitution included these American rights.

The U.S. Senate adopted the Platt Amendment on February 27, 1901. Fourteen senators who had voted for the Teller Amendment (promising Cuban independence) also voted for the Platt Amendment. Foner claims that anti-imperialist senators who could have defeated the Platt Amendment supported

Senator Orville Platt authored the Platt Amendment, which demanded, among other things, that the United States retain the right to intervene in Cuba's domestic affairs to protect Cuban independence. *Hulton Archive/Getty Images. Reproduced by permission.*

Cuba Libre

When the United States declared war on Spain in April 1898, U.S. president William McKinley and Congress said the country was fighting for Cuban independence. After losing the war, Spain withdrew from Cuba in 1900, leaving an American military government to control things until Cuba formed its own government.

By 1901, the United States said it would not withdraw its military force from Cuba unless the country adopted a constitution that gave the United States many rights that effectively destroyed Cuban independence. The United States wanted military and coaling bases on the island and the right to intervene in Cuban affairs to protect life, liberty, and property. McKinley, Secretary of War Elihu Root (1845–1937), and Secretary of State John Hay (1838– 1905) were leading supporters of this policy. This led social reformer Ernest H. Crosby to write the poem *Cuba Libre* (meaning "Free Cuba"), as printed by Philip S. Foner in *The Spanish-Cuban-American War and the Birth of American Imperialism*:

When we sailed from Tampa Bay,
"Cuba Libre!"
And our ships got under weigh,
"Cuba Libre!"
As we floated down the tide,
Crowding to the steamer's side,

You remember how we cried,
"Cuba Libre!"

When we spied the island shore,
"Cuba Libre!"
Then we shouted loud once more,
"Cuba Libre!"
As we sank Cervera's ships,
Where the southern sea wall dips,
What again was on our lips?
"Cuba Libre!"

These are foreign words you know—
"Cuba Libre!"
That we used so long ago,
"Cuba Libre!"
And in all the time between
Such a lot of things we've seen,
We've forgotten what they mean
"Cuba Libre!"

Let us ask the President,
"Cuba Libre!"
What that bit of Spanish meant,
"Cuba Libre!"
Ask McKinley, Root, and Hay
What on earth we meant to say,
When we shouted night and day
"Cuba Libre!"

But alas! They will not speak,
"Cuba Libre!"
For their memories are weak,
"Cuba Libre!"
If you have a lexicon,
Borrowed from a Spanish don,
Send it down to Washington,
"Cuba Libre!"

it in exchange for special federal projects for their states. The House of Representatives approved the Platt Amendment a few days later and McKinley signed it into law on March 2.

Popular reaction in the United States was unfavorable. In an article entitled "The Theft of Cuba," the *Social Democratic*

Herald made a strong point against the Platt Amendment by saying, "The independence of [the United States during the American Revolution] could not have been accomplished without the aid of France, and we search in vain for a clause in our constitution giving France any special rights," according to Foner. McKinley, Root, and supporters of the Platt Amendment defended it by saying Cuba might quickly descend into political chaos without supervision by the United States of America.

On March 3, 1901, Cubans in the capital city of Havana protested against the Platt Amendment. The Cuban Constitutional Convention voted 18 to 10 to reject the amendment on April 12. The next day, however, a committee of five convention delegates left for Washington, D.C., to discuss the situation with President McKinley and War Secretary Root. During conversations on April 25 and 26, Root suggested that if the convention accepted the Platt Amendment, the United States would negotiate a trade agreement favorable to Cuban businesses. This bribery and America's refusal to remove its military led the convention to approve the Platt Amendment on June 12, 1901, by a vote of 16 to 11.

Cuba's first president, Tomás Estrada Palma (1835–1908), took office in May 1902. Estrada Palma was an attorney who had been instrumental in helping the Cuban Revolutionary Party get started in the United States in 1892. The Platt Amendment, however, allowed the United States to intervene in domestic Cuban affairs many times in upcoming years. As an editorial in the *Washington Post,* reprinted by Foner, declared in the wake of the Spanish-American War, money drove everything:

> Foolishly or wisely, we want these newly acquired territories, not for any missionary or altruistic purpose, but for the trade, the commerce, the power, and the money that are in them. Why beat around the bush and promise and protest all sorts of things? Why not be honest? It will pay. Why not tell the truth and say what is the fact—that we want Cuba, Porto Rico, Hawaii, and Luzon...because we believe they will add to our national strength and because they will someday be purchasers at our bargain counters?

For More Information

Beisner, Robert L. *Twelve Against Empire*. New York: McGraw-Hill Company, 1968.

Collins, Mary. *The Spanish-American War.* New York: Children's Press, 1998.

Dolan, Edward F. *The Spanish-American War.* Brookfield, CT: Millbrook Press, 2001.

Foner, Philip S. *The Spanish-Cuban-American War and the Birth of American Imperialism.* New York: Monthly Review Press, 1972.

Gay, Kathlyn, and Martin K. Gay. *Spanish American War.* New York: Twenty First Century Books, 1995.

Golay, Michael. *The Spanish-American War.* New York: Facts On File, 1995.

Graves, Kerry A. *The Spanish-American War.* Mankato, MN: Capstone Books, 2001.

Greene, Theodore P, ed. *American Imperialism in 1898.* Boston, MA: D. C. Heath and Company, 1955.

Langellier, John P. *Uncle Sam's Little Wars: The Spanish-American War, Philippine Insurrection, and Boxer Rebellion, 1898–1902.* Philadelphia, PA: Chelsea House, 2001.

Linderman, Gerald F. *The Mirror of War: American Society and the Spanish-American War.* Ann Arbor, MI: The University of Michigan Press, 1974.

Musicant, Ivan. *Empire by Default: The Spanish-American War and the Dawn of the American Century.* New York: Henry Holt and Company, 1998.

O'Toole, G. J. A. *The Spanish War: An American Epic–1898.* New York: W. W. Norton & Company, 1984.

Smith, Angel, and Emma Dávila-Cox, eds. *The Crisis of 1898: Colonial Redistribution and Nationalist Mobilization.* New York: St. Martin's Press, 1999.

Somerlott, Robert. *The Spanish-American War: Remember the Maine!* Berkeley Heights, NJ: Enslow Publishers, Inc., 2002.

Wukovits, John F. *The Spanish-American War.* San Diego, CA: Lucent Books, 2001.

Zinn, Howard. *A People's History of the United States: 1492–Present.* 20th anniversary ed. New York: HarperCollins, 1999.

Biographies

Clara Barton

Born December 25, 1821
North Oxford, Massachusetts
Died April 12, 1912
Glen Echo, Maryland

American relief worker, founder and first president of the American National Red Cross

Clara Barton broke age and gender stereotypes as a relief worker and nurse during the Spanish-American War (April–August 1898). In February 1898, the seventy-seven-year-old Barton traveled with Red Cross workers to Cuba. The mission's purpose was to help provide food and medical aid to Cuban civilians during a colonial revolution against Spain. In June and July of that year, during some of the fiercest battles of America's war with Spain, Barton tended to wounded American soldiers behind battle lines near Santiago, Cuba. Barton returned to Cuba in 1899 to help malnourished children suffering during America's post-war military rule.

Childhood and teaching career

Clara Barton was born in North Oxford, Massachusetts, on Christmas Day, 1821. She acquired the discipline necessary for hard work by growing up on a farm, where she learned to drive nails, ride ponies, make soap, and raise a vegetable garden. Teaching self-reliance to suffering people

"U.S. Admiral Sampson says openly and truthfully that my aim and efforts are exactly opposed to those of the government from which he takes his orders; that while my effort…is to get food into Cuba, his object, which is the object of the Government, is to keep food out."

Clara Barton quoted in Clara Barton: Professional Angel

Clara Barton. *Courtesy of the Library of Congress.*

would become an important part of Barton's relief work with the American National Red Cross.

At age fifteen, Barton began a teaching career, partly to overcome shyness. Success put her in high demand in North Oxford and surrounding villages. From 1850 to 1851, Barton took a break from teaching to attend the Liberal Institute in Clinton, New York, for her own education.

Barton resumed teaching in 1852 in Bordentown, New Jersey, at a school that grew from a handful of students to hundreds under her guidance as instructor and administrator. School authorities then replaced Barton with a male principal, afraid that a woman could not administer a large operation. Refusing to put up with such ignorance, and suffering from depression, Barton left teaching permanently.

The American Civil War

When the American Civil War (1861–65) broke out in April 1861, Barton was in Washington, D.C., working for the U.S. Patent Office. Surprised that there were no plans for caring for the wounded, Barton placed advertisements for donations in the Worcester *Daily Spy,* a newspaper in Massachusetts. At first Barton distributed the goods from Massachusetts at her home in Washington, D.C., where she also cared for soldiers and made them food. In July 1862, after much effort, she convinced Surgeon-General William A. Hammond to let her go to the front (the areas where battle was taking place).

Once in the thick of the action, Barton worked mostly near battlefields in Maryland, Virginia, and South Carolina. Although legend remembers her as a nurse, Barton worked primarily to bring medical supplies and food to the soldiers, bandaging and comforting them in the field instead of working in army hospitals. Her compassion earned her the nickname "Angel of the Battlefield."

The Franco-Prussian War

During the late 1860s, Barton traveled to Europe to take care of another bout of her recurring depression. While in Geneva, Switzerland, she learned about the International Red Cross. Created by the Treaty of Geneva (an international agreement that the United States did not sign until 1882), the Red Cross worked to relieve wounded soldiers in times of war.

When the Franco-Prussian War (1870–1871) broke out in 1870 between France and several German states, led by Prussia, Barton gained firsthand knowledge about the Red Cross by working with the organization. While distributing relief supplies in French cities such as Strasbourg, Paris, Lyons, Belfort, and Montpellier, Barton became impressed with the effectiveness of Red Cross operations. Trained nurses worked with large stores of supplies that stood ready for relief, protected from attack in buildings painted with bright scarlet crosses, which signified the international agreement not to harm such sites in wartime.

The American Red Cross

After the Franco-Prussian War, Barton experienced another bout of depression and the death of her sister, Sally, before checking herself into a sanitarium (a health resort for those recovering from illness) in Dansville, New York, in 1876. Recovered the following year, Barton wrote to Dr. Louis Appia asking for permission to start a Red Cross organization in the United States. Appia appointed Barton the Red Cross representative in the United States.

Barton served as president of the American National Red Cross (originally called the American Association of the Red Cross) from its birth in 1881, when she was fifty-nine, until 1904. For most of this time she was active in relief work throughout the United States and around the world. In 1882, after years of hard work, Barton finally convinced the United States to sign the Treaty of Geneva, binding the country to international laws concerning Red Cross operations during wartime. In September 1884, while attending the Third International Conference of the Red Cross in Geneva, Barton convinced the entire organization to expand its duties to include peacetime relief work. All along, she conducted the American National Red Cross with complete authority but without a good system of recordkeeping, which eventually led to her downfall in the organization.

The Second Cuban War for Independence

In February 1895, rebels in the Spanish colony of Cuba, an island, launched a revolution against Spain to reform poor economic conditions. By the end of the year, the revolutionaries controlled the rural regions on the eastern end of the island. Success came largely through help from rural civilians, who provided food and shelter to the rebels as they burned sugar plantations, destroyed refineries, and carried out violent attacks on other assets of the Cuban economy.

Spain responded by sending a vicious general, Valeriano Weyler y Nicolau (1838–1930), to command military operations in Cuba in early 1896. Weyler adopted a concentration policy, imprisoning Cuban civilians in crowded camps and burning their homes and fields so they could not help the rebels. Hundreds of thousands of civilians died of starvation and disease in these camps.

Barton was initially hesitant about taking the Red Cross to Cuba to assist the Cuban *pacificos,* as the civilians were called. The Cuban conflict caused tense relations between the United States, Spain, and Cuba, and Barton was unsure of the Red Cross's rights under the Treaty of Geneva in such a political atmosphere. In July 1897, however, Barton met with President **William McKinley** (1843–1901; served 1897–1901; see entry) to discuss the possibility of going to Cuba to help the Cuban pacificos. McKinley liked the idea and made public assistance to the pacificos a topic in his State of the Union message in December 1897.

On January 1, 1898, the Central Cuban Relief Committee formed in New York to raise money and supplies for the Red Cross to distribute in Cuba. On February 6, Barton left for Havana, Cuba, to begin relief work on the island. Upon arriving at a hospital at Los Fosos, Barton saw sights that, compared to the religious warfare and massacres she had seen in Armenia in 1896, "seemed merciful by comparison," according to Ishbel Ross in *Angel of the Battlefield.* People as skinny as skeletons or bloated from malnutrition were dying at the rate of a dozen a day. Children in concentration camps were barely alive.

Barton set to work doing what she did best, organizing the distribution of food from Red Cross warehouses to the concentration centers. On February 13, she had lunch with Captain Charles D. Sigsbee, who commanded the U.S. warship *Maine* in the harbor at Havana, Cuba. The warship was there to protect American interests and to pressure Spain to end the revolution. When the *Maine* exploded mysteriously two days later, killing more than 250 people aboard, Barton visited the wounded sailors in the hospital.

U.S. senator **Redfield Proctor** (1831–1908; see entry in Primary Sources section) visited the island shortly thereafter to assess conditions with his own eyes. Barton took Proctor on a tour during his stay. Later, in a Senate speech that motivated Congress to seek war with Spain, Proctor said of Barton, "The American people may be assured that their bounty will reach the sufferers with the least possible cost and in the best manner in every respect," according to Elizabeth Brown Pryor in *Clara Barton: Professional Angel.* Unfortunately, Barton soon had to return to the United States to clear up political problems with the Central Cuban Relief Committee.

The Spanish-American War

On April 19, 1898, while Barton was back in the United States, Congress authorized President McKinley to prepare for war with Spain. Four days later, Barton found herself stuck on a ship—the *State of Texas*—in Tampa, Florida, with fourteen hundred tons of supplies for the suffering Cubans. U.S. admiral William T. Sampson (1840–1902) would not allow the *State of Texas* to take food to Cuba, where American soldiers had yet to land. Barton did what she could for American soldiers and Spanish prisoners-of-war in Tampa until she finally got official clearance to travel to Cuba at the end of June.

Meanwhile, Barton visited Washington, D.C., to have the McKinley administration clarify the Red Cross's role in relief operations. It was the first American war for the American National Red Cross, and U.S. surgeon-general George M. Sternberg was trying to take control of its operations. Getting approval from the McKinley administration to operate independently of the federal government was one of Barton's crowning achievements in her long years of work for the Red Cross. It allowed the Red Cross to minimize, to the extent possible, political constraints on its relief operations.

Receiving the long-awaited orders to depart from Tampa on June 20, the *State of Texas* finally headed for Cuba with her anxious crew and passengers. When Barton arrived on the island, her role immediately changed from helping the Cubans in concentration camps to helping the wounded American and Cuban soldiers at the front near Santiago de Cuba. Deadly, day-long battles at San Juan Heights and El Caney on July 1, 1898, made it necessary for Barton to tend to wounded and dying soldiers in army hospitals. The hospitals, in Barton's opinion, were as unprepared to treat casualties as American military hospitals had been during the Civil War thirty years earlier.

At the same time, Barton coordinated distribution of supplies and prepared food such as gruel and Red Cross cider for the soldiers. (Her famous cider was a fermented mixture made from stewed apples, prunes, and lime juice.) Barton was working with food supplies when **Theodore Roosevelt** (1858–1919; see entry), who led a volunteer regiment called the Rough Riders, arrived to purchase milk, oatmeal, beefsteak, fruits, and other food. When the Red Cross gave him the food for free, Roosevelt gratefully slung the sack over his shoulder and disappeared back into the jungle, emerging from the war to later become the governor of New York and president of the United States.

After the U.S. Navy defeated Spain at Santiago on July 3 and the city surrendered on July 17, the *State of Texas* led the naval procession to the city's docks, much to Barton's delight. When she later thanked Admiral Sampson for the honor, Commodore Winfield S. Schley (1839–1909) joked that Barton should not be too thankful, for the navy had thought there might be mines in the harbor.

In Santiago, Barton displayed her characteristic skill at organization by dividing the city into districts for distributing food to hungry civilians. Controversy erupted, however, as the Red Cross got blamed for spreading a disease called yellow fever by operating in a contaminated building. In fact, on a night prior to entering Santiago, Barton and others had picked up the disease when they were forced to take shelter in an abandoned building near the Cuban shore because waves prevented them from reaching their ship.

The *State of Texas* became quarantined (made off-limits) and was sent back to New York. This left Barton without transportation for five weeks until she got onto a commercial ship headed for Havana on August 21, nine days after Spain and the United States signed a peace agreement to end the war. Heading home, Barton took comfort in the fact that she had supervised the distribution of six thousand tons of provisions worth half a million dollars.

Back to Cuba

In the United States, Barton began to face criticism about the way she was running the Red Cross. Some felt Barton had misdirected Red Cross resources to Spaniards during the war. Others were concerned that her inadequate record-keeping made it hard to monitor the organization. Hurt by such charges, Barton retreated to her home in Glen Echo, Maryland, to write a book, *The Red Cross in Peace and War*. Published in 1899, half of the book describes the Red Cross's role in Cuba during the Spanish-American War.

In his State of the Union message in December 1898, President McKinley praised the work of Clara Barton and the Red Cross during the Cuban crisis. Barton again approached McKinley, proposing to return to Cuba to help orphan children who had lived in the concentration camps. Barton met resistance from the New York chapter of the Red Cross, which felt she was getting too old for such work. McKinley disagreed and approved Barton's plan, so she sailed back to Cuba in the spring of 1899.

When Barton arrived, Red Cross workers had already been there for a couple of months. Disagreement soon erupted between Barton and people who felt she could better serve the organization in an administrative capacity from Washington, D.C. Barton resented such treatment, which made her last trip to Cuba her most unpleasant. Barton did what she could for the children while she was there, but she left Cuba discouraged about the future of the Red Cross.

Retirement

Growing criticism of her administration led Barton to resign from the Red Cross on June 16, 1904. She lived the rest of her life at her homestead in Glen Echo, Maryland, writing two more books, *A Story of the Red Cross* (1905) and *Story of My Childhood* (1907). Barton died in Glen Echo on April 12, 1912. Thirty-nine years later, the Cuban Red Cross unveiled a marble bust of Clara Barton in Santiago to honor her wartime work in the region.

For More Information

Barton, Clara. *The Red Cross in Peace and War.* Washington, D.C.: American Historical Press, 1899.

Hamilton, Leni. *Clara Barton.* New York: Chelsea House, 1987.

Pryor, Elizabeth Brown. *Clara Barton: Professional Angel.* Philadelphia, PA: University of Pennsylvania Press, 1987.

Rose, Mary Catherine. *Clara Barton: Soldier of Mercy.* New York: Chelsea House, 1991.

Ross, Ishbel. *Angel of the Battlefield: The Life of Clara Barton.* New York: Harper & Row, 1956.

Wheeler, Jill C. *Clara Barton.* Minneapolis, MN: Abdo & Daughters, 2002.

Pascual Cervera y Topete

Born February 18, 1839
Medina Sidonia, Spain
Died April 3, 1909
Puerto Real, Spain

Spanish naval officer

The Spanish-American War (April–August 1898) marked the end of an empire that had spanned the globe. In the historic blink of an eye, Spain lost its colony Cuba to independence and surrendered its control of Puerto Rico, Guam, and the Philippines to the United States. Spain's navy had played an essential role in building its empire. Crushing naval defeats in the Philippines and Cuba during the war, however, sent Spain back to Europe. The man with the misfortune to lead Spain's last naval grasp for empire in Cuba was Rear Admiral Pascual Cervera y Topete.

"We cannot go to war without meeting with a certain and frightful disaster."

Pascual Cervera y Topete quoted in "Leaders Who Lost: Case Studies of Command under Stress"

Naval career

Pascual Cervera y Topete was born in Medina Sidonia, Spain, on February 18, 1839. He attended the Spanish naval academy in San Fernando from 1848 to 1851. Cervera then spent the rest of his life as an officer in the Spanish navy. This included service at Spain's West Indian naval station at the beginning of the Ten Years' War (1868–1878), a rebellion in which Cubans sought better government from Spain.

In 1885, Cervera received command of a ship called the *Pelayo*. Seven years later, Práxedes Mateo Sagasta (1825–1903) became prime minister of Spain. Sagasta appointed Cervera minister of the marine, the head of the naval department of the Spanish government. On October 30, 1897, Rear Admiral Cervera became commander of the entire Spanish squadron stationed at Cadíz, Spain. The man he replaced, Segismundo Bermejo, took Cervera's place in the government as minister of the marine.

The Second Cuban War for Independence

Spain faced another rebellion in its island colony of Cuba beginning in February 1895. This time, the Cuban rebels wanted independence from Spain, protesting the government's economic policies that favored privileged classes on the island and wealthy businessmen back in Spain. Cuban workers, shopkeepers, and farmers wanted more say in their government and better social conditions for the island's working and lower classes.

When Cervera became a squadron commander in October 1897, many Americans and members of Congress were asking President **William McKinley** (1843–1901; served 1897–1901; see entry) to enter the conflict in Cuba. Newspapers in the United States carried stories of Cuban civilians dying from disease and starvation, thanks to Spain's wartime policies. American investment in and trade with Cuba was suffering from the rebels' strategy of destroying plantations, sugar mills, and other means of economic production.

Spain did not think the United States would intervene in the conflict, for President McKinley had said he would strive for peace at all costs. But when McKinley sent the U.S. warship *Maine* to Havana, Cuba, in January 1898, Cervera sought instructions from Bermejo on what to do in the event of war. Bermejo said Cervera's mission would be to destroy American military facilities at Key West, Florida, and blockade the entire U.S. Atlantic coast to contain the U.S. Navy.

Cervera knew this plan was absurd. Two of his squadron's ships, the *Pelayo* and the *Carlos V,* were unavailable. His newest ship, the *Cristóbal Colon,* did not have its four main guns, and his fastest ship, the *Vizcaya,* had a dirty hull that would slow the ship considerably. Turrets that housed mounted guns on the *Infanta Maria Teresa* and *Oquendo* were broken. Cervera warned the Spanish government of his fleet's poor condition in correspondence in early 1898.

Spain, however, failed to correct the problems reported by Cervera. Its government was in great debt from the ongoing Cuban revolution and had neither the time nor the money to bring its naval fleet up to battle conditions. National pride may also have prevented government officials from seeing the true condition of its squadrons. This pride caused Spain to refuse to do the one thing that could prevent a war with United States: leave Cuba entirely.

Preparing for war with the United States

On February 15, the *Maine* exploded mysteriously in the harbor at Havana, hurtling the United States toward a declaration of war. Around April 14, Cervera and the ship captains in his squadron gathered at St. Vincent, Cape Verde, off the west coast of Africa, where the Spanish fleet would assemble for battle. When they sought coal for fuel, the officers found that the U.S. consul had bought almost all that was available in the area. Only after much difficulty—and at twice the regular price—were they able to obtain seven hundred tons of coal from England, a small amount of fuel for a squadron.

Cervera then called a meeting of his staff. Spain planned to keep six ships with heavy guns near the European continent for protection, and to send the other six with Cervera to Cuba. Cervera and his men decided this would be suicide, especially as the United States had enough battleships and smaller vessels to assemble two to four squadrons for action in the Atlantic.

On April 20, Cervera sent a telegram to the Spanish government saying he and his men thought they should return to the Canary Islands and use the Spanish navy to protect the mother country, Spain. In another telegram on April 22, the chief of Cervera's torpedo boat flotilla informed Prime Minister Mateo Sagasta that destruction of the squadron was certain and useless. According to Cervera's chief of staff, Víctor Concas y Palau, in *The Squadron of Admiral Cervera,* the Spanish minister of colonies replied with a telegram written in English, saying, "God bless you."

Heading for Cuba

After the United States declared war on April 25, Cervera and his doomed squadron sailed for the West Indies on April 29. Ironically, this news alarmed residents of the Atlantic coast of the United States. Ignorant of the weak condition of the Spanish fleet, these Americans imagined deadly attacks on their coastal cities and homes. U.S. Navy secretary John D. Long (1838–1915) had to dispatch coastal patrols to calm citizens' fears.

Meanwhile U.S. admiral William T. Sampson (1840–1902) set up a blockade around Havana, Cuba, while U.S. commodore Winfield S. Schley (1839–1909) and his Flying Squadron looked for Cervera in the waters around Cuba and Puerto Rico. Guessing that this would be the American strategy, Cervera and his fleet headed for the port at Santiago de Cuba at the southeastern end of the island, opposite from Havana. Much to Long's annoyance, the Spanish squadron slipped into Santiago untouched, though running low on coal, the morning of May 19.

Unknown to Cervera at the time, his government had issued an order on May 12 that the fleet return to Spain. The crushing defeat of a Spanish squadron by U.S commodore **George Dewey** (1837–1917; see entry) in the Philippines on May 1 had showed Spain how unprepared it was for a naval war. The Spanish governors at Cuba and Puerto Rico, however, convinced Spain to make Cervera's squadron stay before it could refuel and return. According to Concas, one of the governors felt that defeat of Cervera's fleet would rally the Spanish army to repel the U.S. invasion and win the war.

Death on the horizon

Upon learning of Cervera's whereabouts, Admiral Sampson directed the U.S. Atlantic fleet to move its blockade to the mouth of Santiago harbor. Unsure of whether mines protected the port, Sampson kept his fleet in the sea, waiting for Cervera to come out.

Meanwhile, U.S. general **William R. Shafter** (1835–1906; see entry) landed American forces a few miles from Santiago on June 22 and 23. From June 24 to July 1, American troops marched and fought alongside Cuban rebels until they had captured the town of El Caney and the hills of San Juan Heights just outside of Santiago. Cervera sent one thousand men from his ships to help defend Santiago at the beginning of July.

The moment Admiral Cervera had been dreading since April then arrived. While the fighting raged outside Santiago on July 1, Cervera received orders from the Spanish governor of Cuba, General Ramón Blanco y Erenas (1831–1906), to leave the harbor as soon as possible. According to A. B. Feuer in *The Spanish-American War at Sea,* Blanco said, "If we should lose the squadron without a battle, the effect on Spanish morale would be disastrous."

Cervera called his officers together for a final meeting on July 2. He informed them of their orders and advised that the fleet try to outrun the American blockade and sail for the Cuban harbors at Havana or Cienfuegos, fighting only if necessary. According to Concas:

> [The Admiral] stated to us that the time for discussion had passed, that we had done all that was within human power to avoid the catastrophe, and that nothing was left now but to obey, to which we all agreed.... The words of the Admiral were received with enthusiasm, and we all clasped each other's hands fervently, as soldiers who knew how to meet death and destruction, from which no power could save us. There were harsh and well-merited denunciations of many statesmen who remain as calm as if they owed nothing either to God or their country, and we swore that if anyone of us should survive he would defend the memory of those who perished in the encounter.

The naval battle at Santiago

After the fighting sailors had returned to their vessels and rested, Cervera's fleet steamed from port the morning of July 3. The harbor entrance was narrow, crowded further by a ship that the United States had sunk inside it. This forced the Spanish ships to sail single file, each meeting the full brunt of the American attack alone as it emerged into the Caribbean Sea.

The U.S.S. *Brooklyn,* center, participated in the Battle of Santiago Bay on July 3, 1898, in which Admiral Cervera's entire fleet was captured or destroyed.
Hulton Archive/Getty Images. Reproduced by permission.

Aboard the *Infanta Maria Teresa,* Cervera, Concas, and the officers and crew led the fleet into battle. The U.S. fleet was lined up outside the harbor, with the *Brooklyn* farthest to the west. Cervera thought of ramming the *Brooklyn* to give the rest of his squadron a chance to escape westward. U.S. maneuvers, however, put the *Infanta Maria Teresa* in danger of colliding with two American vessels. With his vessel on fire and severely damaged, Cervera eventually decided to strand it on a Cuban beach to prevent the crew from drowning and to protect the boat from being captured.

The battle was over in just four hours. Cervera's entire fleet was beached, captured, or destroyed. Of the Spaniards, 323 died and 151 suffered severe wounds, all for national pride. As Concas described it:

> There was missing the excellent Villaamil, the commander of the destroyers, killed by a shell on the bridge of the *Furor;* also five of the officers of the *Maria Teresa,* and four of the *Vizcaya,* whose survivors related how the poor gunner, Francisco

Zaragoza, with gaping wounds, asked for a piece of the silk flag which the flames were devouring, and, wrapping it about him, gave up his soul to the Creator; and with tears in their eyes they told how the midshipman, Enrique Cheriguini, with both legs shot off close to the trunk, after making preparations to die like a Christian, wrote a letter to his parents, to whom he gave his last thoughts, knowing that God receives in His arms all good children, and that his soul would be united with Him, and with his last breath he wrote the last letter of his name.

Rescue and return

Stranded on a beach, Cervera and his crew tried to organize their camp and tend to their wounded. An American ship appeared amidst this activity to pick up the admiral and some officers and assistants to hold as prisoners-of-war. The sailors Cervera left behind organized themselves into groups of fifty and, using dry branches, dug graves to bury their dead comrades.

Practically naked, Cervera and his men arrived at the U.S. ship *Gloucester,* where the Americans received them honorably. After feeding and caring for their prisoners, the Americans transferred Cervera and his comrades to the *Iowa* and eventually transported them, along with eighteen hundred other prisoners, to confinement on the American mainland.

The war ended on August 12, 1898. On September 12, Cervera boarded a vessel with his men to sail back to Spain. "Every face on board expressed the joy that filled every heart," according to Cervera in *The Spanish-American War.* In Concas's words, "on the 13th of September the shores of the continent which [Christopher] Columbus had discovered, in an evil hour for Spain, faded from our view."

Back in Spain, Cervera and his officers faced a military trial for their defeat. Although the trial ended in Cervera's favor, he assembled a collection of documents to tell his side of the story and published them in 1899 in *The Spanish-American War.* The following year, Concas published *The Squadron of Admiral Cervera* to add to the squadron's defense.

Cervera continued service to his country after the war, first as a vice admiral, then as chief of staff of the navy, and finally as a senator. He died in Puerto Real, Spain, on April 3, 1909.

For More Information

Books

Cervera y Topete, Pascual, ed. *The Spanish-American War: A Collection of Documents Relative to the Squadron Operations in the West Indies.* Washington, D.C.: Government Printing Office, 1899.

Concas y Palau, Víctor. *The Squadron of Admiral Cervera.* Washington, D.C.: Government Printing Office, 1900.

Feuer, A. B. *The Spanish-American War at Sea.* Westport, CT: Praeger Publishers, 1995.

Golay, Michael. *The Spanish-American War.* New York: Facts On File, Inc., 1995.

Musicant, Ivan. *Empire by Default: The Spanish-American War and the Dawn of the American Century.* New York: Henry Holt and Company, 1998.

Notes on the Spanish-American War. Washington, D.C.: Government Printing Office, 1900.

Periodicals

Smith, Eric M. "Leaders Who Lost: Case Studies of Command under Stress." *Military Review,* vol. LXI, April 1981, no. 4, pp. 41–45.

Richard Harding Davis

Born April 18, 1864
Philadelphia, Pennsylvania
Died April 11, 1916
Mount Kisco, New York

American journalist

Richard Harding Davis was one of the world's most popular journalists at the time of the Spanish-American War (April–August 1898). Although raised in upper-middle-class comfort, he relished the chance to join the U.S. Army in the hot, humid jungles during the fighting in Cuba. Davis's coverage of the Rough Riders helped put that regiment in the history books and its leader, **Theodore Roosevelt** (1858–1919; see entry), in the White House. With a knack for finding the human drama in the stories he reported, Davis created war accounts that shocked and entertained Americans back home.

"I claim that trained writers are just as important to this war as trained fighters."

Richard Harding Davis quoted in The Reporter Who Would Be King.

Early life and education

Richard Harding Davis was born on April 18, 1864, in Philadelphia, Pennsylvania. His mother, Rebecca Blaine Harding Davis, was a successful novelist who was very close to Davis and helped him with his writing until her death in 1910. Davis's father, Lemuel Clarke Davis, was the editor of the *Philadelphia Public Register*. Davis grew up comfortably in Philadelphia with a younger brother named Charles and a

Richard Harding Davis.
Courtesy of the Library of Congress.

younger sister named Nora. He attended Lehigh University and then Johns Hopkins University before dropping out without a degree to pursue a writing career.

From Philadelphia to the world

In 1886, Davis's father got him a job as a reporter at the *Philadelphia Record*. In the ensuing years Davis wrote for the *Philadelphia Press* and the *Philadelphia Evening Telegraph* before becoming the managing editor of *Harper's Weekly* in New York in 1890. His work there took Davis around the world, writing stories about the American West and many European and Latin American countries.

Throughout this time Davis developed a dramatic style of writing about controversial subjects such as abortion, execution, and suicide. He also developed the strong belief that writers should be independent of their publishers and hold personal opinions about their subjects. In 1890 he published a short story called "Gallegher" in *Scribner's Magazine*. Over his career, Davis published twelve collections containing a total of around eighty stories. Meanwhile, a war between two New York newspapers and a revolution in Cuba took Davis to that island in 1897.

Looking for war in Cuba

Spain had been fighting rebels in its colony of Cuba since February 1895. By late 1897, two New York newspapers, the *Journal* and the *World,* were engaged in their own war—a fight for readership. *Journal* owner **William Randolph Hearst** (1863–1951; see entry) devised the strategy of hiring the best talent to write sensational stories about shocking events. At the end of 1896, Hearst offered Richard Harding Davis $3,000 to report on the Cuban revolution for a month.

Along with illustrator Frederic Remington (1861–1909), Davis planned to sneak into the Cuban jungles to join Cuban general **Máximo Gómez** (1836–1905; see entry), who was leading the military effort for the rebels. Thanks to travel problems, the men found themselves in the city of Havana instead, along with Spanish general Valeriano Weyler y Nicolau (1838–1930). Weyler gave the men a pass to tour the island as reporters, but they found no fighting, so Remington returned home out of boredom.

Davis remained, however, capturing images in his stories of the suffering on the island. One rebel military strategy included economic destruction, and thus Davis saw beautiful tropical scenery marred by plumes of smoke rising from burning sugarcane fields. In a *Journal* article printed on January 31, 1897, Davis described the awful conditions in the concentration camps that Weyler used to prevent civilians from helping the rebels. Davis used his pass to get to the famous Spanish *trocha*, a military barrier that crossed the entire island at its narrowest point. In a story entitled "The Death of Rodriquez," Davis described the Spanish firing squad execution of a Cuban rebel soldier who met his death with apparent bravery.

Davis breaks from Hearst

While in Cuba, Davis ran into fellow reporters George Bronson Rea and Sylvester Scovel, who carried a copy of the *Journal* from January 17. In it, Hearst reported that Davis and Remington were in Cuba with Gómez and the rebel fighters. Hearst often used lies to create sensational stories, and this one infuriated Davis, who soon decided to return home.

Traveling aboard the commercial ship *Olivette* from Havana, Davis met a Cuban woman named Clemencia Arango. Arango had been arrested for helping the rebels and expelled from the colony by Spain. Upon Arango's arrival at the dock for departure, Spanish authorities had strip-searched her, once in an inspection house and again in a cabin on the ship. Outraged by such treatment of a woman, especially on an American vessel, Davis filed a story about the incident as soon as he reached Tampa, Florida.

Davis failed to report whether it had been a man or a woman who had searched Arango's naked body. Hearst, however, rewrote the article and included a Remington illustration that depicted three Spanish men in straw hats inspecting a naked woman. The story had the intended effect of angering Americans, who became increasingly interested in war with Spain. The rewritten story also infuriated Davis, who vowed never to write for Hearst again.

Finding war in America

In February 1898, the U.S. warship *Maine* mysteriously exploded in the harbor at Havana, Cuba. Two months later, the United States declared war on Spain. This time, Davis would cover the action for the *Times* of London, which was the most popular newspaper in the world. He also wrote stories for the *New York Herald,* a paper that, unlike the *Journal,* was not using stunts and falsifying stories to compete for readership.

On April 25, the day the United States declared war, Davis persuaded Admiral William T. Sampson (1840–1902) to let him board the flagship of the fleet that would patrol the waters around Cuba. This allowed Davis to witness the first military engagement of the war when the Spanish artillery at Matanzas, Cuba, fired upon the *New York* on April 27. The flagship and two others returned fire immediately, ending the attack in less then twenty minutes.

After U.S. Navy secretary John D. Long (1838–1915) ordered all correspondents but one off the *New York,* Davis headed to Tampa, Florida, where the U.S. Army was assembling an invasion force for Cuba. The chaotic process took weeks to complete; during the preparations, army officers stayed in the Tampa Bay Hotel. In his book *The Cuban and Porto Rican Campaigns,* Davis wrote, "This was the rocking-chair period of the war. It was an army of occupation, but it occupied the piazza of a big hotel."

The officers may have been sleeping comfortably in a hotel, but the soldiers stayed in nearby camps, where food was scarce at worst and bad at best. The men could smell their latrine pits (holes dug in the ground that served as communal toilets) as they tried to sleep at night. Among them was the First Volunteer Cavalry Regiment, led by Colonel Leonard Wood (1860–1927) and Lieutenant Colonel Theodore Roosevelt (1858–1919). Davis, sensing that covering Roosevelt would further his own career, reported that the Rough Riders, a cavalry of volunteer soldiers in Cuba during the Spanish-American War famous for their ferocity and bravery, was the best-trained regiment in the Fifth Corps (or V Corps) invasion force.

Returning to Cuba

When the V Corps finally left Tampa on June 14, Davis was one of just seven reporters who traveled on the *Se-*

gurança, the ship that also carried invasion force leader General **William R. Shafter** (1835–1906; see entry). Shafter planned to invade Cuba at Santiago, located near the southeastern end of the island. Navy admiral Sampson had trapped the fleet of Spanish admiral **Pascual Cervera y Topete** (1839–1909; see entry) in the harbor there.

On June 20, Davis and four other journalists accompanied Shafter and Sampson to a meeting with Cuban general **Calixto García** (1839–1898; see entry) to decide where to land the American army. Davis had to ride on a horse because his sciatica (pain in his lower back) had flared up, making it difficult for him to walk. At the meeting, Shafter took García's advice to land at Daquirí, a small town twelve miles east of Santiago.

As the V Corps began to land two days later, Davis had a disagreement with Shafter that soured his already poor opinion of the military leader. Although the navy had bombarded the landing spot and a Cuban rebel had signaled that the coast was clear, Shafter ordered that only army personnel be allowed to participate in the initial landing, in case fighting was necessary. Prohibited from participating, Davis became very angry, for if fighting occurred, someone had to be there to capture it in writing. Davis protested to Shafter that he actually was more of an historian than a news reporter. According to Charles H. Brown in *The Correspondents' War,* Shafter snapped back, "I do not care a damn what you are, I'll treat you all alike."

Riding with Roosevelt

On June 24, American soldiers began the trek from their landing point toward Santiago. Davis, riding atop a mule while suffering from another attack of sciatica, followed along with Roosevelt and the Rough Riders. As the army reached a point called Las Guásimas, an invisible Spanish ambush opened fire from trees and jungle perches. The U.S. Army suffered many losses until it detected the Spanish soldiers's hats, a feat that Roosevelt credited to Davis. This finally allowed the army to fire back with some effect.

During the battle, Davis borrowed a carbine—a light rifle—and fired at the Spaniards. Afterwards, he saw the horrible results of war, including a captain with a wound in his chest, a boy dying from a gunshot between his eyes, and a wealthy New Yorker dead from a bullet through his heart.

The army rested for six days before marching on June 30 to its next battles at El Caney and San Juan Heights—Spain's last lines of defense before Santiago. The fighting began early the next morning when General H. W. Lawton's (1843–1899) division began its assault on El Caney. When that battle lasted beyond its expected duration of two hours, the army began the assault on San Juan Heights as well.

The result was deadly. American regiments marched down a narrow trail before emerging into a clearing at San Juan Heights, where the Spaniards fired upon them. Unable to fire back, thanks to orders from Shafter (who was miles behind in a camp), and unable to retreat, thanks to the regiments marching behind them, American soldiers died by the hundreds. In *The Cuban and Porto Rican Campaigns,* Davis described the scene as follows:

> This was endured for an hour, an hour of such hell of fire and heat, that the heat itself, had there been no bullets, would have been remembered for its cruelty. Men gasped on their backs, like fishes in the bottom of a boat, their heads burning inside and out, their limbs too heavy to move. They had been rushed here and rushed there wet with sweat and wet with fording streams, under a sun that would have made moving a fan an effort, and they lay prostrate, gasping at the hot air, with faces aflame, and their tongues sticking out, and their eyes rolling. All through this the volleys from the rifle-pits sputtered and rattled, and the bullets sang continuously like the wind through the riggings in a gale, shrapnel whined and broke, and still no order came from General Shafter.

After painful waiting, the troops finally got the order to charge. General Hamilton S. Hawkins led troops up the largest hill, San Juan Hill, while Roosevelt, who had been promoted to lead his regiment, led the charge up nearby Kettle Hill. The U.S. Army took San Juan Heights more on the strength of its charge than by its firepower. As Roosevelt was one of the few men sitting high atop a horse, Davis wrote that nobody expected him to survive. When the Spaniards fled down the hills toward Santiago, Davis rushed to the top of San Juan Hill, only to flee quickly to avoid gunfire from the valley below.

From Shafter to Miles

The Americans won the battles of July 1 at the heavy cost of over sixteen hundred casualties, or one out of every six of the soldiers who fought. Defending their position at San Juan Heights was difficult with Spanish soldiers firing from below. In an article printed in the *Herald* on July 7 titled "Our Brave Men Defy Hardships," Davis called the situation "exceedingly grave." He described the American soldiers as tired and weary and barely able to hold out a few more hours. Shafter was to blame for the whole situation, in Davis's opinion: "Truthfully the expedition was prepared in ignorance and conducted in a series of blunders. Its commanding general has not yet even been within two miles of the scene of operation."

The story ran at a time when the United States was trying to negotiate terms of surrender with Spain. Newspapers accused Davis of disloyalty for writing the story under such tense diplomatic conditions. After the war, Shafter said he would have arrested Davis and thrown the reporter off the island if he had seen the article with his own eyes.

As things went, Spain surrendered Santiago and the surrounding region on July 17. Davis had left the island by then to follow Major-General Nelson A. Miles (1839–1925) on an expedition to capture nearby Puerto Rico from Spain. The highlight of the trip for Davis was the day he rode into Coamo with three other correspondents and accepted the town's surrender. Spain and the United States signed a peace agreement soon afterward, on August 12.

End of a writing life

Davis spent the rest of his life publishing as much as he could. Over his career, he wrote seven popular novels and twenty-five dramatic plays. In 1901, his short story "A Derelict" told the tale of two reporters covering the Spanish-American War. It is believed Davis based the characters on himself and his fellow correspondent **Stephen Crane** (1871–1900; see entry in Primary Sources section). Davis became ill in the last months of his life and died, after a heart attack, on April 11, 1916. His war reports live on as recommended reading for students of journalism.

For More Information

Brown, Charles H. *The Correspondents' War: Journalists in the Spanish-American War.* New York: Charles Scribner's Sons, 1967.

Davis, Richard Harding. *Cuba in War Time.* New York: R. H. Russell, 1897.

Davis, Richard Harding. *The Cuban and Porto Rican Campaigns.* New York: Charles Scribner's Sons, 1898.

Lubow, Arthur. *The Reporter Who Would Be King.* New York: Charles Scribner's Sons, 1992.

Musicant, Ivan. *Empire by Default: The Spanish-American War and the Dawn of the American Century.* New York: Henry Holt and Company, 1998.

Osborn, Scott C., and Robert L. Phillips Jr. *Richard Harding Davis.* Boston, MA: Twayne Publishers, 1978.

George Dewey

Born December 26, 1837
Montpelier, Vermont
Died January 16, 1917
Washington, D.C.

American naval officer

George Dewey served in the U.S. Navy for over sixty-two years before his death at age seventy-nine. The Spanish-American War (April–August 1898) launched him to national fame. Without the war, Dewey might have retired without a battle command victory and without being remembered in the storybooks of American history. Victorious as he was, Dewey helped the United States capture the Philippines from Spain and become an imperialist nation.

Early life and education

George Dewey was born in Montpelier, the state capital of Vermont, on December 26, 1837. Dewey mixed the hard work of chores and the regularity of Sunday prayers and sermons with schoolboy pranks and an interest in battle tactics. In his autobiography, *Autobiography of George Dewey: Admiral in the Navy,* he credited the strict, righteous upbringing supplied by his father for his success.

Dewey entered military school at Norwich University at age fourteen and later attended the U.S. Naval Academy in An-

"Gentlemen, a higher power than we has won this battle today."

George Dewey quoted in The Admiral.

George Dewey. *Courtesy of the Library of Congress.*

napolis, Maryland, in 1854. During each of his four years there, Dewey's academic performance improved until he graduated fifth out of fifteen students in 1858. After two years at sea and successful completion of a final examination, Dewey boarded the steam-frigate *Wabash* for service in the Mediterranean Sea.

Building a naval career

At the outset of the American Civil War (1861–65), the navy made the twenty-three-year-old Dewey a lieutenant and assigned him to the *Mississippi* as an executive officer. Dewey served under Admiral David G. Farragut (1801–1870) and participated in naval battles at New Orleans and Port Hudson.

Dewey received his first onshore duties at the naval academy in 1867. That same year, he married Susan Boardman Goodwin, with whom he had a son, George Goodwin Dewey. Susan died in 1872 five days after giving birth to the boy. Dewey, who had lost his own mother early in his life, became especially close to his son. He spent the next twenty-four years rising to the rank of commodore, receiving his promotion on May 23, 1896, while working in Washington, D.C., at the Navy Board of Inspection and Survey.

Appointment to the Asiatic Squadron

Dewey was thinking about retirement by 1897 and worrying that he would never get to command a squadron in battle. **William McKinley** (1843–1901; served 1897–1901; see entry) became president of the United States in March 1897. Also at this time, Spain was involved in an ongoing war with Cuban rebels who had launched a revolution for independence. Stirred up by prejudice and newspaper accounts of Spain's brutal treatment of Cuban civilians, most Americans sympathized with the rebels.

Theodore Roosevelt (1858–1919; see entry) was the assistant secretary of the U.S. Navy under McKinley. Roosevelt was a jingo—someone who wanted to wage war in order to expand the territory of the United States. His boss, U.S. Navy secretary John D. Long (1838–1915), was less aggressive than Roosevelt, so the two often disagreed on matters of foreign policy.

In September 1897, Long went on vacation and left Roosevelt in charge. Before Long returned, Roosevelt intercepted a letter addressed to Long from Senator William Chandler. Chandler wanted Long to appoint Commodore John Adams Howell to replace the commander of the U.S. Asiatic Squadron, who was about to retire. Roosevelt was friends with Dewey and wanted him to get the appointment.

Roosevelt called Dewey down from the inspection office and advised him to ask Senator **Redfield Proctor** (1831–1908; see entry in Primary Sources section) to ask McKinley to appoint Dewey to the command. According to his own account of the event, as reprinted in *The Admiral* by Laurin Hall Healy and Luis Kutner, Long already had decided to appoint Dewey without instructions from McKinley. The politics of the situation, however, angered Long. When he appointed Dewey on October 21, 1897, Long called Dewey into the office and said, according to Healy and Kutner, "I am glad to appoint you, Commodore Dewey. But you won't go as rear admiral [the next higher ranking up from commodore]. You'll go as a commodore. Perhaps you used too much political influence." The insult angered Dewey.

Preparing for war

Dewey purchased every book he could find about the Philippines, where the action would take him if war came with Spain. He then boarded a vessel in San Francisco, California, on December 7, 1897, to set out into the Pacific Ocean. By New Year's Day, he had reached Nagasaki, Japan, where the flagship *Olympia* awaited him. Two days later, Rear Admiral Frederick V. McNair turned command of the U.S. Asiatic Squadron over to Commodore Dewey.

Dewey was sailing for Hong Kong to get close to the Philippines when the U.S. warship *Maine* exploded mysteriously in the harbor at Havana, Cuba, on February 15. The ship was in Cuba to protect American interests and to pressure Spain to end the revolution there. Newspapers in the United States quickly blamed Spain for the disaster, which killed more than 250 people, but no evidence ever surfaced to prove Spain was at fault.

Back in Washington, D.C., Roosevelt needed no evidence to hold Spain responsible. On February 25, when Long took a day off, Roosevelt sent a telegram to Dewey that said, according to Healy and Kutner, "Order the squadron except the *Monocacy* to Hong Kong. Keep full of coal. In the event declaration of war with Spain, your duty will be to see that the Spanish squadron does not leave the Asiatic coast, and then offensive operations in Philippine islands. Keep *Olympia*

until further orders." Long was furious when he found the order, but he did not retract it because war with Spain felt close at hand.

Over the next two months, Dewey assembled his squadron of seven warships in Hong Kong, stocked them with supplies, and worked the crews in battle drills. He also contacted the U.S. consul at Manila, O. F. Williams, to gather information about Spain's forces in Manila Bay. Spanish admiral Patricio Montojo y Pasaron commanded a fleet there with fewer guns than Dewey's squadron. Montojo, however, had the added benefit of many smaller gunboats plus land artillery at the entrance to Manila Bay, the city of Manila, and the nearby naval station on Cavité island. Spain also was putting mines at the entrance to Manila Bay. Fearless, Dewey wrote letters to Long and family members in which he boasted that he could defeat Spain in less than a day.

The Battle of Manila Bay

Unable to avoid war as he had wanted to, President McKinley sent a message to Congress on April 11, 1898, asking for authority to end the conflict in Cuba. Congress supported McKinley and officially declared war on Spain on April 25. Dewey received a telegram the next day from Long that said, according to Ivan Musicant in *Empire by Default,* "War has commenced between the United States and Spain. Proceed at once to Philippine islands. Commence operations particularly against the Spanish fleet. You must capture vessels or destroy. Use utmost endeavors."

Painted in gray battle colors, Dewey's squadron steamed for the Philippines as soon as it was ready. At the entrance to Manila Bay, just three shots silenced the Spanish artilleries at El Fraile, and not one mine exploded as Dewey's ships glided into the bay.

The Asiatic Squadron reached the capital city of Manila by daybreak on May 1. To Dewey's surprise, Montojo's fleet guarded not the city but the nearby naval station at Cavité. Montojo, who did not want Manila to be damaged in the ensuing battle, began firing on the Americans as they aligned their ships for battle. At 5:41 A.M., Dewey turned to the captain of the *Olympia* and, as told by Healy and Kutner, uttered his famous, calm command, "You may fire when you are ready, Gridley."

The battle was not even close. Dewey's squadron took just two hours to make five devastating passes along the line of Montojo's ships. Montojo's flagship, the *Reina Christina,* was the only one to charge during the encounter. Dewey repelled Montojo with blasts that killed many Spaniards, including eighty who were already in the ship's hospital. Warned that he was running out of ammunition, Dewey called for a break in the action at 7:35 A.M., retreated out of range of enemy fire, and ordered breakfast for his men.

As the smoke cleared, Dewey's troops saw that Spain's vessels hung on by a thread. Dewey also learned that instead of running out of ammunition, his ships had more rounds remaining than they had fired. At 11:14 A.M., the Asiatic Squadron resumed attacking Montojo's fleet, which surrendered shortly thereafter at 12:30 P.M.

Unable to secure Spanish permission to use the telegraph cable at Manila for sending news of his victory, Dewey dredged up the cable from the harbor floor and cut it. A couple days later he sent a boat to Hong Kong with a telegram announcing that he had lost not a single sailor while killing 167 Spaniards. When the telegram reached Washington, D.C., on May 7, Dewey was an instant hero.

The siege of Manila

Congress responded to Dewey's victory by promoting him to rear admiral. As the theatre of war shifted to Cuba and Puerto Rico over the next few months, Dewey and the U.S. Army made plans to take the Philippine capital city of Manila, which had strong artillery defenses.

Meanwhile, Dewey faced a growing problem with Germany. The European powers in general were surprised by the American victory over Spain in the Philippines. Germany, whose navy was superior to that of the United States, sent warships to Manila to try to prevent the United States from taking the islands. German ships ignored international rules of war, which required them to obey Dewey's blockade of the bay and to come and go only after receiving permission from Dewey.

On July 17, a lieutenant from a German ship boarded the *Olympia* to present a list of grievances to Dewey. Angered, Dewey replied, according to Healy and Kutner, "Do you want war with us?"

"Certainly not," said the German officer.

Dewey shot back, "Well it looks like it. And you are very near it; and, you can have it, sir, as soon as you like."

The German officer left the *Olympia* and returned to his ship. Dewey knew all along that in the event of war with Germany, the British fleet at Manila Bay would fight with the Americans. As soon as they learned this, too, the Germans began to cooperate with Dewey's blockade.

On August 13, the U.S. Army and Navy staged a fake attack on Manila, after which Spain said it would surrender after pretending to fight for its honor. Thanks to the cut telegraph cable, everyone was unaware that Spain and the United States had already signed a peace protocol in Washington, D.C., hours earlier. The fake battle killed many real Americans and Spaniards.

The Filipino Revolution of 1899

Spain had ended a revolution in the Philippines by reaching an agreement with rebel leader Emilio Aguinaldo (1869–1964) in December 1897. Living in Singapore at the outbreak of the Spanish-American War, Aguinaldo now had a chance to resurrect the revolution. Some historians say Aguinaldo contacted Dewey for support. Others say that Dewey, through U.S. consul general E. Spencer Pratt, contacted Aguinaldo and asked him to assemble rebel land forces to attack Spain in Manila.

Aguinaldo arrived in Manila Bay on May 19, 1898, aboard the American warship *McCulloch*. Aguinaldo believed Pratt had promised American support for Filipino independence in exchange for military assistance against the Spaniards. Dewey supposedly made similar promises at Manila Bay, according to the rebel leader, though Dewey later denied this.

Aguinaldo quickly assembled a force of about one thousand soldiers and fought to take the Cavité region from

Spanish troops, who had retreated into the city of Manila. The rebels also assembled a small navy, which sailed around Manila harbor with Dewey's permission. As Dewey received land forces from the United States at the end of June, however, his patience with the rebels faded. In a meeting with Filipino naval officers in July, Dewey said the United States did not recognize the Filipino flag and asked them to keep their boats away from his fleet.

After winning the Spanish-American War, the United States forced Spain to sell the Philippines to the U.S. government for $20 million as part of the Treaty of Paris on December 10, 1898. Aguinaldo severed relations with the Americans the following month. Responding to the growing threat of war with the Filipino rebels, Dewey telegraphed Long and asked for a diplomatic committee to negotiate for peace.

President McKinley appointed a peace committee but he received war instead. On February 4, 1899, fighting broke out between the Americans and Filipinos. It is uncertain which side fired the first shot. Two days later, in a very close vote, the U.S. Senate approved the Treaty of Paris and the purchase of the Philippines.

Dewey commanded the American naval activities during the beginning of the revolution until McKinley recalled him from the Philippines on May 1, 1899, the first anniversary of his victory over Montojo. The Filipino revolution seemed to be dying down then, but it actually lasted until April 1902.

Sailing into the sunset

From May through September 1899, Dewey enjoyed a leisurely, westward journey home through the Mediterranean Sea, visiting foreign diplomats along the way. His arrival in the United States on September 26 began weeks of parades, parties, and welcome-home addresses.

On November 9, 1899, Dewey married his second wife, a widow named Mildred McLean Hazel. Dewey agreed to seek the U.S. presidency in early 1900, but he failed to receive a nomination from any party. Instead, he became president of the General Board of the Navy, where he served until his death seventeen years later on January 16, 1917.

For More Information

Dewey, George. *Autobiography of George Dewey: Admiral in the Navy.* New York: Scribner, 1913.

Healy, Laurin Hall, and Luis Kutner. *The Admiral.* Chicago, IL: Ziff-Davis Publishing Company, 1944.

Long, L. *George Dewey, Vermont Boy.* Indianapolis, IN: Bobbs-Merrill Co., 1963.

Musicant, Ivan. *Empire by Default: The Spanish-American War and the Dawn of the American Century.* New York: Henry Holt and Company, 1998.

Spector, Ronald H. *Admiral of the New Empire: The Life and Career of George Dewey.* Columbia, SC: University of South Carolina Press, 1988.

West, Richard S. *Admirals of American Empire: The Combined Story of George Dewey, Alfred Thayer Mahan, Winfield Scott Schley, and William Thomas Sampson.* Westport, CT: Greenwood Press, 1971.

Máximo Gómez y Báez

Born November 18, 1836
Baní, Santo Domingo (now part of the Dominican Republic)
Died June 17, 1905
Havana, Cuba

Cuban military officer

"[Americans] continually fill their newspapers with sympathy for our cause, but what do they do? They sell us arms at good round prices—as readily as they sell supplies to the Spaniards, who oppress us; but they never gave us a thing—not even a rifle."

Máximo Gómez y Báez quoted in Marching with Gomez.

Máximo Gómez y Báez.
Courtesy of the Library of Congress.

The very name of the Spanish-American War (April–August 1898) ignores the Republic of Cuba's important role in the conflict. Spain fought many battles against its Cuban colony, both in the Ten Years' War (1868–1878) and in the Second Cuban War for Independence (1895–1898), before the United States entered the fray. Cubans provided military information and assistance to the United States in its effort to drive Spain back to Europe. One of the rebel leaders throughout these struggles was a Dominican farmer named Máximo Gómez y Báez.

Childhood and early military career

Máximo Gómez y Báez was born in Baní, Santo Domingo, on November 18, 1836. (Santo Domingo occupied the eastern part of the island called Hispaniola, east of Cuba. Gómez's birthplace became the Dominican Republic in 1844.) Gómez grew up in a middle-class family and entered a religious seminary to study to become a priest. In the mid-1850s, however, invaders from neighboring Haiti (on the western part of Hispaniola) swept Gómez into a fighting career.

From 1861 to 1865, at the invitation of the leader of the Dominican Republic, Spain tried to reconquer the country, which had been a Spanish colony until 1795. Gómez served the Spanish during the conflict as a captain in the army reserve. Military life suited the strict, serious young man, but the way Spain treated the civilians and black slaves of Santo Domingo disgusted him.

The Ten Years' War

On October 10, 1868, rebels on the nearby island of Cuba launched a revolution against Spain, which still held Cuba as a colony. *Peninsulares*—emigrants from Spain—controlled government and wealth on the island. The middle and lower classes in Cuba wanted more power to shape economic and trade policies. Slavery was still legal, but slaves, naturally, wanted freedom and full participation in government.

Aligned against Spain because of his experiences in the Dominican Republic, Gómez joined the Cuban rebels to help with the military effort. Gómez soon was promoted to the rank of general and commander of Oriente Province, along the eastern end of the island.

By 1871, Spain had confined the Cuban rebels to Oriente. Gómez met with the president of the Republic of Cuba, Carlos Manuel de Céspedes, to recommend a strategy of economic destruction. Gómez wanted the rebels to invade the western half of the island, destroy the sugar and tobacco plantations, and set the slaves free. This would add black soldiers to the ranks of the rebel fighters and also deprive Spain of tax revenue that came from sugarcane and tobacco.

Céspedes rejected the plan and removed Gómez from command. Many of the rebels did not want freedom for the slaves, and many were landowners who did not want to see economic destruction. In fact, the rebels could not agree on whether their goal was better treatment from Spain or complete freedom from the motherland. Although Gómez eventually returned to his command in 1875, disunity led the rebels to settle for a truce called the Pact of Zanjón in 1878. Under the agreement, Spain promised to reform the colonial government.

Preparing for revolt

Reform never happened, however, because Spain did not want to lose the money it was receiving from controlling the Cuban economy and its people. Efforts to launch another rebellion failed until the early 1890s, when Spanish tariffs—taxes—on goods imported from the United States raised the cost of living and discontent for the Cuban middle and lower classes. This time, a Cuban patriot named Jose Martí (1853–1895) organized a second revolution that would succeed.

Working from New York City, Martí began assembling military leadership for the revolution in 1892. With his military capability and previous experience in the Ten Years' War, Gómez was an obvious choice to lead the rebel army. In September 1892, Martí visited Gómez in the Dominican Republic to offer him the role of commander in chief. Gómez, who had settled in his homeland to work as a farmer, gladly accepted. Next, Martí asked Antonio Maceo (1845–1896) to join the rebel army as Gómez's second-in-command. Maceo, a Cuban of African ancestry, had fought in the Ten Years' War and later had become a plantation owner in Costa Rica. Maceo initially resisted resuming his military service, but he finally agreed to join Martí's forces in June 1893.

The Second Cuban War for Independence begins

After much anticipation and many delays, Cuban rebels launched the revolution on February 25, 1895, at Baire, Cuba. Spanish authorities quickly crushed the rebels in the western provinces near the capital of Havana. Meanwhile, the military leaders had encountered travel problems and had not yet reached the island. Maceo finally arrived in Cuba on March 31; Gómez met Martí in the Dominican Republic and they followed on April 11.

On May 4, the three men met at La Mejorana to discuss military strategy. They appointed Gómez commander in chief of the Cuban Liberating Army, Maceo chief of operations in the Oriente Province, and Martí head of the revolution outside Cuba. Martí did not live to continue in his role, however; he was killed in a Spanish attack at Don Ríos on May 19, 1895. Gómez and the rebels now had a martyr to inspire their cause.

Plotting military strategy

Prime Minister Antonio Cánovas del Castillo (1828–1897) and the rest of Spain were not too worried at first when the revolution broke out in February. They became concerned, however, when they learned that Maceo and Gómez were headed for the island. On March 31, Spain announced that it was sending Arsenio Martínez de Campos (1834–1900), a general who had fought in the Ten Years' War, to defend Spain's interests in Cuba.

Martínez de Campos's plan was to repeat the defense that had foiled the rebels in the Ten Years' War. This meant confining the rebels to the eastern, poorer end of the island, and eventually surrounding and overwhelming them with large numbers of Spanish soldiers. The main Spanish tool for confinement was the *trocha*—a barrier two hundred yards wide and fifty miles long consisting of fallen trees, barbed wire, and military forts that stretched across the narrowest part of the island.

Up against this defense, Gómez got to try his strategy of economic destruction, which was proposed unsuccessfully decades before. According to Philip S. Foner in *The Spanish-Cuban-American War and the Birth of American Imperialism*, Gómez said, "The chains of Cuba have been forged by her own richness, and it is precisely this which I propose to do away with soon."

On July 1, 1895, Gómez prohibited Cubans from transporting industrial or agricultural products to areas containing Spanish troops. He also ordered all sugarcane plantations and mills to stop production. When, in spite of his order, harvest and production continued, Gómez issued a new command on November 6 for the complete destruction of all sugarcane plantations and their buildings and railroad connections. He planned to enlist dislocated plantation workers in the rebellion.

Knocking on Havana's door

On November 29, Gómez and Maceo accomplished a major feat—crossing the *trocha*. Maceo and fifteen hundred rebel troops did so in an early morning fog near the town of

Ciego de Avila. Gómez and nine hundred of his soldiers also made the crossing a little farther to the north, assembling on the other side with Maceo for a victory celebration. Perched atop a horse on November 30, Gómez gave a stirring speech to prepare his troops for the fighting and death ahead.

At this point, the Liberating Army in the east got a new ally—the Invading Army in the west. Gómez confirmed the appointment of Maceo as commander of the Invading Army. Maceo, whom the Spaniards called "the lion" for his great strength, had never lost a battle in all his years of fighting for the Cuban cause. Maceo would lead the charge across the western end of Cuba to the capital city of Havana and the province of Pinar del Rio.

While Maceo made his march, Gómez concentrated on economic destruction and diversionary tactics. The Spanish called Gómez "the fox" because he was skilled at evading their forces. He also instilled fear by using firing squads to murder Cubans who disobeyed his orders.

On January 22, 1896, Maceo reached Mantua, the westernmost town in Cuba. Along the way he had passed Havana, raising fears there but declining to attack its strong defenses with his small forces. The invasion of the west still marked the high point of the entire revolution for the Cuban rebels.

Battling "the butcher"

Days before Maceo reached Mantua, Spanish general Martínez de Campos resigned under pressure due to his failing military effort. Prime Minister Cánovas replaced Martínez de Campos with General Valeriano Weyler y Nicolau (1838–1930), a military man known for ruthlessness and referred to as "the butcher" by the American press.

Arriving in Cuba in February, Weyler lived up to his infamous reputation by relocating all Cuban civilians from the countryside into concentration camps to prevent them from helping the rebels. Weyler's troops burned the homes and fields left behind by the civilians. Hundreds of thousands of Cubans died from starvation and disease in the crowded, dirty camps over the next two years.

Gómez and Maceo met on February 19 and again on March 10 to discuss their next move. Both agreed that Maceo should continue attacking in the west while Gómez concentrated on the central provinces. They felt that defeating Weyler would require an increased tempo of economic destruction to make the war ever more expensive for Spain. The meeting on March 10 would be the last time the two Cuban leaders saw each other.

After an extended campaign against Weyler's troops in the west, Maceo headed east for more meetings with Gómez and was killed in a nighttime battle at San Pedro de Hernádez on December 7, 1896. Gómez's son, Francisco Gómez Toro, also died in the same battle while trying to rescue Maceo.

From January 1897 to April 1898, three thousand troops under Gómez's command had forty-one encounters with Spanish soldiers in the central province of Las Villas. During this time, the rebel forces controlled the eastern provinces of Camagüey and Oriente, except for a few large cities. Cuban residents there called each other *ciudadano*, which means citizen. Despite the ongoing economic hardship it was suffering, however, Spain refused to give up the fight.

In August 1897, Prime Minister Práxedes M. Sagasta had to replace Cánovas, who had been assassinated. Sagasta recalled Weyler from Cuba and sent General Ramón Blanco (1831–1906) to command the Spanish army on the island. Blanco only modified Weyler's concentration policy slightly by allowing some people to return home if they had the means to support themselves. As a result, Cuban civilians continued to die in the prison camps.

The United States declares war

As Blanco arrived in Cuba, U.S. president **William McKinley** (1843–1901; served 1897–1901; see entry) was under pressure from Congress and the American public to enter the war. Americans sympathized with the rebels's desire for independence. McKinley resisted the pressure because he wanted to negotiate for peace and did not want a war to disrupt America's booming economy.

Things changed on February 15, 1898, however, when the U.S. warship *Maine* exploded mysteriously in the harbor at Havana, Cuba, killing 268 men aboard. Although there was no evidence that Spain was responsible, Americans blamed the Spanish government for failing to safeguard the vessel. In March and April, McKinley began preparing for war.

As the United States threatened to come to Cuba's aid, Spain talked about ending the fighting and giving Cuba freedom to govern itself, although still as a Spanish colony. Gómez flatly rejected these offers. According to Foner, Gómez and rebel leader **Calixto García** (1839–1898; see entry in Primary Sources section) said, "The names of our champions who have fallen and those of the 150,000 defenseless Cubans pitilessly murdered by General Weyler would condemn us from Heaven if we were to treat with Spain." Gómez said the only way to end the war was for Spain to leave Cuba.

Gómez and the Spanish-American War

When the United States declared war on April 25, Gómez asked America to send guns instead of troops. He feared that U.S. involvement would lead to American control of the island. McKinley decided to send troops instead, and he turned to the Cubans for military information. On May 1, 1898, U.S. Army lieutenant Andrew S. Rowan met with García in Bayamo, Cuba. García and Rowan decided to land fifteen thousand American troops on the north coast of Cuba and to attack Holguín, one of the few cities in Oriente Province that Spain still controlled.

Meanwhile, Gómez corresponded with General Blanco, who said it was time for Spain and Cuba to end their differences and repel the American invaders together. Blanco suggested that Spain would give Cuba complete freedom if the rebels assisted the mother country. According to Foner, Gómez responded to Blanco saying:

> Your audacity *[boldness]* in proposing peace terms to me again dumbfounds me when you know that Cubans and Spaniards can never live in peace on the soil of Cuba. You represent on this continent an old and discredited monarchy, and we are fighting for an American principle, the principle of Bolívar and Washington. You say that we belong to the same race and invite me to fight against a foreign invader, but you are again mistaken because there are no differences of blood or race.

I believe in only one race: humanity, and for me there are only good and evil nations. Spain has been until now an evil one, while the United States at this time is fulfilling for Cuba a duty for humanity and civilization. From the dark savage Indian to the refined blond Englishman, a man for me deserves respect according to his honesty and feelings whatever may be the country or race to which he belongs or the religion which he practices.

In the end, Gómez did not get to fight with the Americans to send Spain back to Europe. Gómez was preparing to receive American troops on the northern coast when the Spanish navy sailed into Santiago de Cuba on May 19, moving the theatre of war to the southeastern coast of the island. In land and sea battles at the end of June and beginning of July, forces under Cuban general Calixto García, U.S. admiral William T. Sampson (1840–1902), and U.S. general **William R. Shafter** (1835–1906; see entry) forced Spain to surrender the entire region around Santiago. This led to a cease-fire on August 12, 1898, under which Spain finally agreed to set Cuba free.

Cuba Libre?

During the revolution, *Cuba Libre* (Free Cuba) had been a rallying cry for the rebels. Now, when they expected to finally get control of their island, the United States took over instead—just as Gómez had feared. In December, McKinley set up a military government under Major-General John R. Brooke, resolving to remain in power there until America decided that Cuba was ready to govern itself. On January 1, 1899, Spain officially left the island, turning control over to the United States.

In ceremonies at Havana that day, Gómez wished to be received by the army in which he had served. Brooke, however, insulted the Cubans by refusing to allow rebel soldiers into the city. Brooke did not trust the rebels to behave themselves around Spanish soldiers. He instead invited some Cuban generals to the ceremonies, eight of whom attended. Gómez refused to be present in Havana that day, but he finally got to march victoriously into Havana with his troops on February 24. Months later, on June 7, he gave a farewell address to the Liberating Army and returned to his homeland.

Over the next three years, Cuba made plans to adopt a constitution and set up its own government. Gómez was a popular choice to be the republic's first president, but he did not want the job; instead, he supported Tomás Estrada Palma (1835–1908). On May 20, 1902, ceremonies in Havana marked the end of the American military government and the beginning of the Cuban Republic. This time, Gómez attended the celebration, helping to raise the Cuban flag over the government palace in Havana with tears streaming down his cheeks. Gómez died three years later, on June 17, 1905, while visiting his beloved city.

For More Information

Books

Flint, Grover. *Marching with Gomez: A War Correspondent's Field Note-Book Kept During Four Months with the Cuban Army.* Boston, MA: Lamson, Wolffe and Company, 1898.

Foner, Philip S. *The Spanish-Cuban-American War and the Birth of American Imperialism.* New York: Monthly Review Press, 1972.

Golay, Michael. *The Spanish-American War.* New York: Facts On File, 1995.

Musicant, Ivan. *Empire by Default: The Spanish-American War and the Dawn of the American Century.* New York: Henry Holt and Company, 1998.

Periodicals

Smith, Joseph. "Heroes of the Cuban Revolution: Martí, Maceo, and Gómez." *Historian,* No. 44, Winter 1994, pp. 3–8.

William Randolph Hearst

Born April 29, 1863
San Francisco, California
Died August 14, 1951
Beverly Hills, California

American newspaper publisher

The Spanish-American War (April–August 1898) pitted the United States against Spain in a battle to drive Spain from its colony of Cuba. During the conflict, the owners of two New York newspapers fought each other to increase circulation and readership. Joseph Pulitzer (1847–1911) had been running the *New York World* for twelve years when William Randolph Hearst bought the *New York Journal* in 1895. A rivalry quickly developed between Pulitzer and Hearst, and they used the Second Cuban War for Independence (1895–1898), and later the Spanish-American War, to fuel their fight. In the end, America won its war, Hearst won his, and the Cuban rebels found themselves at the mercy of an American military government.

Early career

William Randolph Hearst was born in San Francisco on April 29, 1863. His father, George Hearst, owned and operated profitable gold, silver, and copper mines; consequently, the younger Hearst grew up with the privileges that wealth often brings. After getting expelled from Harvard University

"Please remain. You furnish the pictures and I'll furnish the war."

William Randolph Hearst quoted in The Correspondents's War: Journalists in the Spanish-American War.

William Randolph Hearst.
Courtesy of the Library of Congress.

in 1885 thanks to poor grades, Hearst wanted to enter the newspaper business. He asked his father to give him the *San Francisco Examiner,* a daily newspaper that George Hearst had bought to help advance his own political career. George refused his son's request, and Hearst instead went to work for Joseph Pulitzer's *New York World* beginning in 1886.

Pulitzer had purchased the *World* three years earlier, when he was just thirty-six, and he used it to create a reporting style called "new journalism." The *World* catered to readers from the immigrant and working classes. It featured sensational stories about crime and corruption in business and government. The Sunday edition carried a comics section that included cartoonist Richard Outcault's popular character, The Yellow Kid.

Hearst studied Pulitzer's methods while working as his apprentice (a person who works for another, often without pay, in return for learning a trade). In 1887, George Hearst became a U.S. senator. No longer able to work on the *Examiner,* he transferred control of the newspaper to his son. Hearst headed west, as his father had done before him in 1849. And, like his father, he struck gold— building newspaper readership using a combination of sensational stories, high-paid writers and artists, publicity stunts, and old-fashioned hard work.

Yellow journalism

By 1895, Hearst needed money for a new journalistic challenge. Already a success in San Francisco, he set his sights on New York by purchasing the *New York Journal* for $150,000. Hearst got the money from his mother, who had inherited a large fortune when George Hearst died in 1891.

Hearst published his first issue of the *Journal* on November 7, 1895, immediately creating a rivalry with Pulitzer's *World.* The papers fought each other for greater circulation with sensational stories and dirty business tactics. After Hearst stole cartoonist Richard Outcault to write Yellow Kid comic strips for the *Journal,* Pulitzer substituted artist George Luks to continue creating the strip for the *World.* "Yellow journalism" became a term commonly used to describe both Hearst and Pulitzer's tactics and journalistic styles.

The Cuban revolution

When Hearst published his first issue of the *Journal* in November 1895, Cuba was nine months into a revolution against colonial rule by Spain. The revolution began in part because the United States had raised the tariff—import tax—on sugar, Cuba's main product; in return, Spain had raised tariffs on United States imports. The small farmers and working people of Cuba suffered from these tariffs and struggled with rapidly rising costs of living. By rebelling, they hoped to free Cuba from Spanish control in order to improve their lives financially and socially.

The U.S. government refused to take sides officially in the Cuban revolution. Supporting Spain would make the United States seem heartless. On the other hand, supporting Cuba would make the United States appear to be too friendly with the working classes and black rebels who fought among Cuba's revolutionary ranks. American businesses and their pro-business president, **William McKinley** (1843–1901; served 1897–1901; see entry), did not want to see the working classes prevail in Cuba.

As a champion of the working classes, Hearst wanted the United States to help the Cuban rebels in their cause. In January 1897, he hired writer **Richard Harding Davis** (1864–1916; see entry) and illustrator Frederick Remington (1861–1909) to travel to Cuba to capture scenes of the rebellion. (Davis and Remington were only two of the many correspondents that Hearst, Pulitzer, and others sent to Cuba.) Soon after he arrived, Remington got bored and sent a telegram to Hearst saying, according to Charles H. Brown in *The Correspondents' War,* "Everything is quiet. There is no trouble. There will be no war. I wish to return."

Hearst's response to Remington became one of the most famous quotes of the war: "Please remain. You furnish the pictures and I'll furnish the war." While Hearst denied ever saying this, he clearly wanted action in Cuba to help the *Journal* grow.

The Dupuy de Lôme letter

In February 1898, McKinley was still avoiding war with Spain, which had installed a reform government in

Cuba. Spanish reform may have been a response to McKinley's State of the Union message in December 1897, in which McKinley had urged Spain to end the fighting and clean up the corrupt government on the island. Revolution continued, however, because the rebels wanted independence, not reform (improvement or change). In January 1898, after riots in the Cuban capital of Havana, McKinley sent the U.S. warship *Maine* to protect American interests in the region.

Sometime after McKinley's message, the Spanish minister to the United States, Enrique Dupuy de Lôme, wrote a letter to a friend in Cuba. In it he said, "McKinley is weak and catering to the rabble and, besides, a low politician who desires to leave a door open to himself and to stand well with the jingoes of his party," according to Philip S. Foner in *The Spanish-Cuban-American War and the Birth of American Imperialism."* (A jingo was a person who wanted America to wage war in order to expand its power worldwide.) Dupuy de Lôme also said that military victory was the only acceptable result for Spain in Cuba, which meant that the reform government was a fake.

Rebels in Cuba stole the letter and sent it to New York to the Cuban *Junta* (pronounced HOON-ta), which was the revolutionaries' public relations organization in the United States. The *Junta* turned the letter over to Hearst's *Journal*. Not waiting to verify its accuracy, Hearst printed it on February 9, 1898, under the headline, "Worst Insult to the United States in Its History."

Remember the *Maine*

Six days later, the *Maine* exploded mysteriously in the Havana harbor the evening of February 15, killing over 250 people. In correspondence with officials in Washington, D.C., *Maine* captain Charles D. Sigsbee asked the public to withhold opinion on the disaster until after a full investigation.

Hearst needed no investigation, however. Awakened in the middle of the night with news of the explosion, Hearst said, "This means war," according to David Nasaw in *The Chief*. On February 17, the front page of the *Journal* had a blazing headline: "Destruction of the Warship *Maine* Was the Work of An Enemy." A caption under a drawing of the warship read,

"The Spaniards, it is believed, arranged to have the *Maine* anchored over one of the Harbor mines. Wires connected the mine with a power magazine and it is thought the explosion was caused by sending an electric current through the wire."

Hearst played up the event for all it was worth over the next several weeks. He offered a $50,000 reward for identification of the culprit and began a fundraising drive for a *Maine* memorial. While McKinley patiently waited until the end of March for the official naval investigation to issue its report, Hearst criticized the president for siding with the American business leaders who wanted to avoid war. Across the nation Americans cried, "Remember the *Maine,* to hell with Spain!"

The *Journal's* war arrives

At the end of March, a naval board concluded that an external mine had destroyed the *Maine.* (A follow-up naval investigation, completed in 1976, concluded that it actually was more likely to have been an internal explosion in the ship's ammunition magazines, while a National Geographic Society-sponsored computer study in 1997 said external and internal causes were equally likely.) While the board could not identify the culprit, the United States was already on a course for war with Spain. On April 11, the president asked Congress for permission to use the U.S. Army and Navy to end the rebel conflict in Cuba. Congress granted this permission on April 19. The following day, the *Journal* headline read, "NOW TO AVENGE THE *MAINE*!" Only one week after the United States declared war on April 25, the front page of Hearst's paper asked, "How do you like the *Journal's* war?"

After calling loudly for war for over a year, Hearst decided he had to fight in it. After all, **Theodore Roosevelt** (1858–1919; see entry) had called for war and later resigned as assistant secretary of the navy to be second-in-command of a volunteer cavalry regiment called the Rough Riders. In late May 1898, Hearst wrote to President McKinley offering to equip an army regiment with his own money and fight with the regiment as a soldier. McKinley, whom Hearst had opposed in the presidential election of 1896, rejected the idea.

Undaunted, Hearst approached the navy, offering to donate one of his yachts, arm it for action, and serve on it as a commander. The navy took the *Buccaneer* but refused to let Hearst serve aboard it. Meanwhile, rumors spread that a Spanish fleet was sailing from Spain to attack U.S. admiral **George Dewey** (1837–1917; see entry) in the Philippines. Hearst asked a colleague in Europe, James Creelman, to buy a vessel to sink in the Suez Canal in order to block the Spaniards. When the Spanish fleet turned back to Spain, however, Hearst's daring and illegal plan became unnecessary.

Hearst in Cuba

Rejected for military service by both the army and the navy, Hearst appointed himself as a correspondent to cover the war in Cuba for the *Journal*. In the middle of June 1898, Hearst and a team of colleagues boarded the steamship *Sylvia,* which Hearst had equipped with a printing press, dark room for photographs, kitchen, and telegraph equipment.

Once in Cuba, Hearst got to interview several of the war's top military leaders, including U.S. general **William R. Shafter** (1835–1906; see entry), Cuban general **Calixto García;** (1839–1898; see entry in Primary Sources section), and Spanish admiral **Pascual Cervera y Topete** (1839–1909; see entry). On July 1, 1898, near Santiago, Hearst watched American soldiers and volunteers storm the Spanish ground troops in the longest, deadliest battle of the war.

Two days later, on July 3, the Spanish navy tried to escape the harbor at Santiago, only to be crushed by an American fleet led by Commodore Winfield S. Schley (1839–1909). On American Independence Day, July 4, Hearst and the other passengers on the *Sylvia* steamed among the wrecked Spanish vessels in search of a story. What they found were twenty-nine Spanish sailors stranded on a nearby beach. Approaching closely in a small boat, Hearst leapt into the water to reach the beach and captured the men as prisoners of war. Back onboard the *Sylvia,* Hearst convinced the prisoners to give three cheers for the United States while capturing the stunt in a photograph. When Hearst finally turned the prisoners over to military authorities, he got a receipt to prove that the story was true.

Hostilities between Spain and the United States ended soon after the two countries signed a peace protocol on August 12, 1898. Back in New York, Hearst celebrated victory with the same theatrical flair with which he had called for war. When Admiral William T. Sampson (1840–1902) sailed the Atlantic fleet up the Hudson river in a naval parade, the *Journal* declared a holiday for the celebration, much to the anger of local authorities.

On August 21, 1898, Hearst declared that the daily circulation of the *Journal* exceeded that of its nearest competitor by over two hundred thousand. By the end of the year, he claimed that his New York papers had reached a combined daily circulation of 1.25 million readers—the largest readership in the world. Hearst had won the circulation war.

Aftermath

Hearst spent the rest of his life displaying the flair that had made him famous. He built a diversified media empire that included newspapers, magazines, news services, and movies. Hearst died on August 14, 1951, remembering his time in Cuba as one of the greatest adventures of his life.

For More Information

Brown, Charles H. *The Correspondents' War: Journalists in the Spanish-American War*. New York: Charles Scribner's Sons, 1967.

Foner, Philip S. *The Spanish-Cuban-American War and the Birth of American Imperialism*. New York: Monthly Review Press, 1972.

Frazier, Nancy. *William Randolph Hearst: Modern Media Tycoon*. Woodbridge, CT: Blackbirch Marketing, 2001.

Nasaw, David. *The Chief: The Life of William Randolph Hearst*. Boston, MA: Houghton Mifflin Company, 2000.

Procter, Ben. *William Randolph Hearst: The Early Years, 1863–1910*. New York: Oxford University Press, 1998.

Whitelaw, Nancy. *William Randolph Hearst and the American Century*. Greensboro, NC: Morgan Reynolds, 1999.

George Hoar

Born August 29, 1826
Concord, Massachusetts
Died September 30, 1904
Worcester, Massachusetts

American politician

"I can see no difference in the lynching of a Southern [African American] postmaster and lynching [the Filipinos] because they think a government derives its just powers from the consent of the governed, and got those ideas from the Constitution of the United States."

George Hoar quoted in Twelve Against Empire.

George Hoar. *Hulton Archive/Getty Images. Reproduced by permission.*

Before the Spanish-American War (April–August 1898), the domain of the United States stretched no farther then the shores of the Atlantic and Pacific Oceans and the borders of Canada and Mexico. Led by President **William McKinley** (1843–1901; served 1897–1901; see entry), the United States ended the war by acquiring the Spanish colonies of Puerto Rico in the Caribbean, Guam in the Pacific Ocean, and the Philippines in Asia, and by establishing military control over newly independent Cuba. McKinley's Republican Party led this mission of imperialism, or control of foreign people who lack representation in government. By acquiring colonies, many Americans hoped to provide foreign markets for their manufactured goods.

In the nineteenth century, Massachusetts was one of America's industrial centers, particularly in the manufacture of shoes and textiles. Yet one of the most vocal opponents of the Republican Party's imperialistic policies was an otherwise loyal Republican senator from Massachusetts. His name was George "Frisbie" Hoar, and his crusade against imperialism put personal values ahead of party loyalty.

Childhood

George Frisbie Hoar was born in Concord, Massachusetts, on August 29, 1826. Fifty-one years earlier, at North Bridge, three of Hoar's ancestors had fought in the second battle of the American Revolutionary War (1775–83). In 1776, Hoar's grandfather, Roger Sherman, was one of the signers of the American Declaration of Independence. This connection with history helped Hoar develop a love for democracy, upon which he believed the country had been founded.

Hoar grew up in Concord with four older siblings in a hard-working New England family. His father, Samuel Hoar, was a successful attorney. His mother, Sarah (Sherman) Hoar, founded a school to teach reading and sewing to African American children in New Haven, Connecticut. George shared his mother's respect for education and acceptance of people of different races.

Attorney and politician

After graduating from Harvard University with both an undergraduate degree in 1846 and a law degree in 1949, Hoar opened a law practice in Worcester, Massachusetts. The debate over slavery that would lead to the American Civil War (1861–65) in 1861 was heating up at the time. The Free Soil Party had formed in 1848 to give people an alternative to the Whig Party, which did not oppose the extension of slavery into new American territories in the West. Free Soilers opposed slavery, mostly because it was hard for non-slaveowners to compete against farms and businesses that used slaves for labor. Hoar, however, thought slavery was immoral.

"Frisbie," as Hoar's friends called him, spent twenty years practicing law in Worcester, a town he would call home until he died. In 1852, at age twenty-five, Hoar spent one term in the Massachusetts House of Representatives as a member of the Free Soil Party. In 1857 he served a term in the state senate as a member of the Republican Party, which had recently formed to replace the Free Soil Party. To Hoar's great approval, the Republican Party made morality part of its opposition to slavery while also seeking to protect the interests of businesses in the North.

From the House to the Senate

In 1869, the people of Massachusetts elected Hoar to the U.S. House of Representatives. He served four terms there until his election in 1877 to the U.S. Senate, where he served until his death in 1904. As a Republican, Hoar voted in favor of measures to build American industries and to protect them from foreign competition. He believed that hard work in a system of capitalism (an economic system where goods are owned by private businesses and price, production, and distribution are privately determined based on competition in a free market) was God's plan for the progress of civilization.

Yet Hoar also supported a number of social and economic policies that were more popular with the Democratic Party than with his colleagues. Viewing education as the key to personal improvement, Hoar proposed a national plan for public education, especially to help newly freed slaves in the South. (Congress did not pass his plan, however.) Hoar also supported the Sherman Antitrust Act, which was designed to prevent businesses from getting big enough to reduce competition. He also supported the right of women to vote and the right of workers to form labor unions to bargain for fair working conditions. Thanks to his positions on these issues, Hoar became known as a "Half-Breed Republican."

The Spanish-American War

Spain faced a rebellion in its colony of Cuba beginning in February 1895. Led by General **Máximo Gómez y Báez** (1836–1905; see entry), the Cuban rebels wanted freedom to govern their country and control their economic and foreign trade policies. While both sides engaged in violent tactics, newspapers in the United States focused on the Spanish practice of executing prisoners and imprisoning civilians in concentration camps, where hundreds of thousands died from starvation and disease. This swayed Americans to favor the Cubans and call for war with Spain.

Senator Hoar resisted war. Publicly, he said the United States should negotiate for peace, as President McKinley was doing. Privately, he knew that Boston capitalists opposed war, because war might upset the strong U.S. economy, which had finally recovered from the severe depression of 1893. In December 1897, Hoar asked Boston business leader T. Jefferson Coolidge to rally Bostonians to contribute to a presidential relief fund for starving Cubans. Hoar hoped the fund would help the United States stay out the war while still expressing sympathy for the oppressed.

On February 15, 1898, the U.S. warship *Maine* exploded mysteriously in the harbor at Havana, Cuba, killing more than 250 people aboard. A U.S. naval investigation concluded that a mine had caused the explosion, but the naval court could not assign blame for the incident. Frenzied Americans blamed Spain and cried "Remember the *Maine*" to push McKinley to declare war. In this environment, the American business community finally came to support U.S. intervention in the war. On April 11, McKinley asked Congress to give him authority to use American forces to send Spain back to Europe.

Loyal to his party whenever his conscience did not strongly object, Hoar publicly supported McKinley's decision to go to war. He also supported the Teller Amendment, a statement by Congress that the United States intended to leave Cuba to govern itself after securing peace for the island. Yet Hoar refused to support a resolution recognizing the Cuban government as legitimate, and when the Senate met on April 25 to officially declare war, Hoar was absent.

The annexation of Hawaii

McKinley used the war as an opportunity to seize the independent country of Hawaii for the United States. American naval action against Spain in the Philippines (located south of China) on May 1 made Hawaii appear to be a valuable stepping stone to Asia. Moreover, American businesses, especially the sugar, pineapple, and banana industries, would profit greatly from U.S. control of the Hawaiian islands. The capitalist Hawaiian government—run by Sanford B. Dole, who had organized a revolt against the Hawaiian monarchy in 1893—was favorable to American intervention, although the majority of native Hawaiians opposed it.

Senator Hoar had great concerns about taking Hawaii. In December 1897, he had submitted a petition to Congress opposing annexation (adding territory to an existing country) that had been signed by more than twenty-one thousand

Hawaiians. Hoar saw annexation as the first step on the path to U.S. imperialism. This path might open wide if the United States won the war with Spain, which had colonies around the globe. In a conversation in the summer of 1898, McKinley assured Hoar that he wanted only to protect Hawaii from Japan, which had its eye on the islands, and had no intention of using its annexation to begin to build a global empire.

In a speech before the Senate on July 5, 1898, Hoar revealed that he would support the resolution to annex Hawaii. According to Frederick H. Gillett in *George Frisbie Hoar,* however, Hoar warned the country not to look beyond Hawaii for other possessions:

> If this be the first step in the acquisition of barbarous arch-ipelagoes *[large group of islands]* in distant seas; if we are to enter into competition with the great powers of Europe in the plundering of China, in the division of Africa; if we are to quit our own to stand on foreign lands; if our commerce is hereafter to be forced on unwilling people at the cannon's mouth; if we are ourselves to be governed in part by peoples to whom the Declaration of Independence is a stranger; or worse still, if we are to govern subject and vassal states, trampling, as we do it, on our own great character which recognizes alike the liberty and the dignity of individual manhood, then let us resist this thing in the beginning, and let us resist it to the death. I do not agree with those gentlemen who think we should wrest the Philippine Islands from Spain and take charge of them ourselves.

The Treaty of Paris

Fighting between Spain and the United States ended on August 13, 1898, the day after the two countries signed a peace protocol. The U.S. Navy had defeated Spain at Manila in the Philippines and at Santiago in Cuba. These victories allowed the U.S. Army to force surrenders at both islands, as well as at the Spanish colony of Puerto Rico. In addition, the U.S. Army had captured the Pacific island of Guam on its way to reinforce the U.S. Navy in the Philippines.

The peace protocol forced Spain to give freedom to Cuba and to give Puerto Rico and Guam to the United States. The fate of the Philippines would be decided later in treaty negotiations in Paris beginning October 1. To represent the United States, McKinley appointed five members to a peace commission: three imperialists, one moderate, and only one anti-imperialist. Filipinos were not invited to the negotiations, even though they had been fighting for independence from Spain. Despite this fact, and contrary to his promise to Hoar, McKinley said Americans had a duty first to Christianize (teach the ways of the Christian religion) and educate the Filipinos before leaving them to govern themselves.

Hoar opposed colonization of the Philippines. He believed that under the Declaration of Independence and the U.S. Constitution, governments get their power only from the consent of the governed. Seizing a foreign colony that wanted to govern itself would violate the very principle of democracy upon which the United States had separated itself from Great Britain in 1776. Indeed, Hoar compared imperialism to slavery, saying that neither should exist in a free society.

Spain and the United States signed the Treaty of Paris to end the war on December 10, 1898. Spain agreed to sell the Philippines to the United States for $20 million. (The United States got Puerto Rico and Guam at no charge to compensate for its war expenses.) Under the U.S. Constitution, the Senate had to ratify the treaty by a two-thirds majority before it could become American law. A majority of American business journals published that winter favored ratification.

The battle for ratification

McKinley submitted the treaty to the Senate on January 4, 1899. Five days later, Hoar spoke in the Senate to urge his colleagues to reject it. According to the *Congressional Record*, Hoar said, "The question with which we now have to deal is whether Congress may conquer and may govern, without their consent and against their will, a foreign nation, a separate, distinct, and numerous people, a territory not hereafter to be populated by Americans, to be formed into American States and to take its part in fulfilling and executing the purposes for which the Constitution was framed."

Newspapers printed Hoar's speech under many headlines, including one in the *New York World* that said "No Nation Was Ever Created Good Enough to Own Another," according to Richard E. Welch Jr. in *George Frisbie Hoar and the Half-Breed Republicans*. Andrew Carnegie (1835–1919), the wealthy industrialist who had made his fortune in steel, sent Hoar $1,000 to pay for distributing the speech. Five days later, Hoar introduced a Senate resolution that would require the United States to support the right of the Filipinos to govern themselves.

Senator Henry Cabot Lodge (1850–1924), also from Massachusetts, gave a speech in response to Hoar and other anti-imperialists on January 24, 1899. One of his most effective arguments was that the Treaty of Paris did not amount to imperialism because it only ended the war and gave the United States time to decide what was best for the Philippines. He also suggested that "civilizing" the Filipinos would benefit America's economy.

On February 6, 1898, the Senate approved the treaty by a vote of 57 to 27—barely over the required two-thirds majority. Only two more votes in opposition would have defeated it. Hoar and Senator Eugene Hale were the only Republicans to oppose the McKinley administration by voting against the treaty. In gratitude, Hoar sent Hale a gift that he inscribed, according to Gillett, "To the Honorable Eugene Hale, who alone of my colleagues voted with me against the repeal of the Declaration of Independence."

The Philippine rebellion

Two days before the Senate voted on the treaty, fighting broke out between Filipino rebels and the American military. It was the start of a bloody war that lasted three years and cost tens of thousands of lives. Hoar, who had been in contact with Filipino representatives in London, believed the rebel leader Emilio Aguinaldo (1869–1964) and his government were perfectly capable of running the country.

Despite the break with his party over the Philippines, Hoar ran for reelection in 1900 as a Republican and won. Four years later, on September 30, 1904, he died at his home in Worcester, Massachusetts. The Philippines had to wait until 1946 to get the full independence that Hoar wanted for the country in 1898. Writing about the incident in his autobiography, *Autobiography of Seventy Years,* a year before his death, Hoar said:

> When I think of my party, whose glory and whose service to Liberty are the pride of my life, crushing out this people in

their effort to establish a Republic, and hear people talking about *giving* them good government, and that they are better off than they ever were under Spain, I feel very much as if I had learned that my father, or some other honored ancestor, had been a slave-trader in his time, and had boasted that he had introduced a new and easier kind of hand-cuffs or fetters to be worn by the slaves during the horrors of the middle passage.

For More Information

Books

Beisner, Robert L. *Twelve Against Empire: The Anti-Imperialists, 1898–1900.* New York: McGraw-Hill, 1968.

Gillett, Frederick H. *George Frisbie Hoar.* Boston, MA: Houghton Mifflin, 1934.

Hoar, George F. *Autobiography of Seventy Years.* 2 vols. New York: Charles Scribner's Sons, 1903.

Musicant, Ivan. *Empire by Default: The Spanish-American War and the Dawn of the American Century.* New York: Henry Holt and Company, 1998.

Welch, Richard E., Jr. *George Frisbie Hoar and the Half-Breed Republicans.* Cambridge, MA: Harvard University Press, 1971.

Periodicals

Congressional Record, 55th Congress, 3rd session. Washington D.C.: Government Printing Office. 1898 (493–503, 958–960.)

William McKinley

Born January 29, 1843
Niles, Ohio
Died September 14, 1901
Buffalo, New York

25th president of the United States

"Self-preservation is the first law of nature, as it is and should be of nations."

William McKinley quoted in William McKinley.

William McKinley. *Courtesy of the Library of Congress.*

The Spanish-American War and the subsequent acquisition of colonies by the United States were the most important events of William McKinley's presidency. McKinley sought guidance in these matters from two sources that were important to him: his Christian faith and his devotion to business.

Fighting between Spain and the United States took place in the Spanish colonies of Cuba, Puerto Rico, and the Philippines from April until August 1898. After America's decisive military victory, McKinley faced the difficult question of what to do about the Philippines, where America had defeated the Spanish navy. McKinley found an answer only after falling to his knees in the White House and praying to God for guidance. His decision to buy the colony from Spain pleased the American businesses that sought Asian markets for their goods.

Ancestry and boyhood

William McKinley inherited his devotion to God and business from a family of Christian businessmen. McKinley's father, William McKinley Sr., operated a charcoal furnace near

Niles, Ohio. In 1829, the elder McKinley married Nancy Allison, a Methodist whose ancestors hailed from Scotland. Together, the couple had nine children; the seventh, William, was born in the family's wooden cottage on January 29, 1843.

Young William went to school in Niles; after his family moved when he was nine, he attended Poland Academy, a Methodist seminary in Poland, Ohio. There, McKinley made a lifelong commitment to the Methodist faith. At age sixteen, McKinley entered Allegheny College in Meadville, Pennsylvania, but health problems forced him to leave before graduating. McKinley worked as a teacher and a postal clerk until 1861, when he felt a patriotic duty to enlist in the Union army in the American Civil War (1861–1865).

The American Civil War

The Civil War began with the Battle of Fort Sumter on April 12, 1861. The war was fought between the United States and the Confederacy: twelve southern states that had seceded—meaning withdrawn—from the Union. The southern Confederate states sought to protect states' rights, including the practice of slavery, on which their cotton plantation wealth depended. Northern states, on the other hand, wished to end slavery and build the nation around their growing manufacturing industries.

McKinley enlisted in the Union Army on June 11, 1861, as a private in Company E of the Twenty-third Ohio Volunteers. He first served under Commander William S. Rosecrans and First Major Rutherford B. Hayes (1822–1893), who would later become president of the United States. McKinley displayed courage and leadership by helping his fellow soldiers. On one occasion, he led a team of mules through heavy fire to the front lines to feed soldiers in the Battle of Antietam in September 1862. When the Civil War ended in 1865, McKinley left the army and returned to Ohio.

Attorney and husband

Back home, McKinley set out to become a lawyer. He studied as a clerk for a year with a judge and then attended Albany Law School before joining the Ohio bar and opening a practice in the city of Canton. Becoming interested in politics, McKinley received the Republican nomination for the office of prosecuting attorney in Stark County, Ohio. He won the election in 1869. McKinley fought crime in that position for two years until losing the next election in 1871. For the next five years, he practiced law until he was elected to Congress in 1876.

Meanwhile, McKinley had become a husband, marrying Ida Saxton on January 25, 1871. Together, McKinley and Saxton had two daughters, Katherine and Ida. Both daughters died young, causing considerable grief for the McKinleys.

U.S. congressman

McKinley won election to the U.S. House of Representatives from his district in Ohio in 1876. His old friend from the Civil War, the newly elected President Hayes, advised McKinley to make the tariff—or tax—issue his specialty in Congress because it promised to be one of the most important issues for the nation. By taxing imports, tariffs would give American manufacturing industries a competitive advantage. McKinley thought tariffs were necessary not only to protect businesspeople but also to keep wages high for American workers.

Except for a two-year period after losing a reelection bid in 1882, McKinley stayed in the House until 1891. In May 1890, the House passed the McKinley Tariff Act, which raised some tariffs to all-time highs and replaced others with direct subsidies, meaning payments, to American producers. These tariffs resulted in higher prices for consumers, making McKinley and other Republicans unpopular with many citizens. McKinley lost his bid for reelection that year and returned to Ohio.

From the governor's mansion to the White House

Back home again, McKinley served two terms as governor of Ohio from 1892 to 1896. During this time, he nurtured his friendship with Marcus A. Hanna, a multimillionaire industrialist from Cleveland whose money and connections would later help get McKinley to the White House. After receiving the Republican presidential nomination in June 1896, McKinley campaigned from the front porch of his house in Canton. Tens of thousands of Americans took trains to hear him speak there. McKinley won the election and took the oath of office in Washington, D.C., in March 1897.

American business during McKinley's presidency

Three things drove McKinley's presidential policies and even his approach to the Spanish-American War: the economy was finally strong again after going through a depression that began in 1893; the U.S. Census Bureau had announced that the American frontier was closed because Americans had begun settling all areas of the continent; and American industries were producing more goods than the public could consume.

As a result of these forces, American businesses sought to develop foreign markets for their goods. Imperialists, those who advocated control of foreign people who lack representation in government, believed the United States should acquire colonies for this purpose, as European and Asian powers did. Anti-imperialists opposed colonialism and wanted the United States to negotiate favorable trade agreements with foreign countries.

Speaking in his inaugural address, McKinley opposed imperialism. As told by Edwin P. Hoyt in *William McKinley,* McKinley said, "We want no wars of conquest. We must avoid the temptation of territorial aggression." Yet territorial aggression dominated McKinley's presidency in the form of the Spanish-American War.

The Cuban War for Independence

When McKinley took office in March 1897, Cubans had been rebelling against the government in Spain for two years. The American press carried stories of Spain's brutal treatment of Cuban civilians and rebels. This coverage led to growing public support for U.S. intervention in Cuba. During the prior presidential administration, Grover Cleveland (1837–1908; served 1885–1889 and 1893–1897) had chosen neither to recognize the Cuban insurgents nor to intervene to support them.

When he took office, McKinley was determined to take the same course. As a Christian, he wished to see negotiations lead to peace in Cuba. As a friend of business, he did not want war to disrupt America's recovery from the depression of 1893. Judging from magazines and journals of the time, American businesses shared these concerns. McKinley did work, however, to set up relief funds for Americans and Cuban civilians who suffered under Spain's harsh policies.

Things changed in 1898. On February 15, the U.S. warship *Maine* mysteriously exploded in Havana harbor in Cuba, killing more than 250 people aboard. McKinley had sent the ship there in January to protect American interests after riots had broken out in Havana. The American public blamed Spain for the catastrophe and demanded war. In late March, McKinley learned that bankers, brokers, business leaders, editors, clergy members, and big corporations all were ready for war, too. The Cuban revolution was damaging America's annual trade with the island, valued at around $100 million.

The stress on McKinley was so great that he often burst into tears in the White House. Writing about the president in *The Mirror of War,* Gerald F. Linderman said, "He required drugs in order to sleep. He aged visibly. He paced a path through the White House grounds."

On March 27, McKinley finally demanded that Spain end the hostilities in Cuba immediately. Although Spain was prepared to end the fighting by mid-April, it was still unwilling to set Cuba free. As the Cuban rebels would not stop fighting without gaining their freedom, McKinley ordered a naval blockade of Cuba on April 21, and Congress declared war on April 25. Speaking to his private secretary two years later, according to Linderman, McKinley said, "[D]eclaration of war against Spain was an act which has been and will always be the greatest grief of my life. I never wanted to go to war with Spain. Had I been let [alone] I could have prevented [it]. All I wanted was more time."

The Spanish-American War

The United States faced war with a regular army of only twenty-eight thousand troops compared to Spain's force of two hundred thousand in Cuba. When war appeared imminent, McKinley called for 125,000 Americans to volunteer for army service; over one million volunteers answered the call. Hoping to erase any lingering hostility from the American Civil War, the president selected officers from both the North and the South to lead the growing army. The appointments included ex-Confederate soldiers, such as Alabama native and member of Congress Joseph Wheeler (1836–1906), who would lead an entire division into battle in Cuba.

After setting the wheels of war into motion, McKinley delegated operational control to War Secretary Russell Alger (1836–1907) and the heads of the various military departments. Remaining in Washington, D.C., throughout the summer, the president welcomed the news of naval victories by Commodore **George Dewey** (1837–1917; see entry) in the Philippines on May 1 and by Commodore Winfield S. Schley (1839–1909) in Cuba on July 3. Unsure of its exact location, McKinley had to locate the Philippines on a map torn out of a schoolbook. When his fellow Americans discovered the location, many of them urged the president to seize the islands as the spoils of war.

Hostilities ended after the United States and Spain signed a peace protocol on August 12 (although one last battle took place in Manila, Philippines, on August 13 before news of the truce arrived there). The United States had been victorious in Cuba, the Philippines, Puerto Rico, and Guam. Because Congress had promised not to acquire Cuba when it had voted to declare war, McKinley had to let Cuba become independent. No official promises bound the United States with respect to the other three colonies, however.

According to Ivan Musicant in *Empire by Default: The Spanish-American War and the Dawn of the American Century*, McKinley did not want to give the Philippines back to Spain, for Spain had not governed the colony well, in McKinley's opinion. McKinley personally did not like the idea of taking the colony for commerce, but popular opinion pressured him to pursue this route. Moreover, he thought giving the Philippines independence would result in the country falling into chaos and eventually being conquered by another European power. As reported in Howard Zinn's *A People's History of the United States: 1492–Present,* after falling to his knees and praying to God many times for guidance, McKinley heard God advise him to take the Philippines so that Americans could teach the Filipinos principles of Christian self-governance.

In the Treaty of Paris, signed in December 1898, Spain gave Guam and Puerto Rico to the United States to cover its war costs. The United States bought the Philippines from Spain for just $20 million. Although McKinley got the islands at a bargain price, his country paid heavily afterwards with the blood of its soldiers. In February 1899, a group of Filipinos led by Emilio Aguinaldo (1869–1964) launched a revolution against American colonization. Aguinaldo said that Admiral Dewey, who had been promoted from commodore after his May 1 victory, had promised independence for the island nation in exchange for Filipino rebel assistance during the war in Manila. The Filipino revolt lasted until July 1902 before the U.S. military crushed it.

McKinley never saw the end of the rebellion, however. After starting a second term in 1901, he went on a summer tour of the United States that ended at the Pan-American Exposition in Buffalo, New York. Greeting his fellow citizens there on September 6, McKinley was shot by an anarchist (one who supports the abolition of government, sometimes through violence) named Leon Czolgosz. McKinley clung to life for a week before he died during the early morning hours of September 14. According to Charles H. Grosvenor in *William McKinley: His Life and Work,* McKinley's last words were, "Goodbye all. It is God's way. His will, not ours, be done."

For More Information

Collins, David R. *William McKinley, 25th President of the United States.* Ada, OK: Garrett Educational Corp., 1990.

Foner, Philip S. *The Spanish-Cuban-American War and the Birth of American Imperialism.* New York: Monthly Review Press, 1972.

Gould, Lewis L. *The Spanish-American War and President McKinley.* Lawrence, KA: University of Kansas Press, 1982.

Grosvenor, Charles H. *William McKinley: His Life and Work.* Washington, D.C.: The Continental Assembly, 1901.

Higgins, Eva. *William McKinley: An Inspiring Biography*. Canton, OH: Daring Pub. Group, 1989.

Hoyt, Edwin P. *William McKinley*. Chicago, IL: Reilly & Lee Company, 1967.

Joseph, Paul. *William McKinley*. Edina, MN: Abdo & Daughters, 2000.

Kent, Zachary. *William McKinley*. New York: Children's Press, 1988.

Klingel, Cynthia A., and Robert B. Noyed. *William McKinley: Our Twenty-Fifth President*. Chanhassen, MN: Childs World, 2002.

Linderman, Gerald F. *The Mirror of War: American Society and the Spanish-American War*. Ann Arbor, MI: The University of Michigan Press, 1974.

Morgan, H. Wayne. *William McKinley and His America*. Syracuse, NY: Syracuse University Press, 1963.

Musicant, Ivan. *Empire by Default: The Spanish-American War and the Dawn of the American Century*. New York: Henry Holt and Company, 1998.

Zinn, Howard. *A People's History of the United States: 1492–Present*. 20th anniversary ed. New York: HarperCollins, 1999.

Theodore Roosevelt

Born October 27, 1858
New York, New York
Died January 6, 1919
Oyster Bay, New York

American naval officer; 26th president of the United States

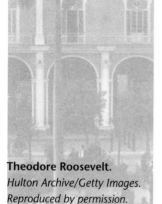

"No triumph of peace is quite so great as the supreme triumphs of war."

Theodore Roosevelt quoted in Theodore Roosevelt: A Life.

Theodore Roosevelt.
Hulton Archive/Getty Images. Reproduced by permission.

Theodore Roosevelt led a cavalry of volunteer soldiers in Cuba during the Spanish-American War (April–August 1898). Famous in the United States for their ferocity and bravery, the cavalry became known as the Rough Riders. For Roosevelt, who was thirty-nine at the time, the war fulfilled his strong desire to engage in military combat. Roosevelt's wartime performance made him popular in the United States and helped him become the twenty-sixth president of the United States (1901–1909).

Childhood

Theodore Roosevelt was born in New York City on October 27, 1858, to Theodore Roosevelt Sr. and Martha (Bulloch) Roosevelt. The second of four children, Roosevelt grew up in great wealth but poor health. Roosevelt was a small, skinny child, and asthma made it difficult for him to breathe. As he grew older, Roosevelt responded to his poor health by exercising vigorously to make his body strong. Throughout his childhood, Roosevelt became an avid hunter, a voracious reader, and studied nature by spending time immersed in it.

Roosevelt was a child when the American Civil War (1861–65) began. Disturbed that his father had decided not to fight in the war, Roosevelt channeled his anger into a prayer to God that the Union Army would smash the Confederate soldiers to powder, according to a biographer. Later in life, Roosevelt would have a chance to prove himself on the battlefield, as his father had chosen not to do.

Early adulthood

After graduating from Harvard College in 1880, Roosevelt married his first wife, Alice Hathaway Lee. The couple had a daughter named Alice. In his search for a profession, Roosevelt tried law school before deciding to become a writer. His first book, *The Naval War of 1812; or, the History of the United States Navy During the Last War with Great Britain,* showed Roosevelt's great interest in the U.S. Navy.

Always interested in politics, Roosevelt spent much of his spare time at the New York offices of the Republican Party. Shortly thereafter, in 1882, Roosevelt was elected to the New York State Assembly, where he earned a reputation as an enemy of corrupt government. On February 14, 1884, Roosevelt's wife and mother died just hours apart. (His father had died six years earlier.) Consumed with grief, Roosevelt tried to return to the assembly but soon left politics to live in the Dakota Territory on a ranch and to continue his writing career.

Roosevelt married his second wife, Edith Kermit Carow, in 1886, and fathered five children with her. Roosevelt's continued passion for politics, devotion to the Republican Party, and interest in reform led President Benjamin Harrison (1833–1901; served 1889–1893) to appoint Roosevelt to the U.S. Civil Service Commission in Washington, D.C., in 1889. Roosevelt's job was to make sure people got federal jobs based on their ability instead of through favoritism or political friendship. Back in New York City in 1895, Roosevelt worked as president of the Board of Police Commissioners. Both jobs allowed Roosevelt to fight the governmental corruption he despised.

Appointment to the Navy Department

In 1896, Roosevelt campaigned on behalf of **William McKinley** (1843–1901; served 1897–1901; see entry), a fellow Republican who was running for president of the United States. When McKinley won, Roosevelt sought the job of assistant secretary of the navy. He thought the United States had to build a strong navy in order to grow into a world power.

While Roosevelt was campaigning for McKinley, Cuban rebels were continuing to fight for independence from Spain in a revolution that had begun in 1895. Americans were horrified at the news reports that Spanish general Valeriano Weyler y Nicolau (1838–1930) had imprisoned Cuban civilians in camps to prevent them from helping the rebels. The Cuban revolution was hurting American businesses, which had invested $50 million in sugarcane plantations and other areas of the Cuban economy. When McKinley became president, many Americans wanted to declare war against Spain and drive the corrupt Spanish government out of Cuba. Roosevelt, a jingo—someone who wanted to wage war in order to expand the territory of the United States—agreed with them.

McKinley appointed Roosevelt to the Navy Department, after being assured that the younger man would not be too aggressive about waging war. Roosevelt, however, was too independent, passionate, and energetic to remain calm. In June 1897, after only three months in office, he gave a rousing speech at the U.S. Naval War College in Newport, Rhode Island. Roosevelt said that preparing for war was the best way to have peace, and building a strong navy was the best way to prepare for war.

His boss, U.S. Navy secretary John D. Long (1838–1915), was less aggressive than Roosevelt, so the two often disagreed on matters of foreign policy. He did not share Roosevelt's opinions and was upset by his public comments. Roosevelt angered Long again at the end of September by persuading Senator **Redfield Proctor** (1831–1908; see entry in Primary Sources section) to help him appoint Commodore **George Dewey** (1837–1917; see entry), a friend of Roosevelt's, to command the navy's Asiatic Squadron. Annoyed by the politics that led to Dewey's appointment, Long sent Dewey to Asia as a commodore rather than promoting him to rear admiral as expected.

The road to war

On February 15, 1898, Americans became outraged when the U.S. warship *Maine* exploded in the harbor at Havana, Cuba. More than 250 Americans lost their lives in the blast. The ship had been sent there to protect American interests on the island. In March, a naval investigation concluded that a mine had destroyed the ship but did not identify those responsible for setting off the mine. Roosevelt was convinced that Spain was responsible, however, and he called for war in Cuba.

McKinley was avoiding war, largely because the American business community feared disruption of its recovery from the economic depression of 1893. This policy angered Roosevelt. According to Nathan Miller in *Theodore Roosevelt: A Life,* Roosevelt wrote a letter to a friend in March 1898 in which he said:

> In the name of humanity and of national self-interest alike, we should have interfered in Cuba three years ago.... The craven fear and brutal selfishness of the mere money-getters, have combined to prevent us from doing our duty. The blood of the Cubans, the blood of women and children who have perished by the hundred thousand in hideous misery lies at our door; and the blood of the murdered men of the *Maine* calls not for indemnity [payment] but for the full measure of atonement which can only come by driving the Spaniard from the New World.

Preparing to fight

The United States eventually declared war on April 25, and War Secretary Russell A. Alger (1836–1907) made plans to send an expedition to drive Spain from the colony. It was Roosevelt's chance to make up for his father's failure to serve in the American Civil War. Full of boyish energy and dreams of combat, Roosevelt resigned from the Navy Department to seek a fighting spot in the army.

Roosevelt became a lieutenant colonel under his friend, Colonel Leonard Wood (1860–1927), in the First U.S. Volunteer Cavalry Regiment. After purchasing a uniform from Brooks Brothers and stuffing it with twelve pairs of eyeglasses for his poor vision, Roosevelt headed for San Antonio, Texas, where his regiment would train. He arrived on May 15. Just two weeks earlier, on May 1, Roosevelt's friend Commodore Dewey had crushed Spain's squadron in the Philip-

Theodore Roosevelt, center, leads his regiment of volunteer soldiers, known as the Rough Riders. *Courtesy of the Library of Congress.*

pines (an island chain in the Pacific Ocean south of China) without losing one sailor to enemy fire.

By the time Roosevelt got to San Antonio, his regiment of one thousand volunteers had been nicknamed the Rough Riders. His fellow soldiers were Native Americans, cowboys, gamblers, lawmen, outlaws, college students, actors, and musicians. The regiment trained by taking long rides on horseback in the sweltering Texan heat. At the end of May, they boarded a train for Tampa, Florida, where the Fifth Corps expedition (called the V Corps) was assembling to head for Cuba.

Roosevelt's men arrived in Tampa amidst disorganization and chaos, typical of the army's conduct during the war. Food and supplies were scarce. There were not enough ships to transport all the soldiers to Cuba; consequently, 440 of the Rough Riders had to stay in Florida, and only the officers could bring their horses on board with them. Afraid of being left behind, Roosevelt stormed up a gangplank to prevent regular army regiments from getting on the ship before him and his volunteers. Once on the ship, the Rough Riders and the V Corps suffered in sweaty, cramped conditions before arriving in Cuba on June 22, 1898.

The battle of Las Guásimas

The U.S. Atlantic Naval Squadron, commanded by Admiral William T. Sampson (1840–1902), had blockaded Spanish admiral **Pascual Cervera y Topete** (1839–1909; see entry) in the harbor at Santiago de Cuba at the southeastern end of the island. After consulting with Sampson and Cuban general **Calixto García** (1839–1898; see entry in Primary Sources section), U.S. Army general **William R. Shafter** (1835–1906; see entry) decided to land the V Corps at Daquirí and march his troops twelve miles along the coast to the Spanish stronghold at Santiago.

After landing in Cuba and sleeping for two nights amongst biting land crabs, the army headed for Santiago on the morning of June 24. General Joseph Wheeler (1836–1906) ordered Wood and Roosevelt to lead the Rough Riders along a narrow path. The Regular First and Tenth Cavalries marched on a wagon road that ran parallel to the path. Both roads converged at Las Guásimas, where the Americans joined forces to meet the Spaniards.

When the Spanish fired from hidden positions, the Rough Riders struggled to take cover in the thick jungle. Then they tried to advance, searching for their enemies, who were hard to find because they used rifles with smokeless gunpowder. According to Nathan Miller in *Theodore Roosevelt: A Life*, Roosevelt later admitted, "All the while I was thinking that I was the only man who did not know what I was about."

When the Rough Riders finally spotted the hats worn by some of the Spanish troops, they were able to fire their own weapons more effectively. This led to a series of Spanish retreats and American advances until the U.S. regiments had chased their opponents from Las Guásimas. Camping near a cool stream on the ridge they had captured, the Rough Riders rested for six days while the U.S. Army planned its next move.

The siege of San Juan

The village of El Caney and a series of hills called San Juan Heights were all that separated the U.S. Army from Santiago. On June 30, General Shafter finally came ashore and met with his senior officers to plan an attack. Colonel Wood was promoted to take over the brigade of a sick officer, so Roosevelt proudly found himself in command of his regiment. According to historians, Roosevelt rose early on the morning of July 1, shaved, ate bad bacon, drank black coffee, and prepared to fight.

The battle began when Captain Allyn K. Capron Sr.'s artillery unit shelled El Caney to clear the way for General H. W. Lawton (1843–1899), who attacked with his infantry division at 7:00 A.M. Shafter had expected Lawton to complete the siege in two hours. It took nine hours, however, and cost many lives.

Around 1:00 P.M., Roosevelt was waiting impatiently when he finally got the order to attack San Juan Heights. The Rough Riders marched toward Kettle Hill, which had gotten its name from an iron sugar refinery kettle that sat on top of it. African American soldiers from the Ninth Cavalry Regiment joined the Rough Riders for the attack. Together, they stormed up the hill, cutting through a barbed wire fence and forcing the Spaniards to retreat with the sheer strength of their surge.

Once atop Kettle Hill, the Rough Riders fired at the Spanish troops on San Juan Hill to help their fellow Americans there. Then they advanced, along with the Ninth Cavalry, to take a spur of San Juan Hill. According to historians, Roosevelt killed a Spanish soldier there with his pistol and later bragged about it in a letter to home.

The battle ended as the Spanish army retreated below San Juan Heights and into Santiago. Of the four hundred Rough Riders who fought that day, eighty-six were killed or wounded. It seemed like a miracle to those like Roosevelt who had survived uninjured. The man who had been small and sick as a child wrote in *The Rough Riders* that he felt as strong as a bull moose.

The Round-Robin Letter

Spain eventually surrendered at Santiago on July 17 and then agreed to a cease-fire on August 12. Roosevelt was already becoming a hero back home as people read reports of his accomplishments in newspapers. Republicans urged him to return to America to run for governor of New York, but Roosevelt said he could not leave his soldiers behind.

The situation was dire for the entire V Corps. Thousands of soldiers became sick with malaria or got yellow fever. War Secretary Alger did not want to bring infected troops home to spread disease in the United States; however, staying in Cuba's tropical environment meant almost certain death.

On August 3, Shafter and his officers in Cuba met to discuss the situation. With Shafter's permission, the officers decided to send a letter to Shafter, the officer in charge, suggesting that whoever failed to evacuate the V Corps out of Cuba would be responsible for the deaths to come. It came to be called the Round-Robin Letter because everyone at the meeting signed it before sending it to Shafter, who planned to forward it to Alger at the War Department. Roosevelt, who did not fear the military officials back home because he was technically a civilian, sent another letter of his own reiterating the concerns in the Round-Robin letter.

President McKinley read the letters in the newspapers as both were leaked to the press before Shafter sent them to Secretary Alger. McKinley and Alger were furious because they felt the written criticism weakened the United States' position as it was negotiating to end the war. Roosevelt's popularity protected him from official punishment, but Alger prevented Roosevelt from receiving the Congressional Medal of Honor for his wartime service.

The governorship and the presidency

Roosevelt's fame and popularity launched him into the governor's office in New York in January 1899. From there, he became vice-president of the United States under McKinley in April 1901. Five months later, an assassin took McKinley's life, elevating Roosevelt to the presidency on September 14.

The Navy grew under the Roosevelt administration until it could assemble a battle fleet of sixteen ships. In 1906, Roosevelt ordered a military occupation of Cuba to squash a rebellion on the island. After leaving the White House in 1909, Roosevelt returned to hunting and writing. He tried unsuccessfully to return to the White House in the election of 1912. A favorite to get the Republican nomination for president in 1920, Roosevelt died in his sleep at his home in Oyster Bay, New York, on January 6, 1919. According to Gerald F. Linderman in *The Mirror of War,* Roosevelt concluded shortly before his death, "San Juan was the great day of my life."

For More Information

Foner, Philip S. *The Spanish-Cuban-American War and the Birth of American Imperialism.* New York: Monthly Review Press, 1972.

Fritz, Jean. *Bully for You, Teddy Roosevelt.* New York: G. P. Putnam's Sons, 1991.

Linderman, Gerald F. *The Mirror of War: American Society and the Spanish-American War.* Ann Arbor, MI: The University of Michigan Press, 1974.

Miller, Nathan. *Theodore Roosevelt: A Life.* New York: William Morrow and Company, 1992.

Musicant, Ivan. *Empire by Default: The Spanish-American War and the Dawn of the American Century.* New York: Henry Holt and Company, 1998.

Samuels, Peggy. *Teddy Roosevelt at San Juan: The Making of a President.* College Station, TX: Texas A&M University Press, 1997.

Roosevelt, Theodore. *The Rough Riders.* New York: Charles Scribner's Sons, 1899.

William Shafter

Born October 16, 1835
Comstock Township,
Kalamazoo County, Michigan
Died November 12, 1906
Bakersfield, California

American military officer

William Shafter was the commanding officer of the U.S. Army in Cuba during the Spanish-American War (April–August 1898). His obesity and medical problems forced Shafter to direct military operations from miles behind the front lines. Hundreds of men died in the fighting, and thousands more died from diseases they contracted during Cuba's steamy summer season. Yet Shafter's troops worked with the U.S. Navy to force Spain to surrender an entire region of Cuba just twenty-five days after landing on the island. This led to a negotiated cease-fire, Cuba's freedom from Spain, and American military control of the island.

"I don't care a damn what you are, I'll treat you all alike."

William Shafter quoted in Pecos Bill: A Military Biography of William R. Shafter.

Shafter's early years and military career

William Rufus Shafter was born in Comstock Township, Kalamazoo County, Michigan, on October 16, 1835. The oldest of four children, Shafter had a large physique that grew strong as he worked on his family's pioneer farm. Shafter also did well in school, winning many spelling bees.

William Shafter. *Hulton Archive/Getty Images. Reproduced by permission.*

155

In 1856, Shafter became a country schoolteacher in Galesburg, Michigan, where he had attended school as a boy. Four years later, he landed a teaching job in Athens, Michigan. He married one of his pupils, Harriet Grimes, in 1862. Just before his marriage, Shafter enrolled in the Union Army at the outbreak of the American Civil War (1861–65).

Shafter fought in many Civil War battles, including those at Ball's Bluff and Nashville, and he also spent time as a prisoner of war. Several years after the war, on April 14, 1869, he became lieutenant colonel of the 24th United States Infantry. Shafter spent the next three decades as a career man in the army, serving mostly in frontier situations and rising to the rank of brigadier general by 1897, just before the outbreak of the Spanish-American War.

The Spanish-American War begins

The United States declared war on Spain on April 25, 1898. Spain's colony of Cuba—a tropical island ninety miles south of Florida—was the source of the conflict. Spain had been fighting a war against Cuban rebels there since February 1895. The rebels, tens of thousands of them, wanted independence from Spain and freedom to control their own government.

Led by General **Máximo Gómez y Báez** (1836–1905; see entry), the rebels sought to destroy the island's sugarcane plantations and mills, thus cutting off Spain's primary source of colonial revenue. This destruction also hurt American businesses, which had invested $50 million in the island. Spain fought back by herding Cuban civilians into concentration camps, where hundreds of thousands of them died from disease and starvation. The mysterious explosion of the American warship *Maine* in Havana, Cuba, in February 1898 led the United States to declare war on Spain the following April.

Unprepared for war, U.S. president **William McKinley** (1843–1901; served 1897–1901; see entry) had to select someone to lead the U.S. Army on its Cuban expedition. The man he settled upon was William Shafter, who weighed around three hundred pounds and suffered from varicose veins and gout, both painful and debilitating medical conditions. Despite these physical limitations, however, Shafter's record of leading troops on successful frontier missions against Native Americans gave him the necessary experience to fight Spanish troops in Cuba's hot tropical climate.

Landing at Daquirí

After receiving his orders, Shafter traveled to Tampa, Florida, where his troops assembled for action. Before Shafter could take them safely to Cuba, however, the U.S. Navy had to locate the Spanish fleet of Vice Admiral **Pascual Cervera y Topete** (1839–1909; see entry), who had sailed from Spain for an unknown destination. Americans living on the East Coast nervously scanned the Atlantic Ocean, but Cervera did not attack the United States. Instead, his fleet slipped into port at Santiago, Cuba, on May 19. U.S. admiral William T. Sampson (1840–1902) and his Atlantic Fleet then trapped Cervera's ships in Santiago, clearing the way for Shafter's ground invasion.

On June 14, 1898, the Fifth Army Corps (or V Corps) steamed out from Tampa destined to land somewhere near Santiago. Working with Admiral Sampson and the U.S. Navy, Shafter planned to defeat Cervera's fleet and then to capture the city, two victories that would give the United States a firm foothold on Cuba. Commanding the three divisions of Shafter's V Corps were Brigadier General J. Ford Kent, Brigadier General Henry W. Lawton (1843–1899), and Major General Joseph W. Wheeler (1836–1906).

On the morning of June 20, U.S. Army ships reached the waters outside Santiago. Sampson boarded Shafter's flagship, the *Seguranca,* for a conference before both military leaders went ashore to meet with Cuban generals **Calixto García** (1839–1898; see entry in Primary Sources section) and Jesús Rabí.

García had recommended that Shafter's troops land at Daquirí, about twelve miles east of Santiago. Early on June 22, the U.S. Navy bombarded Daquirí to make way for the landing. After a Cuban rebel signaled that the coast was clear, Shafter's men began to disembark. Lieutenant Colonel, and future president of the United States, **Theodore Roosevelt** (1858–1919; see entry) and his volunteer regiment of Rough Riders were among the first to reach the shore. Suffering from gout, Shafter stayed aboard the *Seguranca* rather than land with his soldiers.

One of Shafter's first orders was to keep news correspondents on the transport vessels until the soldiers had landed. This made Shafter very unpopular with the correspondents, who feared they might miss the V Corps's first battles with Spain. Shafter also alienated the Cuban rebels by suggesting that they carry supplies and dig trenches for the Americans rather than fight with them. When he learned of this, General García objected, saying his men were not just "pack-mules," according to Philip S. Foner in *The Spanish-Cuban-American War and the Birth of American Imperialism*. It was not the last time that Shafter would insult the Cubans.

The Siege of Santiago

After setting up a telegraph connection to Washington, D.C., the V Corps began its march to Santiago on June 24. Fearful that tropical diseases such as malaria and yellow fever would overtake his troops, Shafter resolved to get them to Santiago as fast as possible.

The V Corps' first battle occurred that day at Las Guásimas, a few miles from the landing point. Led by General Wheeler and Colonel Leonard Wood (1860–1927), the American troops ran into Spanish soldiers retreating toward Santiago. Death totals were low by military standards, but the Americans learned how hard it is to fight an enemy in jungle terrain. For example, most Spaniards used rifles with smokeless powder, but many American volunteers, including the Rough Riders, used rifles that revealed a soldier's location with a puff of smoke as soon as he pulled the trigger.

After the battle at Las Guásimas, a series of hills called San Juan Heights and the town of El Caney were all that separated the Americans from Santiago. Meeting with his officers on June 30, Shafter said his plan was simply to storm those city defenses. Finally ashore, Shafter traveled to high ground at a place called El Pozo, where he could see Santiago two-and-a-half miles away. Communication problems, however, prevented Shafter from having any real input during the day-long battle on July 1.

The battle proved to be the deadliest of the war. Shafter expected General Lawton's regiment to take El Caney in two hours. It took nine. Meanwhile, Generals Kent and

Wheeler stormed San Juan Heights, an operation that included the Rough Riders as well as two African American army regiments. By the end of the day, hundreds of Americans and Spaniards were dead as the surviving Spanish soldiers retreated to temporary safety in Santiago.

Surrender and suffering

Two days later, on July 3, Admiral Cervera's fleet tried to escape Santiago harbor to go to Havana or Cienfuegos. As Admiral Sampson was on his way to a meeting with Shafter, Commodore Winfield S. Schley (1839–1909) led the Atlantic Fleet to victory against Cervera. With no naval defenses and hundreds of people starving in the city, Spanish commander José Torál surrendered Santiago and all twelve thousand of his troops in the surrounding region on July 17.

Surrender gave Shafter another chance to insult the Cubans and disgruntle the news correspondents. Although the Cuban rebels had been fighting against Spain for over three years, Shafter refused to let them participate in the surrender ceremonies on July 17. This snub led Calixto García to resign from the Cuban army the next day. At the ceremony, while U.S. soldiers raised the American flag over the palace in Santiago, Shafter ordered his troops to remove American news correspondent Sylvester Scovel from the palace roof. Scovel refused to get down voluntarily upon Shafter's order to do so and allegedly struck at Shafter in an ensuing argument.

The V Corps then found itself stuck in Cuba during the deadly summer months, when tropical diseases such as malaria and yellow fever were at their worst. According to Foner, when asked to identify his best generals during the revolution against Spain, Cuban general Gómez had named June, July, and August. But those months had attacked American soldiers also, who were not used to the muggy climate. The majority of the fifty-five hundred American casualties of the war came about as a result of sickness and disease rather than from combat.

The Round-Robin Letter

In this disease-ridden environment, Shafter called his division and brigade commanders and medical officers to-

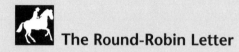

The Round-Robin Letter

The Round-Robin Letter, as reprint-
ed from Paul H. Carlson's *Pecos Bill: A Military Biography of William R. Shafter.*

> *To Major-General William R.
> Shafter, Commanding United States Forces
> in Cuba:*
>
> *We, the undersigned General Offi-
> cers, commanding various Brigades, Divi-
> sions, etc., of the United States Army of
> Occupation in Cuba, are of the unanimous
> opinion that this army must at once be
> taken out of the Island of Cuba, and sent
> to some point on the northern sea-coast of
> the United States; that this can be done
> without danger to the people of the United
> States; that there is no epidemic of yellow
> fever in the army at present, only a few
> sporadic cases; that the army is disabled
> by malarial fever to such an extent that its
> efficiency is destroyed, and it is in a condi-
> tion to be practically entirely destroyed by
> the epidemic of yellow fever sure to come*

> *in the near future. We know from reports
> from competent officers, and from person-
> al observations, that the army is unable to
> move in the interior, and that there are no
> facilities for such a move if attempted, and
> will not be until too late; moreover, the
> best medical authorities in the island say
> that with our present equipment we could
> not live in the interior during the rainy sea-
> son, without losses from malarial fever, al-
> most as deadly as from yellow fever. This
> army must be removed at once, or it will
> perish as an army. It can be safely moved
> now. Persons responsible for preventing
> such a move will be responsible for the un-
> necessary loss of many thousands of lives.
> Our opinions are the result of careful per-
> sonal observation, and are also based upon
> the unanimous opinion of our medical of-
> ficers who are with the army, and under-
> stand the situation absolutely.*

gether for a meeting on August 3, 1898. With Shafter's approval, the commanders and officers decided to write a letter
to Shafter, which he would then forward to U.S. war secretary
Russell Alger (1836–1907), demanding that the troops be returned to the United States immediately. The Round-Robin
Letter, as it came to be called because it circulated among all
the officers, was signed by division commanders Kent, Lawton, and Wheeler; regimental commander Theodore Roosevelt; and Shafter's other officers.

American newspapers printed the letter, which infuriated President McKinley and War Secretary Alger. They were
trying to supervise peace negotiations with Spain. If the Spanish position in Cuba had been stronger, the letter might have
weakened America's negotiating stance by suggesting that its
military could not capture and hold the entire island. As it
turned out, however, the Spanish military felt it was facing

inevitable defeat. Consequently, Spain signed a peace protocol on August 12, 1898, agreeing to free Cuba and to turn over its other island colonies of Puerto Rico and Guam to the United States.

Retirement

After disbanding the V Corps at Camp Wikoff on Long Island, New York, Shafter led a quiet life in the army before retiring in 1901. In retirement, he made his home on a ranch near Bakersfield, California. Shafter's unhealthy weight kept him fairly inactive during this time; he died at his ranch on November 12, 1906.

For More Information

Books

Carlson, Paul H. *Pecos Bill: A Military Biography of William R. Shafter.* College Station, TX: Texas A&M University Press, 1989.

Cosmas, Graham A. *An Army for Empire: The United States Army in the Spanish-American War.* Columbia, MO: University of Missouri Press, 1971.

Feuer, A. B. *The Santiago Campaign of 1898: A Soldier's View of the Spanish-American War.* Westport, CT: Praeger Publishers, 1993.

Foner, Philip S. *The Spanish-Cuban-American War and the Birth of American Imperialism.* New York: Monthly Review Press, 1972.

Golay, Michael. *The Spanish-American War.* New York: Facts On File, 1995.

Miley, John D. *In Cuba with Shafter.* New York: Charles Scribner's Sons, 1899.

Musicant, Ivan. *Empire by Default: The Spanish-American War and the Dawn of the American Century.* New York: Henry Holt and Company, 1998.

Sargent, Herbert H. *The Campaign of Santiago de Cuba.* Chicago, IL: A. C. McClurg & Co., 1907.

Wheeler, Joseph. *The Santiago Campaign.* Philadelphia, PA: Drexel Briddle, 1899.

Periodicals

Rhodes, Charles D. "William Rufus Shafter." *Michigan History Magazine* 16 (Fall, 1932): 370–83.

Shafter, William R. "The Capture of Santiago de Cuba." *Century* 57 (February, 1899): 612–30.

Primary Sources

Stephen Crane

Excerpt from "Marines Signalling Under Fire At Guantánamo,"
McClure's Magazine, February 1899.

Reprinted in *The War Dispatches of Stephen Crane*
Edited by R. W. Stallman and E. R. Hagemann
Published in 1964

Writer Stephen Crane (1871–1900) was a war journalist during the Spanish-American War (April–August 1898). Crane had achieved international popularity in 1895 with the publication of his novel *The Red Badge of Courage,* a fictional tale of a soldier's journey from fear to courage during an un-named battle of the American Civil War (1861–65). While reporting the Spanish-American War from Cuba, Crane got to see, hear, feel, and smell the fear and death he had described so well in his novel.

Crane had tried to reach war-torn Cuba in January 1897, before the United States had entered the conflict. Cuban rebels had been fighting to win their independence from Spain since February 1895. When the boat carrying Crane to Cuba sank, he and four other men crowded into a small dinghy and navigated a return voyage in choppy waters for over thirty hours before reaching shore in Florida. Crane later turned the ordeal into one of his most famous short stories, "The Open Boat."

In April 1898, fifteen months after his failed attempt to visit Cuba, Crane was in London, England, when the Unit-

"With a thousand rifles rattling; with the field-guns booming in your ears; with...bullets sneering always in the air a few inches over one's head, and with this enduring from dusk to dawn, it is extremely doubtful if anyone who was there will be able to forget it easily."

War journalist Stephen Crane reported from Cuba during the Spanish-American War.
©*Bettmann/CORBIS. Reproduced by permission.*

ed States declared war on Spain. America wanted to help the rebels win the Cuban revolution, which had been hurting American business interests on the island and causing great suffering for Cuban civilians. When he heard the news, Crane headed for New York to arrange to report the war for *Blackwood's Magazine* and the *New York World. World* owner Joseph Pulitzer (1847–1911) was engaged in a battle for greater readership with **William Randolph Hearst** (1863–1951; see entry in Biographies section) and the *New York Journal.* Crane preferred writing fiction to reporting news, however, so he did not turn out as much material as Pulitzer wanted.

From a boat called *The Three Friends,* Crane saw the U.S. Marines land at Guantánamo Bay, on the southeastern end of the island, on June 10, 1898. The United States set up a coaling station there for the U.S. Navy, which had bottled up the Spanish navy in a bay at nearby Santiago. Once ashore, Crane joined the Marines, some of whom were bathing naked, when Spanish soldiers fired from the jungles. Bullets whizzed through the air for two days and nights, which Crane spent in a trench alongside Marines who signaled messages to their ships with lanterns. Crane described the ordeal in an article that was first published in *McClure's Magazine* in February 1899.

Things to remember while reading "Marines Signalling Under Fire At Guantánamo"

- **Richard Harding Davis** (1864–1916; see entry in Biographies section) was another popular and respected journalist who covered the Spanish-American War in Cuba. Writing in *Stephen Crane: A Bibliography,* author Ames W. Williams says Davis considered Crane's story "one of the finest examples of descriptive writing of the war."

"Marines Signalling Under Fire At Guantánamo"

They were four Guantánamo marines, officially known for the time as signalmen, and it was their duty to lie in the trenches of Camp McCalla, that faced the water, and, by day, signal the **Marblehead** with a flag and, by night, signal the Marblehead with lanterns. It was my good fortune—at that time I considered it my bad fortune, indeed—to be with them on two of the nights when a wild storm of fighting was pealing about the hill; and, of all the actions of the war, none were so hard on the nerves, none strained courage so near the panic point, as those swift nights in Camp McCalla. With a thousand rifles rattling; with the field-guns booming in your ears; with the diabolic **Colt** automatics clacking; with the roar of the Marblehead coming from the bay, and, last, with **Mauser** bullets sneering always in the air a few inches over one's head, and with this enduring from dusk to dawn, it is extremely doubtful if anyone who was there will be able to forget it easily. The noise; the impenetrable darkness; the knowledge from the sound of the bullets that the enemy was on three sides of the camp; the infrequent bloody stumbling and death of some man with whom, perhaps, one had **messed** two hours previous; the weariness of the body, and the more terrible weariness of the mind, at the endlessness of the thing, made it wonderful that at least some of the men did not come out of it with their nerves hopelessly in shreds....

The signal squad had an old cracker-box placed on top of the trench. When not signalling they hid the lanterns in this box; but as soon as an order to send a message was received, it became necessary for one of the men to stand up and expose the lights. And then—oh, my eye, how the **guerrillas** hidden in the gulf of night would turn loose at those yellow gleams!...

How, in the name of wonders, those four men at Camp McCalla were not riddled from head to foot and sent home more as **repositories** of Spanish ammunition than as marines is beyond all comprehension. To make a confession—when one of these men stood up to wave his lantern, I, lying in the trench, invariably rolled a little to the right or left, in order that, when he was shot, he might not fall on me. But the squad came off **scatheless**, despite the best efforts of the

Marblehead: An American cruiser that bombed the Spanish soldiers from its position in Guantánamo Bay.

Colt: A weapons manufacturer and type of firearm.

Mauser: A weapons manufacturer and type of firearm.

messed: Dined.

guerrillas: Soldiers.

repositories: Places where things are stored.

scatheless: Unharmed.

The 1st U.S. Marine Battalion lands at Guantánamo, Cuba, on June 10, 1898, and raises the American flag. It is the first unit to establish a military position on Cuban soil. *Hulton Archive/Getty Images. Reproduced by permission.*

most formidable corps in the Spanish Army—the *Escuadra de Guantánamo....*

Possibly no man who was there ever before understood the true eloquence of the breaking of the day. We would lie staring into the east, fairly ravenous for the dawn. Utterly worn to rags, with our nerves standing on end like so many bristles, we lay and watched the east—the unspeakably **obdurate** and slow east. It was a wonder that the eyes of some of us did not turn to glass balls from the fixity of our gaze....

One midnight, when an important message was to be sent to the Marblehead, Colonel Huntington came himself to the signal-place with Adjutant Draper and Captain McCauley, the quartermaster. When the man stood up to signal, the colonel stood beside him. At sight of the lights, the Spaniards performed as usual. They drove enough bullets into that immediate vicinity to kill all the marines in the corps.

obdurate: Stubborn.

Lieutenant Draper was agitated for his chief. "Colonel, won't you step down, sir?"

"Why, I guess not," said the grey old veteran in his slow, sad, always gentle way. "I am in no more danger than the man."

"But, sir—" began the adjutant.

"Oh, it's all right, Draper."

So the colonel and the private stood side to side and took the heavy fire without either moving a muscle.

Day was always obliged to come at last, punctuated by a final exchange of scattering shots. And the light shone on the marines, the dumb guns, the flag. Grimy yellow face looked into grimy yellow face, and grinned with weary satisfaction. Coffee!

Usually it was impossible for many of the men to sleep at once. It always took me, for instance, some hours to get my nerves combed down. But then it was great joy to lie in the trench with the four signalmen, and understand thoroughly that that night was fully over at last, and that, although the future might have in store other bad nights, that one could never escape from the prison-house which we call the past.

What happened next...

Once the Marines secured the base at Guantánamo, the theatre of battle moved up the coast of Cuba to the area around Santiago. During this time, Crane displayed such a disinterest in reporting that he lost his freelance job with the *World*. At the U.S. Army's first major battle at Las Guásimas on June 24, Crane stayed in the rear while most reporters marched to the front lines with **Theodore Roosevelt** (1858–1919; see entry in Biographies section) and his Rough Riders cavalry regiment. Nervous and fearful, Crane even stayed behind during the famous battle at San Juan Heights on July 1, which led to a Spanish surrender at Santiago weeks later.

After that battle, however, Crane described the pain and misery he had seen at "Bloody Bend," a place in the San

Juan River where dead bodies clogged the murky red water. According to Linda H. Davis in *Badge of Courage*, Crane described himself as feeling like "a mere corpse. My limbs were of dough and my spinal cord burned within me as if it were a red-hot wire."

Did you know...

- Crane caught malarial fever, a tropical disease, while reporting from Cuba. Because of his illness, he returned to the United States on July 8. After recovering, Crane was fired by the *World* and hired by the *Journal* to report on the fighting in Puerto Rico in August. When the war ended on August 12, soon after Crane had arrived, he traveled to Havana, Cuba, where he spent months in exile (voluntary absence from one's own country) writing about lost love and the Cuban war in poems and short stories. Crane died two years later, on June 5, 1900, from tuberculosis, an infectious disease, complicated by the malarial fever he had caught during the war.

For More Information

Davis, Linda H. *Badge of Courage: The Life of Stephen Crane.* Boston, MA: Houghton Mifflin Company, 1998.

Foner, Philip S. *The Spanish-Cuban-American War and the Birth of American Imperialism.* New York: Monthly Review Press, 1972.

Golay, Michael. *The Spanish-American War.* New York: Facts on File, 1995.

Musicant, Ivan. *Empire by Default: The Spanish-American War and the Dawn of the American Century.* New York: Henry Holt and Company, 1998.

Stallman, R. W., and E. R. Hagemann, eds. *The War Dispatches of Stephen Crane.* New York: New York University Press, 1964.

Wertheim, Stanley, and Paul Sorrentino, eds. *The Correspondence of Stephen Crane.* New York: Columbia University Press, 1988.

Williams, Ames W., and Vincent Starrett. *Stephen Crane: A Bibliography.* Glendale, CA: J. Valentine, 1948.

Antonio Eulate

Excerpt from "The Report of the Vizcaya*"*

**Reprinted from *Notes on the Spanish-American War*
Published by the Office of Naval Intelligence in 1900**

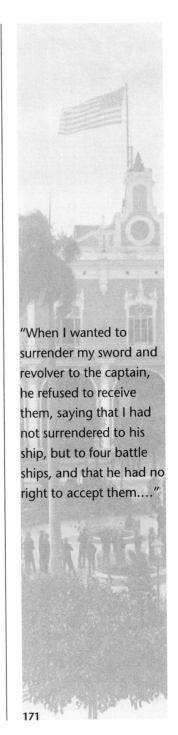

"When I wanted to surrender my sword and revolver to the captain, he refused to receive them, saying that I had not surrendered to his ship, but to four battle ships, and that he had no right to accept them...."

Spanish admiral **Pascual Cervera y Topete** (1839–1909; see entry in Biographies section) sensed death on the horizon as his fleet headed for Cuba in April 1898 to wage war with the United States. Two of his squadron's ships were not available for service, and problems plagued the remaining six. As Cervera's chief of staff, Víctor Concas y Palau, said in *The Squadron of Admiral Cervera,* the admiral wrote to the Spanish government and "insisted time and time again on the danger that was threatening us, on the unfinished condition of our ships that were being fitted out abroad, on the impossibility of going to war, and on the probable results." According to A. B. Feuer in *The Spanish-American War at Sea,* future British prime minister Winston Churchill (1874–1965) wrote at the time, "With only a week's supply of provisions, Cervera was turned loose by his government quite as pitilessly as his fellow countrymen are in the habit of pushing a bull into a ring."

By the end of May, the U.S. Navy had trapped Cervera and his fleet in the harbor at Santiago, Cuba, on the southeastern end of the island. U.S. general **William R. Shafter** (1835–1906; see entry in Biographies section) then spent the

Wreck of the *Reina Mercedes,* one of the Spanish fleet lost to U.S. attack in Santiago harbor on July 3, 1898. *Courtesy of the Library of Congress.*

month of June landing American soldiers near Santiago. The soldiers marched and killed their way through the Cuban jungles, reaching Santiago's defenses after bloody, day-long battles at El Caney and San Juan Heights on July 1. The next day, Cervera received orders from the Spanish governor of Cuba, General Ramón Blanco y Erenas (1831–1906), to break the U.S. naval blockade at Santiago and head for another city. Blanco hoped that either victory or defeat for Cervera would rally the Spanish soldiers in Santiago to repel the American land invasion.

On the morning of July 3, Cervera's ships steamed solemnly, one by one, out of Santiago harbor. Each passed through a narrow channel into the Caribbean Sea, only to have to face a six-ship enemy fleet led by U.S. commodore Winfield S. Schley (1839–1909). Antonio Eulate, captain of one of Cervera's ships, the *Vizcaya,* sent the following report to Cervera three days after his fleet's crushing defeat.

Things to remember while reading "The Report of the *Vizcaya*":

- The force of the attack on the *Vizcaya* was second only to that suffered by the *Infanta Maria Teresa*, the flagship carrying Cervera, which was the first to face the enemy. Eulate and the *Vizcaya* emerged from the bay next.

"The Report of the Vizcaya *"*

In compliance with the instructions received from your excellency, I got my ship ready on the morning of the 2d instant, to go out at 4 P.M. But as the **reembarkation** *of the first company did not begin until that time, it was 6:30 P.M. before the ship was ready to put to sea. At that moment the battle flag was hoisted by the officers, whom I addressed, reminding them of the obligations imposed upon them by the* **Ordinances**, *and the heroic deeds of our ancestors in our honorable career. After a prayer, we received, kneeling, the* **benediction** *of the chaplain.*

With the flag hoisted, we were awaiting your excellency's last orders, and at 9 o'clock A.M. of the day following, July 3, the ship was ready to follow in the wake of the flagship. At 9 o'clock (true time) she started up, following the Teresa, *and at 9:30, after passing the Punta Socapa, we went full speed ahead, steering in conformity with the instructions previously issued by your excellency. At the same moment we opened fire on the hostile ships, very heavy at first, but gradually decreasing in the 5.5-inch* **battery**, *owing to the defects of the guns and ammunition, of which your excellency is aware.*

In spite of these defects, the enthusiasm and intelligence of the officers in charge of the battery and the excellent discipline of their crews made it possible to fire during the battle, which lasted two hours and a half, 150 rounds with the port battery, one of the guns alone firing 40 rounds, the others 25 and above, with the exception of one, which only fired 8 rounds. The deficiencies of these guns were numerous, chief among them, as you already know, the fact that the breach could not be closed, the projectiles jammed, and the firing pins failed to act....

reembarkation: Reloading onto a ship of sailors who had gone ashore to fight alongside soldiers in Santiago.

Ordinances: Laws and rules of the Spanish navy.

benediction: Blessing.

battery: The guns on the warship.

Antonio Eulate   173

In the high battery there were so many casualties that, although there was but one gun left that could be fired, there were not men enough to serve it. In the lower battery there were no men left either to serve the guns or to conduct the firing....

I wanted to try [to see] whether we could ram the Brooklyn, which was the ship that harassed us most on port side and which was nearest to us. To that end I put to port, but the Brooklyn did the same, indicating that she was going to use only her guns. The undersigned, with his head and shoulder wounded, was obliged to withdraw to have his wounds dressed. Almost faint from the loss of blood, he resigned his command for the time being to the executive officer, with clear and positive instructions not to surrender the ship, but rather beach or burn her. In the sick bay I met Ensign Luis Fajardo, who has having a very serious wound in one of his arms dressed. When I asked him what was the matter with him he answered that they had wounded him in one arm, but that he still had one left for his country.

When the flow of blood of my wounds had been checked, I went back on deck and saw that the executive officer had issued orders to steer for the coast in order to run ashore, for we had no serviceable guns left and the fire at the stern had assumed such dimensions that it was utterly impossible to control it. This sad situation was still further complicated by a fire breaking out on the forward deck as the result of the bursting of a steam pipe and the explosion of one or more boilers of the forward group...

As soon as the ship had been beached, the executive officer gave instructions to make all arrangements for the immediate rescue of the crews. Attempts were at once made to lower the boats. When I found that only one was in serviceable condition, I ordered that it be used mainly for the transportation of the wounded, and I authorized all those who could swim or who had life-preservers or anything else sufficiently buoyant to keep them above water to jump in and try to gain the reefs of the **shoal**, which was about 98 yards from the bow.

The rescue was effected in perfect order, in spite of the awe-inspiring aspect of the ship on fire, with the ammunition rooms exploding, the flames rising above the fighting tops and smokestacks, and with the side armor red-hot. I was taken ashore by the officers in the last boat that carried wounded, and was subsequently picked up by a United States boat, which carried me to the Iowa....When I wanted to surrender my sword and revolver to the captain, he re-

shoal: A shallow body of water or a sandbar.

fused to receive them, saying that I had not surrendered to his ship, but to four battle ships, and that he had no right to accept them....

*The foregoing is all I have the honor of reporting to your excellency upon the loss of my ship in a battle against four far superior ships without **striking her colors** nor permitting the enemy to set foot upon her deck, not even for the rescue. There are 98 men missing of her crew.*

What happened next...

Cervera's defeat gave the United States a strong advantage in Cuba. Through negotiations and further battles in Cuba, Puerto Rico, and the Philippines, the United States turned this advantage into Spanish surrender in Santiago on July 17 and into a worldwide cease-fire on August 12.

Did you know...

• War with the United States in 1898 caused a surge of national pride, or nationalism, in Spain. Spaniards compared their country to a lion, fierce and brave, defending itself with pride. America was described as a pig, trying to hog foreign markets for itself.

• This nationalism began to fade after Spain lost the battle of Manila Bay in the Philippines on May 1, 1898. Further losses in Cuba during June and July and in Puerto Rico in August turned Spanish pride into anger. Some Spaniards blamed the politicians for fighting a war that Spain could not win. Others blamed the military, laughing at the soldiers who walked Spain's streets in the months after the peace protocol of August 12, 1898. Riots broke out across Spain in the summer of 1899 to protest rising consumer taxes that were required to pay Spain's war debts.

striking her colors:
Surrendering by lowering a ship's flags.

For More Information

Books

Balfour, Sebastian. "The Impact of War within Spain: Continuity or Crisis?" In *The Crisis of 1898: Colonial Redistribution and Nationalist Mobilization,* edited by Angel Smith and Emma Dávila-Cox. New York: St. Martin's Press, 1999.

Cervera y Topete, Pascual, ed. *The Spanish-American War: A Collection of Documents Relative to the Squadron Operations in the West Indies.* Washington, D.C.: Government Printing Office, 1899.

Concas y Palau, Víctor. *The Squadron of Admiral Cervera.* Washington, D.C.: Government Printing Office, 1900.

Feuer, A. B. *The Spanish-American War at Sea.* Westport, CT: Praeger Publishers, 1995.

Golay, Michael. *The Spanish-American War.* New York: Facts On File, 1995.

Musicant, Ivan. *Empire by Default: The Spanish-American War and the Dawn of the American Century.* New York: Henry Holt and Company, 1998.

Office of Naval Intelligence. *Notes on the Spanish-American War.* Washington, D.C.: Government Printing Office, 1900.

Periodicals

Smith, Eric M. "Leaders Who Lost: Case Studies of Command under Stress." *Military Review,* vol. LXI, April 1981, no. 4, pp. 41–45.

Calixto García

Letter of protest to U.S. general William R. Shafter, July 17, 1898

Reprinted from *The Spanish-Cuban-American War and the Birth of American Imperialism*, by Philip S. Foner

Published in 1972

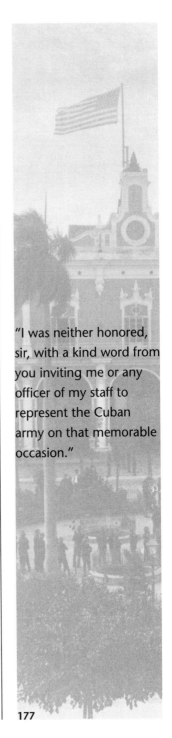

"I was neither honored, sir, with a kind word from you inviting me or any officer of my staff to represent the Cuban army on that memorable occasion."

When the United States declared war on Spain in April 1898, rebels in Cuba already had been fighting for independence from Spain over the previous three years. By intervening, the United States intended to end the revolution, which was hurting American business with the colony. In a show of good faith toward Cuba, the U.S. Congress approved the Teller Amendment, in which the United States promised to leave Cuba to the Cubans after a victory over Spain.

On April 9, 1898, U.S. war secretary Russell A. Alger (1836–1907) and U.S. Army general Nelson A. Miles (1839–1925) sent Lieutenant Andrew S. Rowan on a mission to meet with Cuban general Calixto García (1839–1898). García was in charge of the Cuban Liberating Army's troops in the southeastern province of Oriente. García gave Rowan maps and military data to take back to Alger and Miles. In a letter to Alger, García said he would be happy to coordinate the war effort with the United States. By May 12, the Republic of Cuba had ordered García and the Liberating Army not only to cooperate with the U.S. Army, but also to obey the orders of its commander in Cuba, **William R. Shafter** (1835–1906; see entry in Biographies section).

Under protection from García's army, U.S. troops land at Daiquirí and set up a base camp. *Granger Collection. Reproduced by permission.*

Shafter's troops arrived in Cuba on June 22, 1898. Under protection from García's army, the American soldiers landed at Daiquirí, twelve miles east of the Spanish stronghold at Santiago de Cuba. Shafter's plan was to march his troops to attack Spain at Santiago, where the U.S. Navy had trapped a Spanish fleet in the harbor.

Shafter's Fifth Army Corps and the Cuban rebels accomplished this task over the next few weeks, forcing Spanish general José Torál to surrender at Santiago on July 17, 1898. In a report on the effort, General Miles noted the valuable role played by García's troops in keeping Spanish reinforcements away from the city, as reprinted by Philip S. Foner in *The Spanish-Cuban-American War and the Birth of American Imperialism:*

> It will be observed that Gen. Garcia regarded my requests as his orders, and promptly took steps to execute the plan of operations. He sent 3,000 men to check any movement of the 12,000 Spaniards stationed at Holguin. A portion of this latter force started to the relief of the garrison at Santiago, but was

Spain's surrender at Santiago on July 17, 1898, was due in large part to the hard work of Cuban general Calixto García, center, and his rebel army.
©*Bettmann/CORBIS.*
Reproduced by permission.

successfully checked and turned back by the Cuban forces under Gen. Feria. General Garcia also sent 2,000 men, under Perez, to oppose the 6,000 Spaniards at Guantánamo, and they were successful in their object. He also sent 1,000 men, under General Rios, against 6,000 men at Manzanillo. Of this garrison, 3,500 started to reinforce the garrison at Santiago, and were engaged in no less than 30 combats with the Cubans on their way before reaching Santiago, and would have been stopped had Gen. Garcia's request of June 27 been granted.

In spite of the hard work of the Cuban rebels, Shafter excluded them from negotiations for the surrender of Santiago and did not invite García to the surrender ceremonies on July 17. Then, at the direction of U.S. president **William McKinley** (1843–1901; served 1897–1901; see entry in Biographies section), Shafter allowed the Spanish authorities to remain in charge in Santiago until the United States could set up a military government to control the area. Despite the Teller Amendment, it looked like the United States was not going to be quick in putting Cubans in control of their own country.

These events led García to resign from the Liberating Army on July 17, 1898. In a letter to his General-in-Chief, **Máximo Gómez y Báez** (1836–1905; see entry in Biographies section), García explained that resignation was the only way he could protest America's insults without disobeying his orders to follow Shafter's commands. That same day, García sent a letter to Shafter criticizing America's disrespectful treatment of the Liberating Army.

Things to remember while reading the letter from Cuban general Calixto García to U.S. general William R. Shafter on July 17, 1898:

- Two days before General Toral surrendered at Santiago, General Shafter sent a telegram to Washington, D.C., acknowledging the key role played by García's troops, as reprinted by Foner: "I do not believe that Toral is trying to gain time in hopes of getting reinforcement. Cubans have forces in vicinity of all Spanish troops."

- In spite of their promise to give Cuba to the Cubans, many Americans wrongly believed the Cubans were savages, incapable of self-government. Racism was largely responsible for such attitudes, as over half of Cubans were black.

Letter of protest from Cuban general Calixto García to U.S. general William R. Shafter on July 17, 1898

*Sir: On May 12 the government of the **Republic of Cuba** ordered me, as commander of the Cuban army in the east, to cooperate with the American army following the plans and obeying the orders of its commander. I have done my best, sir, to fulfill the wishes of my government, and I have been until now one of your most faithful **subordinates**, honoring myself in carrying out your orders as far as my powers have allowed me to do it.*

*The city of **Santiago** surrendered to the American army, and news of that important event was given to me by persons entirely*

Republic of Cuba: The government set up by Cuban rebels in September 1895 after beginning their second revolution against Spain.

subordinate: A person under the command of another person.

Santiago: A port city in Cuba in the southeastern province of Oriente, where Spanish General José Toral surrendered to U.S. General William R. Shafter on July 17, 1898.

*foreign to your staff. I have not been honored with a single word from yourself informing me about the negotiations for peace or the terms of the **capitulation** by the Spaniards. The important ceremony of the surrender of the Spanish army and the taking possession of the city by yourself took place later on, and I only knew of both events by public reports.*

I was neither honored, sir, with a kind word from you inviting me or any officer of my staff to represent the Cuban army on that memorable occasion.

*Finally, I know that you have left in power in Santiago the same Spanish authorities that for three years I have fought as enemies of the independence of Cuba. I beg to say that these authorities have never been elected at Santiago by the residents of the city; but were appointed by royal **decrees** of the Queen of Spain.*

*I would agree, sir, that the army under your command should have taken possession of the city, the **garrison** and the forts.*

*I would have given my warm cooperation to any measure you may have deemed best under American military law to hold the city for your army and to preserve public order until the time comes to fulfill the **solemn** pledge of the people of the United States to establish in Cuba a free and independent government. But when the question arises of appointing authorities in Santiago de Cuba under the special circumstances of our thirty years strife against Spanish rule, I cannot see but with the deepest regret that such authorities are not elected by the Cuban people, but are the same ones selected by the Queen of Spain, and hence are ministers appointed to defend Spanish **sovereignty** against the Cubans.*

A rumor, too absurd to be believed, General, describes the reason of your measures and of the orders forbidding my army to enter Santiago for fear of massacres and revenge against the Spaniards. Allow me, sir, to protest against even the shadow of such an idea. We are not savages ignoring the rules of civilized warfare. We are a poor, ragged army as ragged and poor as was the army of your forefathers in their noble war for independence, but like the heroes of **Saratoga and Yorktown,** *we respect our cause too deeply to disgrace it with barbarism and cowardice.*

In view of all these reasons, I sincerely regret being unable to fulfill any longer the orders of my government, and, therefore, I have tendered today to the commander-in-chief of the Cuban army, Maj.

capitulation: Surrender.

decree: A formal order.

garrison: A military outpost.

solemn: Serious.

sovereignty: Royal power.

Saratoga and Yorktown: Sites of important battles during the American Revolution for independence from Great Britain.

*Gen. Máximo Gómez, my **resignation** as commander of this section of our army.*

*Awaiting his **resolution**, I have retired with all my forces to **Jiguaní**.*

I am respectfully yours,

Calixto García, Major General

What happened next...

American papers printed García's letter about one week later. According to Foner, newspaper editorials generally agreed that Shafter should have treated García and the Cuban rebels with more respect. In fact, the letter created such a disturbance that Shafter had to explain his conduct to officials in Washington, D.C. Instead of swallowing his pride, Shafter accused García of expecting to get control of the whole city of Santiago.

Before leaving Santiago, García urged members of the Liberating Army to maintain peace and good order to demonstrate their capability for self-government. He also drew up plans for Cubans to elect mayors and councils for governing Cuban cities and towns. The plans called for voting rights for all people over twenty-one years of age, regardless of race or gender.

Continuing its disrespect for Cuban independence, the United States rejected García's plans. According to Foner, in a dispatch to Washington, D.C., on August 16, 1898, Shafter said that America must have full control over the Cubans. Over the next few months, the United States worked to put its own military government in charge on the island. Cuba did not get its independence until 1902. Even then, the American authorities forced Cuba to include provisions in its constitution giving the United States the right to intervene in Cuba's domestic and foreign affairs.

García did not live to see his country govern itself. In December 1898, he headed a Cuban commission sent to meet with the McKinley administration. The commission intended to negotiate a monetary payment for disbanding the Liberating

resignation: The act of leaving an office or position.

resolution: A formal expression of opinion.

Jiguaní: A Cuban town in the southeastern province of Oriente located inland from and northwest of the port city of Santiago de Cuba.

Army. (After the war ended, the United States had smoothed relations with García by giving him a hero's welcome in Santiago on September 23.) During the visit to Washington, D.C., Senator John T. Morgan told the Cubans that the United States would control their country with a military government until America thought it was time to leave, regardless of the commitment to Cuban independence as described in the Teller Amendment.

In an undated letter to Senator Morgan signed by García, the Cuban commission argued strongly that the Teller Amendment obligated the United States to act according to Cuba's wishes for immediate self-government. Shortly after writing that letter, García contracted pneumonia and died in Washington, D.C., on December 11, 1898.

Did you know...
- Even after Spain surrendered at Santiago de Cuba on July 17, 1898, large numbers of Cubans, Spaniards, and Americans continued to die there. Disease and starvation were the common enemies. At the time of the Spanish surrender, fifteen thousand of Santiago's fifty thousand residents were sick. Smallpox and yellow fever were the most serious diseases. Limited food supplies and dirty, crowded conditions threatened life throughout the city, where two hundred people died each day during the hot summer months in 1898.

For More Information
Foner, Philip S. *The Spanish-Cuban-American War and the Birth of American Imperialism.* New York: Monthly Review Press, 1972.

Golay, Michael. *The Spanish-American War.* New York: Facts on File, 1995.

The *New York World*

Excerpts from daily newspaper coverage of the explosion of the U.S.S. Maine
Published February 16 and 17, 1898

"In the same despatch Capt. Sigsbee said that not more than one hour prior to the explosion the magazines and boilers had been carefully inspected, thus, in his judgment, precluding the possibility of accident...."

By January 1898, Cuba had been fighting a revolution for independence from Spain for nearly three years. Cuban rebels wanted freedom to govern themselves. Spain wanted to hold onto the Cuban colony, whose rich sugarcane and tobacco industries were valuable resources.

On January 12, in the Cuban capital of Havana, a pro-Spanish but anti-military newspaper, *El Reconcentrado,* published an article that criticized a Spanish army officer. Army officers and their civilian friends reacted by destroying the offices of *El Reconcentrado,* as well as those of two newspapers that supported Cuban autonomy—the right of Cuba to govern itself as a free state within the Spanish empire. This event led to riots between Spaniards and Cubans who disagreed on the issue of Cuban freedom.

The United States, which had stayed out of the Cuban conflict, reacted to the riots by sending Captain Charles Sigsbee and the U.S. battleship *Maine* to Havana on January 24. Calling it a friendly mission, U.S. president **William McKinley** (1843–1901; served 1897–1901; see entry in Biographies section) hoped that the naval visit would protect American

To many Americans, the sinking of the U.S.S. *Maine* was a valid reason to declare war against Spain. *Corbis Corporation. Reproduced by permission.*

lives and property in the region and pressure Spain to bring the revolution to an end through peaceful negotiations.

On the evening of Tuesday, February 15, the *Maine* mysteriously exploded while anchored in Havana harbor. Of the 355 people onboard, 252 died in the explosion and eight more died in Havana hospitals from their wounds. Many American newspapers already wanted to wage war with Spain to end the revolution, and the *Maine* disaster fueled that fire. These excerpts from the *New York World,* which was in a war at the time with the *New York Journal* to see which could gain the most readers, contain haunting—but unproven—suggestions that Spain had sabotaged the American battleship.

Things to remember while reading the excerpts from the *New York World*:

- Only six days before the explosion, the *New York Journal* had printed a letter written by the Spanish minister to the United States, Enrique Dupuy de Lôme. In the letter, which had been stolen from a Spanish newspaper editor visiting Cuba, Dupuy de Lôme called President McKinley "weak," according to Ivan Musicant in *Empire by Default.* American hostility toward Spain was thus heightened when the *Maine* exploded.

Excerpts from the New York World on February 16 and 17, 1898

Wednesday, February 16, 1898.

THE U.S. BATTLE-SHIP MAINE BLOWN UP IN HAVANA HARBOR.

More than One Hundred of the Crew Killed by the Explosion Which Occurred While They Were Asleep.

MESSAGE FROM THE WORLD'S STAFF CORRESPONDENT.

Capt. Sigsbee and All but Two Officers Escaped, but a Hundred of the Crew Were Drowned—Cause of Explosion Unknown.

THE EXPLOSION WAS IN THE BOW OF THE VESSEL.

*World Staff Correspondent **Cables** it is Not Known Whether Explosion Occurred On or UNDER the Maine.*

HAVANA, Feb. 15.—At a quarter of ten o'clock this evening a terrible explosion took place on board the United States battle-ship Maine *in Havana harbor.*

Many were killed and wounded.

All the boats of the Spanish cruiser Alfonso XII *are assisting.*

As yet the cause of the explosion is not apparent. The wounded sailors of the Maine *are unable to explain it.*

It is believed that the battle-ship is totally destroyed.

The explosion shook the whole city.

Windows were broken in all the houses.

cables: Telegraphs.

The correspondent of the Associated Press conversed with several of the wounded sailors. They say the explosion took place while they were asleep, so that they can give no particulars as to the cause.

The wildest **consternation** prevails in Havana. The wharves are crowded with thousands of people.

It is believed the explosion occurred in a small **powder magazine**.

The explosion was in the fore part of the vessel and not in the powder magazines, which Capt. Sigsbee says were in perfect order.

Capt. Sigsbee, although badly wounded in the face, was very cool giving orders to officers and men.

The officers also showed great coolness and valor giving orders to men.

They were in their shirt-sleeves, having been hurled from their bunks at this moment.

They are bringing in the wounded to land.

Some are mortally wounded and will probably die.

Five minutes after the explosion, the Spanish warship Alfonso Doce had lowered her boats and was picking up those who were swimming.

United States Consul-General **Lee** is at the Governor-General's palace conferring with Captain-General **Blanco**.

Thursday, February 17, 1898.

MAINE *EXPLOSION CAUSED BY BOMB OR TORPEDO?*

Capt. Sigsbee and Consul-General Lee Are in Doubt—The World Has Sent Special Tug, With Submarine Divers, to Havana to Find Out—Lee Asks for an Immediate Court of Inquiry—260 Men Dead.

IN A SUPPRESSED **DESPATCH** TO THE STATE DEPARTMENT, THE CAPTAIN SAYS THE ACCIDENT WAS MADE POSSIBLE BY AN ENEMY.

Dr. E. C. Pendleton, Just Arrived from Havana, Says He Overheard Talk There of a Plot to Blow Up the Ship—Capt. Zalinski, the Dynamite Expert, and Other Experts Report to The World that the Wreck Was Not Accidental—Washington Officials Ready for Vigor-

consternation: Alarm and confusion.

powder magazine: A compartment for the storage of ammunition.

Fitzhugh Lee: Lead American consul—official—in Cuba.

Ramón Blanco y Erenas: Spanish governor of Cuba.

despatch: Alternative spelling for dispatch, a written message.

ous Action if Spanish Responsibility Can Be Shown—Divers to Be Sent Down to Make Careful Examinations.

Washington, Feb. 16.—A suppressed cable despatch received by Secretary **Long** from Capt. Sigsbee announced the Captain's conclusion, after a hasty examination, that the disaster to the Maine was not caused by accident.

He expressed the belief that whether the explosion originated from without or within, it was made possible by an enemy.

He requested that this **intimation** of his suspicions be considered confidential until he could conduct a more extended investigation.

This despatch was laid before the President, at whose suggestion Assistant Secretary **Day** cabled Consul-General Lee to make whatever examination was possible himself and render assistance to Capt. Sigsbee.

In the same despatch Capt. Sigsbee said that not more than one hour prior to the explosion the magazines and boilers had been carefully inspected, thus, in his judgment, precluding the possibility of accident....

SPANISH OFFICER IN CUBA MAKES A STARTLING PREDICTION.

A Spanish resident of this city, a man of responsible position, recalled a few days ago a letter from a lieutenant in the Spanish army in Cuba. This letter was written in Havana, is dated Jan. 28, 1898, and one section of it reads as follows:

"The visit of the battle-ship Maine has created a very bad feeling among us; it tastes like 'burned horn' in the mouths of the people.

"Though they conceal their anger, the storm is near the surface.

"It is certain that before long that will happen which will astonish the whole world."

HEARD OF A PLOT TO BLOW UP THE MAINE.

Dr. C. E. Pendleton Learns of the Disaster Upon His Arrival on a Steamer from Key West and Hastens to Washington.

Dr. C. E. Pendleton arrived here yesterday on the Mallory liner Lampasas from Key West and departed for Washington on an early

John D. Long: U.S. Secretary of the Navy.

intimation: Suggestion.

William Rufus Day: Assistant U.S. Secretary of State.

afternoon train. As soon as he heard news of the Maine *disaster he became greatly excited and said he had urgent business at the White House.*

A few weeks ago Dr. Pendleton was in Havana. While there he was in constant communication with the New York newspaper correspondents. He left Cuba in the early part of this month and sailed from Key West on the Lampasas *on Saturday afternoon.*

During the trip he was constantly in the company of Capt. Hoswell, who occupied state room No. 25. Just who the Captain was or the nature of his mission no one seemed to know. The crew spoke of him as "the detective."

It was shortly after noon yesterday when the Lampasas *was docked. Before she had been alongside the pier a minute a score of newsboys were surrounding the gangway, shouting the fate of the* Maine *at the top of their voices.*

"What's that they are crying?" asked Pendleton, who was standing at the entrance to the saloon.

"Something has happened to the Maine*," answered a fellow-passenger.*

"What?" shouted the doctor, excitedly. In a minute a copy of The World *was placed in his hands. He read the headlines hurriedly, simply catching a word here and there. But he grasped the situation as if by intuition.*

The paper fell from his hands. He dropped on his knees, and, raising his hands and looking upward, he said in a choking voice:

"My God? Why did I not send them word before?"

Dr. Pendleton rushed on the pier and ordered a carriage. He piled his luggage into the coach and with Capt. Hoswell drove off.

The story of Dr. Pendleton, according to one of the passengers on the Lampasas*, is as follows:*

Dr. Pendleton had been in Havana a few days only when the story of the Maine *having her guns levelled on* **Morro Castle** *began to be circulated and discussed by the frequenters of the cafes. The rumor naturally created excitement.*

The sympathisers with the insurgents were open in their boasts that the United States had at last awakened to the gravity of the situation and was ready to act upon the slightest **provocation.**

Morro Castle: An historic fort at the entrance of Havana harbor.

provocation: The act of intentionally causing anger.

*On the other hand, the Spaniards were by no means **reticent** in their threats and defiance. They did not hesitate to say that if the Americans were not careful their fate would be a matter of history in a very few days.*

Dr. Pendleton paid little attention to these rumors and personal opinions. One day, while walking with a friend, he mentioned the fact that the Maine's *guns were levelled on Morro Castle. The man simply laughed. Pendleton asked him what he thought of it.*

"Why, don't you know?" he replied; "if the Maine *ever attempted to level her guns on Morro she would go up in the air like a balloon. We are prepared for everything and anything. The first warlike move on the part of this American battle-ship will be met with determined and decisive action by our people.*

"We have enough sub-marine wires under and all around the Maine *to blow her to hell whenever we choose."*

At the time Pendleton thought little of the statement. It was only when he learned of the disaster to the battle-ship that the terrible truth dawned on him.

What happened next...

President McKinley appointed a naval court of inquiry to investigate the explosion of the *Maine.* Headed by Admiral William T. Sampson (1840–1902), the court finally issued a report on March 25, concluding that two explosions had destroyed the battleship. The first, as reported in Ivan Musicant's *Empire by Default,* was "a mine situated under the bottom of the ship." The second was one or more ammunition compartments that had been ignited by the first explosion. As for the culprit, Sampson and his colleagues said, again according to Musicant, that they were "unable to obtain evidence fixing the responsibility for the destruction of the *Maine* upon any person or persons." Nonetheless the United States went to war with Spain on April 25.

reticent: Silent and reserved.

Did you know...

- Spain conducted its own investigation in February and March 1898, and concluded that an internal explosion alone had caused the disaster. The most important evidence in this regard was that hull plates from the *Maine* were bent outward. The Spanish report, however, failed to recognize that the keel of the battleship had been bent into an upside-down V, suggesting a external explosion as well.

- In the 1970s, the U.S. Navy reinvestigated the incident and this time concluded that an accidental internal explosion alone was the most likely cause of the disaster. In 1997, the National Geographic Society commissioned a study using computer simulations. The study concluded that either an internal accident or an external mine could have destroyed the *Maine*. Thus, the mystery remains.

For More Information

Books

Blow, Michael. *A Ship to Remember: The* Maine *and the Spanish-American War.* New York: William Morrow and Company, 1992.

Brown, Charles H. *The Correspondent's War: Journalists in the Spanish-American War.* New York: Charles Scribner's Sons, 1967.

Golay, Michael. *The Spanish-American War.* New York: Facts On File, 1995.

Musicant, Ivan. *Empire by Default: The Spanish-American War and the Dawn of the American Century.* New York: Henry Holt and Company, 1998.

O'Toole, G. J. A. *The Spanish War: An American Epic–1898.* New York: W. W. Norton & Company, 1984.

Somerlott, Robert. *The Spanish-American War: 'Remember the* Maine. Berkeley Heights, NJ: Enslow Publishers, Inc., 2002.

Periodicals

New York World. February 16, 17, and 20, 1898.

Web Sites

Newman, Lucia, Cynthia Tornquist, and Reuters. "Remembering the Maine." *CNN.com* http://www.cnn.com/US/9802/15/remember.the.maine/ (accessed on November 15, 2002).

Redfield Proctor

Excerpt from a speech to the U.S. Senate, March 17, 1898

Reprinted from the Congressional Record of the 55th Congress, Second Session, Volume XXXI

Published in 1898

"Torn from their homes, with foul earth, foul air, foul water, and foul food or none, what wonder that one-half have died and that one-quarter of the living are so diseased that they can not be saved?"

In March 1898, U.S. president **William McKinley** (1843–1901; served 1897–1901; see entry in Biographies section) faced pressure to wage war against Spain in Cuba. The month before, on February 15, the U.S. warship *Maine* had exploded mysteriously in the harbor at Havana, Cuba, killing more than 250 people aboard. Spain's three-year-old war with Cuban revolutionaries fighting for their independence was hurting America's $100 million annual trade with the island. American newspapers reported that hundreds of thousands of Cuban civilians had died in concentration camps, imprisoned by Spanish general Valeriano Weyler y Nicolau (1838–1930).

McKinley was desperately avoiding war, however. As a Christian and as one who had seen the horrors of combat in the American Civil War (1861–65), McKinley wanted to negotiate for peace. He also feared that a war would hurt America's booming economy, which had recovered from a depression begun in 1893. Despite the revolution's negative impact on America's trade with Cuba, leading U.S. newspapers and business magazines joined McKinley in opposing war, even after the *Maine* exploded.

That winter, Senator Redfield Proctor (1831–1908), a Republican from Vermont, traveled to Cuba to assess the revolution. While newspapers reported that Proctor went at McKinley's request, Proctor insisted that he went only for himself. When he returned, the horror of what he had seen moved him to prepare a speech to the U.S. Senate, which he delivered at the urging of colleagues on March 17, 1898.

Things to remember while reading Proctor's speech to the U.S. Senate:

- President McKinley neither wanted nor expected Proctor to deliver the speech on March 17. Proctor visited McKinley at the White House to share his statement with the president before going on to the Capitol. When McKinley asked Proctor if he would deliver the speech later that day, Proctor said no because he wanted to have it typewritten first. When Proctor arrived at the cloakroom in the Capitol, however, Senator Frye of Maine urged Proctor to give the speech, literally pushing him into the Senate chamber. Afterwards, a close friend of McKinley's, Senator Mark Hanna, told Proctor, "Had I known what you meant to do, I should have got down on my knees and tried to stop you," according to Gerald F. Linderman in *The Mirror of War.*

Redfield Proctor traveled to Cuba in March 1898 and saw firsthand the negative effects that revolution was having on the Cuban people and their land. *Hulton Archive/Getty Images. Reproduced by permission.*

Speech by Senator Redfield Proctor to the U.S. Senate, March 17, 1898

Mr. President, more importance seems to be attached by others to my recent visit to Cuba than I have given it, and it has been sug-

Mr. President: In this instance, the presiding officer of the Senate.

gested that I make a public statement of what I saw and how the situation impressed me. This I do on account of the public interest in all that concerns Cuba, and to correct some inaccuracies that have, not unnaturally, appeared in reported interviews with me.

My trip was entirely unofficial and of my own motion, not suggested by anyone. The only mention I made of it to the **President** was to say to him that I contemplated such a trip and to ask him if there was any objection to it; to which he replied that he could see none. No one but myself, therefore, is responsible for anything in this statement....

Outside **Habana** all is changed. It is not peace nor is it war. It is desolation and distress, misery and starvation. Every town and village is surrounded by a "trocha" (trench), a sort of rifle pit, but constructed on a plan new to me, the dirt being thrown up on the inside and a barbed-wire fence on the outer side of the trench. These trochas have at every corner and at frequent intervals along the sides what are there called forts, but which are really small blockhouses, many of them more like large **sentry boxes,** loopholed for musketry, and with a guard of from two to ten soldiers in each.

The purpose of these trochas is to keep the **reconcentrados** in as well as to keep the insurgents out. From all the surrounding country the people have been driven in to these fortified towns and held there to subsist as they can. They are virtually prison yards, and not unlike one in general appearance, except that the walls are not so high and strong; but they suffice, where every point is in range of a soldier's rifle, to keep in the poor reconcentrado women and children....

Their huts are about 10 by 15 feet in size, and for want of space are usually crowded together very closely. They have no floor but the ground, no furniture, and, after a year's wear, but little clothing except such stray substitutes as they can **extemporize**; and with large families, or more than one, in this little space, the commonest sanitary provisions are impossible. Conditions are unmentionable in this respect. Torn from their homes, with foul earth, foul air, foul water, and foul food or none, what wonder that one-half have died and that one-quarter of the living are so diseased that they can not be saved? A form of **dropsy** is a common disorder resulting from these conditions. Little children are still walking about with arms and chest terribly **emaciated,** eyes swollen, and abdomen bloated to three times the natural size. The physicians say these cases are hopeless.

President: In this instance, the president of the United States, William McKinley.

Habana: The capital city of Cuba, called Havana in the United States.

sentry boxes: A small structure for sheltering a sentry, or guard, from bad weather.

reconcentrados: Cubans who had been forcibly relocated from the countryside into concentration camps in cities controlled by Spain.

extemporize: To create in a makeshift fashion.

dropsy: Edema, a disease characterized by swelling.

emaciated: Unhealthily thin.

*Deaths in the streets have not been uncommon. I was told by one of our **consuls** that they have been found dead about the markets in the morning, where they had crawled, hoping to get some stray bits of food from the early **hucksters**, and that there had been cases where they had dropped dead inside the market surrounded by food. Before **Weyler's** order, these people were independent and self-supporting. There are not beggars even now. There are plenty of professional beggars in every town among the regular residents, but these country people, the reconcentrados, have not learned the art. Rarely is a hand held out to you for **alms** when going among their huts, but the sight of them makes an appeal stronger than words....*

*I inquired in regard to **autonomy** of men of wealth and men as prominent in business as any in the cities of Habana, Matanzas, and Sagua, bankers, merchants, lawyers, and autonomist officials, some of them Spanish born but Cuban bred, one prominent Englishman, several of them known as autonomists, and several of them telling me they were still believers in autonomy if practicable, but without exception they replied that it was "too late" for that.*

*Some favored a United States **protectorate**, some **annexation**, some free Cuba; not one has been counted favoring the insurrection at first. They were business men and wanted peace, but said it was too late for peace under Spanish sovereignty. They characterized Weyler's order in far stronger terms than I can. I could not but conclude that you do not have to scratch an autonomist very deep to find a Cuban. There is soon to be an election, but every polling place must be inside a fortified town. Such elections ought to be safe for the "ins."*

*I have endeavored to state in not **intemperate** mood what I saw and heard, and to make no argument thereon, but leave everyone to draw his own conclusions. To me the strongest appeal is not the barbarity practiced by Weyler nor the loss of the Maine, if our worst fears should prove true, terrible as are both of these incidents, but the spectacle of a million and a half of people, the entire native population of Cuba, struggling for freedom and deliverance from the worst misgovernment of which I ever had knowledge. But whether our action ought to be influenced by any one or all these things, and, if so, how far, is another question....*

But it is not my purpose at this time, nor do I consider it my province, to suggest any plan. I merely speak of the symptoms as I saw them, but do not undertake to prescribe. Such remedial steps as

consuls: A government official who looks after the welfare of a nation's commerce and citizens in a foreign country.

hucksters: A person who sells food at a market.

Weyler: Valeriano Weyler y Nicolau. The Spanish general who adopted the policy of imprisoning Cuban civilians in concentration camps to prevent them from helping the Cuban rebels.

alms: Donations given to poor people.

autonomy: In this instance, the right of Cuba to govern itself, but still as a possession of Spain.

protectorate: An arrangement under which one nation protects and controls another nation.

annexation: Making Cuba a part of the United States of America.

intemperate: Free from outrage.

may be required may safely be left to an American President and the American people.

What happened next...

According to Gerald F. Linderman in *The Mirror of War,* "Redfield Proctor's half-hour speech so excited the proponents of war and converted the proponents of peace that it supplied the nation's final propulsion to war against Spain." On March 19, the *Wall Street Journal* reported that Proctor had convinced many business leaders on Wall Street to support war. Many conservative journals that had opposed war, such as the *American Banker,* now spoke out in favor of it. By April 11, McKinley reluctantly asked Congress to give him the authority to use America's armed forces to end Spanish control of Cuba.

Did you know...

- Before becoming a senator, Proctor owned the Vermont Marble Company (the world's largest marble company in 1903). Although he resigned as company president and director to serve as senator, he still controlled the company unofficially in 1898. After Proctor delivered his speech to the Senate, antiwar Congressman Thomas Reed accused the senator of serving his business interests by speaking out in favor of war. According to Linderman, Reed said, "Proctor's position might have been expected. A war will make a large market for gravestones."

For More Information

Books

Foner, Philip S. *The Spanish-Cuban-American War and the Birth of American Imperialism.* New York: Monthly Review Press, 1972.

Linderman, Gerald F. *The Mirror of War: American Society and the Spanish-American War.* Ann Arbor, MI: The University of Michigan Press, 1974.

Musicant, Ivan. *Empire by Default: The Spanish-American War and the Dawn of the American Century.* New York: Henry Holt and Company, 1998.

Periodicals

Congressional Record of the 55th Congress, Second Session, Volume XXXI. Washington D.C.: Government Printing Office (daily edition, March 17, 1898).

Theodore Roosevelt

Excerpt from **The Rough Riders**
Published in 1899

The deadliest battle of the Spanish-American War (April–August 1898) took place outside the city of Santiago, Cuba, on July 1, 1898. To capture the city, the U.S. Army needed to fight its way through the town of El Caney and the surrounding hills called San Juan Heights. The evening before, thousands of troops, commanded by U.S. general **William R. Shafter** (1835–1906; see entry in Biographies section), had begun to march down a ten-foot-wide path to attack Spain at those targets.

Colonel **Theodore Roosevelt** (1858–1919; see also entry in Biographies section) was among the troops that arrived outside San Juan Heights in the early morning hours of July 1. Roosevelt led a regiment of volunteers called the Rough Riders. Anxious to begin the assault on San Juan Heights, Roosevelt instead found his regiment in a serious predicament.

General Shafter was miles behind the battle lines because his obesity and gout, a painful medical condition, prevented him from joining the fight. Messengers on horses galloped between Shafter's tent and the front to deliver reports to the general and orders to the officers. As Roosevelt and the other regiments reached San Juan Heights on July 1, their orders were to hold their fire until they were told to attack.

This put the American troops in jeopardy. When they emerged from the narrow jungle path into the clearings near San Juan Heights, they became easy targets for Spanish soldiers hiding atop the hills. Troops marching behind the Americans made retreat impossible. Stuck as they were, the U.S. soldiers began falling dead into a curve in the San Juan River that became known as Bloody Bend. In his history of the war, *The Rough Riders*, Roosevelt recalls the death that surrounded him as his men waited for their orders to attack San Juan Heights.

Things to remember while reading the excerpt from *The Rough Riders:*

- While Roosevelt's men hid from their attackers in the jungle grasses, Roosevelt spent much of his time on horseback, which increased his risk of injury and death. In fact, as a cavalry, the entire volunteer regiment was supposed to be on horseback. A shortage of transport vessels, however, had forced most of the soldiers to leave their horses behind in Tampa, Florida.

Excerpt from The Rough Riders

*The fight was now on in good earnest, and the Spaniards on the hills were engaged in heavy volley firing. The **Mauser** bullets drove*

Theodore Roosevelt, center, was put in command of the Rough Riders on June 30, 1898, just one day before the horrific battles at San Juan Heights and Kettle Hill. *AP/Wide World Photos. Reproduced by permission.*

Mauser: A weapons manufacturer and a type of firearm.

in sheets through the trees and the tall jungle grass, making a peculiar whirring or rustling sound; some of the bullets seemed to pop in the air, so that we thought they were explosive; and, indeed, many of those which were coated with brass did explode, in the sense that the brass coat was ripped off, making a thin plate of hard metal with a jagged edge, which inflicted a ghastly wound. These bullets were shot from a 45-calibre rifle carrying smokeless powder, which was much used by the **guerillas** and irregular Spanish troops. The Mauser bullets themselves made a small, clean hole, with the result that the wound healed in a most astonishing manner. One or two of our men who were shot in the head had the skull blown open, but elsewhere the wounds from the minute steel-coated bullet, with its very high velocity, were certainly nothing like as serious as those made by the old large-calibre, low-power rifle. If a man was shot through the heart, spine, or brain he was, of course, killed instantly; but very few wounded died—even under the appalling conditions which prevailed, owing to the lack of attendance and supplies in the field-hospitals with the army.

While we were lying in reserve we were suffering nearly as much as afterward when we charged. I think that the bulk of the Spanish fire was practically unaimed, or at least not aimed at any particular man, and only occasionally at a particular body of men; but they swept the whole field of battle up to the edge of the river, and man after man in our ranks fell dead or wounded, although I had the troopers scattered out far apart, taking advantage of every scrap of cover.

Devereux was dangerously shot while he lay with his men on the edge of the river. A young West Point cadet, Ernest Haskell, who had taken his holiday with us as an acting second lieutenant, was shot through the stomach. He had shown great coolness and **gallantry**, which he displayed to an even more marked degree after being wounded, shaking my hand and saying, "All right, Colonel, I'm going to get well. Don't bother about me, and don't let any man come away with me." When I shook hands with him I thought he would surely die; yet he recovered.

The most serious loss that I and the regiment could have suffered befell [us] just before we charged. Bucky O'Neill was strolling up and down in front of his men, smoking his cigarette, for he was **inveterately** addicted to the habit. He had a theory that an officer ought never to take cover—a theory which was, of course, wrong, though in a volunteer organization the officers should certainly expose themselves very fully, simply for the effect on the men; our regi-

guerillas: Regular Spanish soldiers.

gallantry: Courage.

inveterately: Firmly.

mental toast on the transport running, "The officers; may the war last until each is killed, wounded, or promoted." As O'Neill moved to and fro, his men begged him to lie down, and one of the sergeants said, "Captain, a bullet is sure to hit you." O'Neill took the cigarette out of his mouth, and blowing out a cloud of smoke laughed and said, "Sergeant, the Spanish bullet isn't made that will kill me." A little later he discussed for a moment with one of the regular officers the direction from which the Spanish fire was coming. As he turned on his heel a bullet struck him in the mouth and came out the back of his head; so that even before he fell his wild and gallant soul had gone out into the darkness.

In the battle of San Juan Heights, Roosevelt's Rough Riders joined with African American soldiers in the 9th and 10th Cavalries for the famous charge up Kettle Hill, July 1, 1898.

What happened next...

Impatience grew among the troops until Roosevelt almost ordered his regiment to charge Kettle Hill without permission from Shafter. Before that happened, as retold by Roosevelt, "Lieutenant-Colonel Dorst came riding up through the storm of bullets with the welcome command 'to move forward and support the regulars in the assault on this hills in front.'" The Rough Riders then made their famous run up Kettle Hill, taking it by the sheer force of their charge along with African Americans in two regular army regiments. By the end of the day, the Americans controlled both San Juan Heights and El Caney, which, together with a July 3 naval victory, led to Spanish surrender on July 17.

Did you know...

- Of the four hundred Rough Riders who fought at San Juan Heights on July 1, eighty-six were killed or wounded.

- General Shafter received much criticism for his conduct of the Cuban operations during the war. According to Ivan Musicant in *Empire by Default,* a soldier of the 16th Infantry wrote, "General Shafter is a fool and I believe he should be shot." After the victory at San Juan Heights on July 1, thousands of American soldiers died from diseases that they had caught in Cuba's humid summer jungles. Roosevelt compared it to the epidemic of malaria that had killed thousands of British soldiers on the island of Walcherin after their failed invasion at the Belgian seaport of Antwerp in 1809: "Not since the campaign of Crassus against the Parthians has there been so criminally incompetent a General as Shafter, and not since the expedition against Walcherin has there been a grosser mismanagement than this," Roosevelt wrote to Senator Henry Cabot Lodge, according to Musicant.

For More Information

Foner, Philip S. *The Spanish-Cuban-American War and the Birth of American Imperialism.* New York: Monthly Review Press, 1972.

Fritz, Jean. *Bully for You, Teddy Roosevelt.* New York: G. P. Putnam's Sons, 1991.

Linderman, Gerald F. *The Mirror of War: American Society and the Spanish-American War.* Ann Arbor, MI: The University of Michigan Press, 1974.

Miller, Nathan. *Theodore Roosevelt: A Life.* New York: William Morrow and Company, 1992.

Musicant, Ivan. *Empire by Default: The Spanish-American War and the Dawn of the American Century.* New York: Henry Holt and Company, 1998.

Roosevelt, Theodore. *The Rough Riders.* New York: Charles Scribner's Sons, 1899.

Samuels, Peggy. *Teddy Roosevelt at San Juan: The Making of a President.* College Station, TX: Texas A&M University Press, 1997.

Carl Schurz

Excerpt from "American Imperialism: An Address Opposing Annexation of the Philippines, January 4, 1899"

Reprinted from *American Imperialism in 1898*
Edited by Theodore P. Greene
Published in 1955

"Let the poor and the men who earn their bread by the labor of their hands pause and consider well before they give their assent to a policy so deliberately forgetful of the equality of rights...."

When the United States declared war on Spain in April 1898, it promised to make Cuba a free and independent country after securing peace there. It made no such promises, however, with respect to the other Spanish colonies involved in the conflict: Puerto Rico, Guam, and the Philippines. During the war, American troops achieved military and naval victories on all these fronts. Under the terms of the cease-fire negotiated on August 12, 1898, Spain promised to give Guam and Puerto Rico to the United States as compensation for its war expenses. The fate of the Philippines would be determined in a second series of negotiations that took place in Paris beginning October 1, 1898.

The end of the war ignited a debate in the United States over imperialism—the act of controlling foreign people who have no governmental rights or powers. Imperialists believed that the United States should grow into a world power by acquiring colonies. Foreign lands would provide markets for American farmers and manufacturers, who already exported over $2 billion worth of goods each year. Colonies would give the United States a base for further economic and political expansion throughout the world. Some imperialists also believed colonialism would help Americans spread Christianity, the dominant religion in the United States.

Anti-imperialists did not want the United States to have foreign colonies. Some believed possessing colonies violated the spirit of the American Declaration of Independence. With that document, in 1776, America's Founding Fathers broke away from British colonialism because they believed that people should govern themselves in a democracy. Other anti-imperialists feared the introduction of foreign races to America. Many also felt the U.S. government should help farmers and manufacturers by negotiating trade agreements with other countries rather than by adding colonies.

One of the most outspoken anti-imperialists was Carl Schurz. Schurz was born in Prussia (now northern Germany and Poland) in 1829. After the Prussian Revolution of 1848 failed to overthrow King Frederick William IV, Schurz sought political freedom in the United States. Over the next fifty years, he participated in the anti-slavery movement, fought for the Union Army in the American Civil War (1861–65), served as a U.S. senator from 1869 to 1875, and worked as a writer, editor, and political activist.

Schurz opposed imperialism. When the United States tried to annex (to add to an existing country or area) Santo Domingo by treaty in 1869, Senator Schurz helped defeat the effort. When the United States thought about acquiring Hawaii when U.S. president **William McKinley** (1843–1901; served 1897–1901; see entry in Biographies section) took office in 1897, Schurz met with McKinley to urge him not to do so. According to Robert L. Beisner in *Twelve Against Empire*, McKinley reassured Schurz by saying, "Ah, you may be sure there will be no jingo nonsense under my Administration. You need not borrow any trouble on that account." (Jingo was a term for people who wanted to use war to expand American territory.) Yet despite his statement, McKinley ended up taking Hawaii in July 1898 during the Spanish-American War.

When the war started in April 1898, Schurz supported the goal of freeing Cubans from colonial rule by Spain. He strongly opposed using the war to take colonies from the enemy, however. When imperialism became a hot topic in the middle of the war, Schurz wrote often to McKinley, urging

him to remain true to the American spirit of democracy by saying "no" to colonialism.

In December 1898, the United States and Spain signed the Treaty of Paris to end the war officially. In the treaty, Spain gave Puerto Rico and Guam to the United States and sold it the Philippines for $20 million. Because treaties need to be ratified—approved—by two-thirds of the U.S. Senate, the debate over imperialism heated up. In this atmosphere, Schurz, a member of the Anti-Imperialist League, gave the following address at the University of Chicago on January 4, 1899.

U.S. senator Carl Schurz strongly opposed the United States taking control of the Philippines after the Spanish-American War.
Courtesy of the Library of Congress.

Things to remember while reading "American Imperialism: An Address Opposing Annexation of the Philippines, January 4, 1899":

- Schurz's opposition to imperialism was not entirely well-principled. Schurz believed that in taking other countries, the United States had a moral obligation to make them states. But Schurz did not want the Spanish colonies to become American states. He thought the Latino and African people in Puerto Rico and the Asian natives in the Philippines and Guam were savages and barbarians. Schurz did not want such people participating in the government of the United States.

embark: To start a project.

republic: A society in which people control the government through elected representatives.

"American Imperialism: An Address Opposing Annexation of the Philippines, January 4, 1899"

*It is proposed to **embark** this **republic** in a course of imperialistic policy by permanently annexing to it certain islands taken, or partly* taken, from Spain in the late war. The matter is near its decision, but not yet decided. The peace treaty made at Paris is not yet ratified by the Senate; but even if it were, the question whether those islands, although **ceded** by Spain, shall be permanently incorporated in the territory of the United States would still be open for final determination by Congress. As an open question therefore I shall discuss it.

If ever, it **behooves** the American people to think and act with calm **deliberation**, for the character and future of the republic and the welfare of its people now living and yet to be born are in **unprecedented** jeopardy. To form a **candid** judgment of what this republic has been, what it may become, and what it ought to be, let us first recall to our minds its condition before the recent Spanish War.

Our government was, in the words of Abraham Lincoln, "the government of the people, by the people, and for the people." It was the noblest ambition of all true Americans to carry this democratic government to the highest degree of perfection and justice, in **probity**, in assured peace, in the security of human rights, in progressive civilization; to solve the problem of popular self-government on the grandest scale, and thus to make this republic the example and guiding star of mankind....

Then came the Spanish War. A few vigorous blows laid the feeble enemy helpless at our feet. The whole scene seemed to have suddenly changed. According to the **solemn proclamation** of our government, the war had been undertaken solely for the liberation of Cuba, as a war of humanity and not of conquest. But our easy victories had put conquest within our reach, and when our arms occupied foreign territory, a loud demand arose that, pledge or no pledge to the contrary, the conquests should be kept, even the Philippines on the other side of the globe, and that as to Cuba herself, independence would only be a **provisional** formality....

What, then, shall we do with such populations? Shall we, according, not indeed to the letter, but to the evident spirit of our constitution, organize those countries as territories with a view to their eventual admission as states? If they become states on an equal footing with the other states they will not only be permitted to govern themselves as to their home concerns, but they will take part in governing the whole republic, in governing us, by sending senators and representatives into our Congress to help make our laws, and by voting for president and vice-president to give our national government its executive. The prospect of the consequences which would follow the admission of the Spanish **creoles** and the **negroes** of West

cede: To surrender.

behooves: To be necessary or worthwhile.

deliberation: Careful consideration and discussion.

unprecedented: Never before known or experienced.

candid: Open and honest.

probity: Honesty.

solemn proclamation: Serious announcement.

provisional: Temporary.

Creole: A person of European descent born in Spanish America or the West Indies.

negro: An outdated term for black people descended from Africans below the Sahara desert.

*India islands and of the Malays and Tagals of the Philippines to participation in the conduct of our government is so alarming that you **instinctively** pause before taking the step.*

*But this may be avoided, it is said, by governing the new possessions as mere dependencies, or subject provinces. I will **waive** the constitutional question and merely point out that this would be a most serious departure from the rule that governed our former acquisitions, which are so frequently quoted as **precedents**. It is useless to speak of the District of Columbia and Alaska as proof that we have done such things before and we can do them again. Every candid mind will at once admit the vast difference between those cases and the permanent establishment of substantially **arbitrary** government over large territories with many millions of inhabitants, and with the prospect of there being many more of the same kind, if we once launch out on a career of conquest. The question is not merely whether we can do such things, but whether, having the public good at heart, we should do them.*

*If we do adopt such a system, then we shall, for the first time since the abolition of slavery, again have two kinds of Americans: Americans of the first class, who enjoy the privilege of taking part in the government in accordance with our old constitutional principles, and Americans of the second class, who are to be ruled in a substantially arbitrary fashion by the Americans of the first class, through congressional legislation and the action of the national executive—not to speak of individual "masters" **arrogating** to themselves powers beyond the law....*

If we do, we shall transform the government of the people, for the people, and by the people, for which Abraham Lincoln lived, into a government of one part of the people, the strong, over another part, the weak. Such an abandonment of a fundamental principle as a permanent policy may at first seem to bear only upon more or less distant dependencies, but it can hardly fail in its ultimate effects to disturb the rule of the same principle in the conduct of democratic government at home. And I warn the American people that a democracy cannot so deny its faith as to the vital conditions of its being—it cannot long play the king over subject populations without creating within itself ways of thinking and habits of action most dangerous to its own vitality—most dangerous especially to those classes of society which are the least powerful in the assertion, and the most helpless in the defense of their rights. Let the poor and the men who earn their bread by the labor of their hands pause and

instinctively: Naturally.

waive: To put aside.

precedents: Prior examples that set the way for doing something.

arbitrary: Uncontrolled by law, random.

arrogating: To claim wrongfully.

consider well before they give their assent to a policy so deliberately forgetful of the equality of rights....

What can there be to justify a change of policy **fraught with** such **direful** consequences? Let us pass the arguments of the advocates of such imperialism candidly in review.

The cry suddenly raised that this great country has become too small for us is too ridiculous to demand an answer, in view of the fact that our present population may be tripled and still have ample elbow-room, with resources to support many more. But we are told that our industries are gasping for breath; that we are suffering from over-production; that our products must have new outlets, and that we need colonies and dependencies the world over to give us more markets. More markets? Certainly. But do we, civilized beings, **indulge** in the absurd and barbarous notion that we must own the countries with which we wish to trade? ...

"But we must civilize those poor people!" Are we not **ingenious** and **charitable** enough to do much for their civilization without **subjugating** and ruling them by criminal aggression?...

It is **objected** that they are not capable of independent government. They may answer that this is their affair and that they are at least entitled to a trial. I frankly admit that if they are given that trial, their conduct in governing themselves will be far from perfect. Well, the conduct of no people is perfect, not even our own. They may try to revenge themselves upon their **tories** in their Revolutionary War. But we, too, threw our tories into hideous dungeons during our Revolutionary War and persecuted and drove them away after its close. They may have bloody civil broils. But we, too, have had our Civil War which cost hundreds of thousands of lives and devastated one-half of our land; and now we have in horrible abundance the killings by **lynch law,** and our battles at **Virden.** They may have troubles with their wild tribes. So had we, and we treated our **wild tribes** in a manner not to be proud of....

No, we cannot expect that the Porto Ricans, the Cubans, and the Filipinos will maintain orderly governments in **Anglo-Saxon** fashion. But they may succeed in establishing a tolerable order of things in their own fashion, as Mexico, after many decades of **turbulent** disorder, succeeded at last, under Porfirio Diaz, in having a strong and orderly government of her kind, not, indeed, such a government as we would tolerate in this Union, but a government answering

fraught with: Full of.

direful: Terrible.

indulge: To allow oneself to do something.

ingenious: Clever.

charitable: Generous.

subjugate: To conquer.

objected: To argue against.

Tories: Member of the Tory party, a political party in power in Great Britain when the American colonies declared their independence in 1776.

lynch law: Not a real law, but an unlawful murder committed by a mob of people. (At the time of Schurz's speech, two African Americans were murdered weekly, on average, by lynch mobs in the United States.)

Virden: A town in southwest-central Illinois. On October 12, 1898, at least ten people had died in a riot at a mine in Virden. Some say the riot helped the labor movement win its struggle to limit the length of the workday to eight hours.

wild tribes: With respect to the United States of America, this is a reference to Native Americans.

Anglo-Saxons: People of English descent.

turbulent: Violent.

Mexican character and interests, and respectable in its relations with the outside world.

This will become all the more possible if, without annexing and ruling those people, we simply put them on their feet, and then give them the benefit of that humanitarian spirit which, as we claim, led us into the war for the liberation of Cuba....

*Ask yourselves whether a policy like this will not raise the American people to a level of moral greatness never before attained! If this democracy, after all the **intoxication** of triumph in war, **conscientiously** remembers its professions and pledges, and **soberly** reflects on its duties to itself and others, and then deliberately resists the temptation of conquest, it will achieve the grandest triumph of the democratic idea that history knows of....*

What happened next...

One month after Schurz's address, the Senate ratified the Treaty of Paris on February 6, 1899 by just two votes. Two days earlier, a revolution had erupted in the Philippines. The U.S. and the Filipino sides accused each other of firing the first shot. The last shot was not fired until April 1902. During those three years, more than two hundred thousand people died in the fighting. After its victory over the rebels, the United States controlled the Philippines from 1902 until it became an independent nation in 1946.

Did you know...

- The United States still has colonies. Neither Puerto Rico nor Guam, islands acquired by America during the Spanish-American War, has a voting representative in Congress or an electoral college member (a person who participates in the selection of the president of the United States). Residents of these U.S. territories thus cannot cast votes for the president, vice-president, or members of Congress during national elections. The same is true for people who live in the U.S. Virgin Islands in the Caribbean Sea and in

intoxication: Overpowering excitement.

conscientiously: Carefully, in a moral sense.

soberly: Carefully, in a clear-headed sense.

the Northern Mariana Islands and American Samoa in the Pacific Ocean.

For More Information

Foner, Philip S. *The Spanish-Cuban-American War and the Birth of American Imperialism.* New York: Monthly Review Press, 1972.

Greene, Theodore P., ed., *American Imperialism in 1898.* Boston, MA: D. C. Heath and Company, 1955.

Langellier, John P. *Uncle Sam's Little Wars: The Spanish-American War, Philippine Insurrection, and Boxer Rebellion, 1898–1902.* Philadelphia, PA: Chelsea House, 2001.

Zinn, Howard. *A People's History of the United States: 1492–Present.* 20th anniversary ed. New York: HarperCollins, 1999.

Where to Learn More

Books

Barton, Clara. *The Red Cross in Peace and War.* Washington, D.C.: American Historical Press, 1899.

Beisner, Robert L. *Twelve Against Empire.* New York: McGraw-Hill Book Company, 1968.

Blow, Michael. *A Ship to Remember: The* Maine *and the Spanish-American War.* New York: William Morrow and Company, Inc., 1992.

Brown, Charles H. *The Correspondent's War: Journalists in the Spanish-American War.* New York: Charles Scribner's Sons, 1967.

Carlson, Paul H. *Pecos Bill: A Military Biography of William R. Shafter.* College Station, TX: Texas A&M University Press, 1989.

Cervera y Topete, Pascual, ed. *The Spanish-American War: A Collection of Documents Relative to the Squadron Operations in the West Indies.* Washington, D.C.: Government Printing Office, 1899.

Collins, David R. *William McKinley, 25th President of the United States.* Ada, OK: Garrett Educational Corp., 1990.

Collins, Mary. *The Spanish-American War.* New York: Children's Press, 1998.

Concas y Palau, Víctor. *The Squadron of Admiral Cervera.* Washington, D.C.: Government Printing Office, 1900.

Cosmas, Graham A. *An Army for Empire: The United States Army in the Spanish-American War.* Columbia, MO: University of Missouri Press, 1971.

Davis, Linda H. *Badge of Courage: The Life of Stephen Crane*. Boston, MA: Houghton Mifflin Company, 1998.

Davis, Richard Harding. *Cuba in War Time*. New York: R. H. Russell, 1897.

Davis, Richard Harding. *The Cuban and Porto Rican Campaigns*. New York: Charles Scribner's Sons, 1898.

Dolan, Edward F. *The Spanish-American War*. Brookfield, CT: Millbrook Press, 2001.

Feuer, A. B. *The Santiago Campaign of 1898*. Westport, CT: Praeger Publishers, 1993.

Feuer, A. B. *The Spanish-American War at Sea*. Westport, CT: Praeger Publishers, 1995.

Flint, Grover. *Marching with Gomez: A War Correspondent's Field Note-Book Kept During Four Months with the Cuban Army*. Boston, MA: Lamson, Wolffe and Company, 1898.

Foner, Philip S. *The Spanish-Cuban-American War and the Birth of American Imperialism*. New York: Monthly Review Press, 1972.

Frazier, Nancy. *William Randolph Hearst: Modern Media Tycoon*. Woodbridge, CT: Blackbirch Marketing, 2001.

Fritz, Jean. *Bully for You, Teddy Roosevelt*. New York: G. P. Putnam's Sons, 1991.

Gay, Kathlyn, and Martin K. Gay. *Spanish American War*. New York: Twenty First Century Books, 1995.

Gillett, Frederick H. *George Frisbie Hoar*. Boston, MA: Houghton Mifflin Company, 1934.

Golay, Michael. *The Spanish-American War*. New York: Facts On File, Inc., 1995.

Gould, Lewis L. *The Spanish-American War and President McKinley*. Lawrence, KA: University of Kansas Press, 1982.

Graves, Kerry A. *The Spanish-American War*. Mankato, MN: Capstone Books, 2001.

Greene, Theodore P, ed. *American Imperialism in 1898*. Boston, MA: D. C. Heath and Company, 1955.

Grosvenor, Charles H. *William McKinley: His Life and Work*. Washington, D.C.: The Continental Assembly, 1901.

Hamilton, Leni. *Clara Barton*. New York: Chelsea House, 1987.

Healy, Laurin Hall, and Luis Kutner. *The Admiral*. Chicago, IL: Ziff-Davis Publishing Company, 1944.

Higgins, Eva. *William McKinley: An Inspiring Biography*. Canton, OH: Daring Pub. Group, 1989.

Hoar, George F. *Autobiography of Seventy Years*. 2 vols. New York: Charles Scribner's Sons, 1903.

Hoyt, Edwin P. *William McKinley*. Chicago, IL: Reilly & Lee Company, 1967.

Joseph, Paul. *William McKinley.* Edina, MN: Abdo & Daughters, 2000.

Kent, Zachary. *William McKinley.* New York: Children's Press, 1988.

Klingel, Cynthia A., and Robert B. Noyed. *William McKinley: Our Twenty-Fifth President.* Chanhassen, MN: Childs World, 2002.

Langellier, John P. *Uncle Sam's Little Wars: The Spanish-American War, Philippine Insurrection, and Boxer Rebellion, 1898–1902.* New York: Chelsea House, 2001.

Linderman, Gerald F. *The Mirror of War: American Society and the Spanish-American War.* Ann Arbor, MI: The University of Michigan Press, 1974.

Long, L. *George Dewey Vermont Boy.* Indianapolis, IN: Bobbs-Merrill Co., 1963.

Lubow, Arthur. *The Reporter Who Would Be King.* New York: Charles Scribner's Sons, 1992.

Miley, John D. *In Cuba with Shafter.* New York: Charles Scribner's Sons, 1899.

Miller, Nathan. *Theodore Roosevelt: A Life.* New York: William Morrow and Company, Inc., 1992.

Morgan, H. Wayne. *William McKinley and His America.* Syracuse, NY: Syracuse University Press, 1963.

Musicant, Ivan. *Empire by Default: The Spanish-American War and the Dawn of the American Century.* New York: Henry Holt and Company, 1998.

Nasaw, David. *The Chief: The Life of William Randolph Hearst.* Boston, MA: Houghton Mifflin Company, 2000.

Notes on the Spanish-American War. Washington, D.C.: Government Printing Office, 1900.

Osborn, Scott C., and Robert L. Phillips Jr. *Richard Harding Davis.* Boston, MA: Twayne Publishers, 1978.

O'Toole, G. J. A. *The Spanish War: An American Epic–1898.* New York: W. W. Norton & Company, 1984.

Procter, Ben. *William Randolph Hearst: The Early Years, 1863–1910.* New York: Oxford University Press, 1998.

Pryor, Elizabeth Brown. *Clara Barton: Professional Angel.* Philadelphia, PA: University of Pennsylvania Press, 1987.

Roosevelt, Theodore. *The Rough Riders.* New York: Charles Scribner's Sons, 1899.

Rose, Mary Catherine. *Clara Barton: Soldier of Mercy.* New York: Chelsea House, 1991.

Rosenfeld, Harvey. *Diary of a Dirty Little War: The Spanish-American War of 1898.* Westport, CT: Praeger Publishers, 2000.

Ross, Ishbel. *Angel of the Battlefield: The Life of Clara Barton.* New York: Harper & Row, Publishers, Inc., 1956.

Samuels, Peggy. *Teddy Roosevelt at San Juan: The Making of a President.* College Station, TX: Texas A&M University Press, 1997.

Sargent, Herbert H. *The Campaign of Santiago de Cuba.* Chicago, IL: A. C. McClurg & Co., 1907.

Smith, Angel, and Emma Dávila-Cox, eds. *The Crisis of 1898: Colonial Redistribution and Nationalist Mobilization.* New York: St. Martin's Press, Inc., 1999.

Somerlott, Robert. *The Spanish-American War: 'Remember the Maine.* Berkeley Heights, NJ: Enslow Publishers, Inc., 2002.

Spector, Ronald H. *Admiral of the New Empire: The Life and Career of George Dewey.* Columbia, SC: University of South Carolina Press, 1988.

Stallman, R. W., and E. R. Hagemann, eds. *The War Dispatches of Stephen Crane.* New York: New York University Press, 1964.

Welch, Richard E., Jr. *George Frisbie Hoar and the Half-Breed Republicans.* Cambridge, MA: Harvard University Press, 1971.

Wertheim, Stanley, and Paul Sorrentino, eds. *The Correspondence of Stephen Crane.* New York: Columbia University Press, 1988.

West, Richard S. *Admirals of American Empire: The Combined Story of George Dewey, Alfred Thayer Mahan, Winfield Scott Schley, and William Thomas Sampson.* Westport, CT: Greenwood Press, 1971.

Wheeler, Jill C. *Clara Barton.* Edina, MN: Abdo & Daughters, 2002.

Wheeler, Joseph. *The Santiago Campaign.* Philadelphia, PA: Drexel Briddle, 1899.

Whitelaw, Nancy. *William Randolph Hearst and the American Century.* Greensboro, NC: Morgan Reynolds, 1999.

Wukovits, John F. *The Spanish-American War.* San Diego, CA: Lucent Books, 2001.

Zinn, Howard. *A People's History of the United States: 1492–Present.* 20th anniversary ed. New York: HarperCollins, 1999.

Periodicals

Congressional Record. 55th Cong., 2d sess., Vol. 31, pp. 2916–19.

Congressional Record. 55th Cong., 3d sess., pp. 493–503, 958–960.

New York World. February 16, 17, and 20, 1898.

Rhodes, Charles D. "William Rufus Shafter." *Michigan History Magazine* 16 (Fall, 1932): 370–83.

Shafter, William R. "The Capture of Santiago de Cuba." *Century* 57 (February, 1899): 612–30.

Smith, Eric M. "Leaders Who Lost: Case Studies of Command under Stress." *Military Review,* vol. LXI, April 1981, no. 4, pp. 41–45.

Smith, Joseph. "Heroes of the Cuban Revolution: Martí, Maceo, and Gómez." *Historian,* No. 44, Winter 1994, pp. 3–8.

Web Sites

Cushing, Lincoln. *1898–1998: Centennial of the Spanish American War.* http://www.zpub.com/cpp/saw.html (accessed January 8, 2003).

Great Projects Film Company, Inc. *Crucible of Empire: The Spanish American War.* http://www.pbs.org/crucible/ (accessed January 8, 2003).

Library of Congress. *The Spanish-American War in Motion Pictures.* http://memory.loc.gov/ammem/sawhtml/sawhome.html (accessed January 8, 2003).

Library of Congress. *The World of 1898: The Spanish-American War.* http://www.loc.gov/rr/hispanic/1898/ (accessed January 8, 2003).

McSherry, Patrick, ed. *The Spanish American War Centennial Website.* http://www.spanamwar.com/ (accessed January 8, 2003).

Newman, Lucia, Cynthia Tornquist, and Reuters. "Remembering the Maine." *CNN.com.* http://www.cnn.com/US/9802/15/remember.the.maine/ (accessed January 8, 2003).

The New York Public Library. *A War in Perspective, 1898–1998: Public Appeals, Memory, and the Spanish-American Conflict.* http://www.nypl.org/research/chss/epo/spanexhib/ (accessed January 8, 2003).

Index

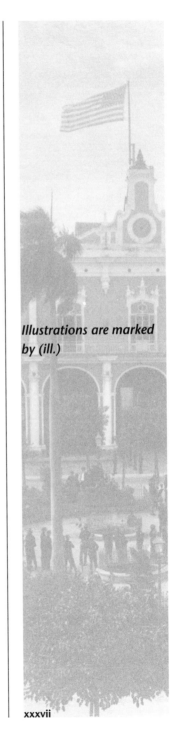

racism and 205, 206, 207–208
slavery compared with 135,
    136–137, 208
Spain and 89
United States and 4–5, 34–35,
    53–54, 65–77, 130
Industrial Revolution 5–6
Infanta Maria Teresa 91, 94
Influence of Sea Power upon History
    32
Invading Army 118–119

J

Japan 34, 134
Jefferson, Thomas 17
Journalists. *See also* Newspapers
    Frederic Remington 22–23, 23
        (ill.), 37, 98–99, 125
    generally 37
    George Bronson Rea 99
    James Creelman 128
    new journalism 124
    Richard Harding Davis (*see*
        Davis, Richard Harding)
    Stephen Crane 37, 103,
        165–170, 166 (ill.)
    Sylvester Scovel 99, 159
    William Randolph Hearst (*see*
        Hearst, William Randolph)
    yellow journalism 20, 124
Juadenes y Alvarez, Fermín 62
Judaism 38

K

Kent, Jacob Ford 47, 48 (ill.), 157,
    158–159, 160
Kettle Hill 47, 102, 152, 201 (ill.),
    202. *See also* San Juan
    Heights, Battle of
Knights of Labor 18

L

La Liga 8
Las Guásimas, Battle of 46 (ill.)
    casualties of 46–47
    conduct of 45–47, 151, 158

Joseph W. Wheeler and 45–46,
    151, 158
Leonard Wood and 46, 151, 158
Liberating Army and 46, 47
Richard Harding Davis and
    101–102
Spain and 158
Stephen Crane and 169
Theodore Roosevelt and 46,
    151, 169
Lawton, Henry W. 47 (ill.)
    appointment of 157
    Battle of El Caney and 47, 102,
        152, 158
    Round-Robin letter and 160
Lee, Fitzhugh 187, 188
Liberating Army
    Battle of Las Guásimas and 46,
        47
    Battles of El Caney and San
        Juan Heights and 47–48, 178
    disbanding of 182–183
    landing at Daiquirí and 178
    Russell A. Alger and 41–42, 177
    Second Cuban War for Inde-
        pendence and 117–119
    surrender of Santiago and 50,
        178–182
    tactics of 11–13, 12, 41, 84, 90,
        117, 156
    United States and 31, 41–42,
        44, 177–183
Lincoln, Abraham 207, 208
Linderman, Gerald F. 37, 142, 196
Little War 10
Lodge, Henry Cabot 28, 136, 202
Long, John D.
    George Dewey and 33, 54,
        106–107, 109, 112, 148
    Richard Harding Davis and 100
    strategy of 33, 92
    Theodore Roosevelt and
        106–107, 108–109, 148
    U.S.S. *Maine* and 56, 188
Luks, George 124
Lynching 19, 209

M

Maceo, Antonio 11 (ill.)
    death of 119
    joins Liberating Army 10–11

N